Women, Work, and Child Welfare in the Third World

AAAS Selected Symposia Series

Published by Westview Press, Inc.
5500 Central Avenue, Boulder, Colorado

for the

American Association for the Advancement of Science
1333 H Street, N.W., Washington, D.C.

Women, Work, and Child Welfare in the Third World

Edited by Joanne Leslie and Michael Paolisso

AAAS Selected Symposium 110

AAAS Selected Symposia Series

This Westview softcover edition is printed on acid-free paper and bound in library-quality, coated covers that carry the highest rating of the National Association of State Textbook Administrators, in consultation with the Association of American Publishers and the Book Manufacturers' Institute.

Published in 1989 in the United States of America by Westview Press, Inc., 5500 Central Avenue, Boulder, Colorado 80301, and in the United Kingdom by Westview Press, Inc., 13 Brunswick Centre, London WC1N 1AF, England

Library of Congress Cataloging-in-Publication Data
Women, work, and child welfare in the Third World / edited by Joanne
Leslie, Michael Paolisso.
   p.   cm. — (AAAS selected symposium : 110)
Includes bibliographies and index.
ISBN 0-8133-7805-2
   1. Child welfare–Developing countries.   2. Children of Working
mothers—Developing countries.   3. Working mothers–Developing
countries.   I. Leslie, Joanne.   II. Paolisso, Michael Jeffrey.
III. Series.
HV804.W65   1989
362.7'09172'4—dc20   89-14683
                                                                          CIP

Printed and bound in the United States of America

 The paper used in this publication meets the requirements of the American National Standard for Permanence of Paper for Printed Library Materials Z39.48-1984.

10   9   8   7   6   5   4   3   2   1

About the Book

Two fields of social action that have received increasing attention in the last decade in much of the developing world are the survival and healthy development of children, and the social and economic roles of women. Researchers, policy makers and program planners in both fields have become increasingly concerned about the relationship between women's work and child welfare, although frequently from differing points of view. The primary focus of those in the women in development field has been on ways to enhance women's economic opportunities; this focus has led to a tendency either to de-emphasize women's child care responsibilities, or to assume that substitute child caretakers would provide equally good care. In a similarly one-sided fashion, those concerned with child survival and development, usually professionals from education and public health, have tended to view women primarily as an instrument to produce healthy children, ignoring or minimizing the opportunity costs of women's time, and the genuine need in most low-income households for mothers to earn income during the same years that they are bearing and raising children.

This book represents one of the first efforts to bring together in a single volume the work of a growing number of researchers interested in simultaneously studying women's roles and child welfare in the Third World. The studies included illustrate not only the multifaceted nature of women's work and child welfare, but also the benefits of using a variety of research approaches and methodologies. The findings from these studies are important to the development of policies and interventions that simultaneously increase women's effectiveness as economic actors and as child care providers.

About the Series

The *AAAS Selected Symposia Series* was begun in 1977 to provide a means for more permanently recording and more widely disseminating some of the valuable material that is discussed at the AAAS Annual National Meetings. The volumes in this *Series* are based on symposia held at the Meetings that address topics of current and continuing significance, both within and among the sciences, and in the areas in which science and technology have an impact on public policy. The *Series* format is designed to provide for rapid dissemination of information, so the papers are reproduced directly from camera-ready copy. The papers published in the *Series* are organized and edited by the symposium arrangers, who then become the editors of the various volumes. Most papers published in the *Series* are original contributions that have not been previously published, although in some cases additional papers from other sources have been added by an editor to provide a more comprehensive view of a particular topic. Symposia may be reports of new research or views of established work, particularly work of an interdisciplinary nature, since the AAAS Annual Meetings typically embrace the full range of the sciences and their societal implications.

ARTHUR HERSCHMAN
Head, Meetings and Publications
American Association for the
Advancement of Science

Contents

Acknowledgments

First and foremost, we want to acknowledge our enormous debt to Dr. Mayra Buvinic´, Director of the International Center for Research on Women (ICRW). In a very real sense, this book is as much hers as ours. From the initiation of ICRW's research program on Women's Work and Child Welfare in 1984, through the organization of the AAAS Symposium at which many of these papers were originally presented, to the lengthy process of selecting, revising, and editing the final collection, Mayra has provided the moral commitment, intellectual leadership, and institutional support that have made preparing this book not just possible, but richly rewarding. In addition, we are deeply appreciative of the untold hours spent by ICRW staff members, both past and present, on checking references, typing, copy editing, proofreading, and then checking everything one last time. They have shown dedication, patience, and a professional attention to detail above and beyond the call of duty, and we sincerely thank each and every one of them. We are also extremely grateful to the Rockefeller Foundation for its early encouragement of ICRW's work in this area and for the financial assistance the Foundation has provided in support of ICRW's work on this book. Many others have provided a sounding board for ideas, a critical reading of particular chapters, sorely needed encouragement along the way, and sometimes all of the above. We are grateful to each of you and hope you will be pleased with the book you have helped to bring into existence.

Joanne Leslie
Michael Paolisso

Foreword

Both the fields of international health and economic development recognize the need to better understand the productive and reproductive responsibilities of women in developing countries. From the health perspective, the concern with primary health care, maternal child health, and child survival focuses attention on the role of women as providers of health for young children. From the economic position, the contribution of women to the economies of developing countries results in an increased interest in ways of integrating women into economic development projects in different sectors.

What has not been addressed adequately to date is how Third World women balance productive and reproductive responsibilities, and what, if any, are the health consequences for children due to women's need to work. This concern with the interactive nature of women's economic work and time spent providing care for children is critically important, given the expansion of women's work responsibilities due to the combined effects of macro-level economic changes—Third World recession, debt, and government austerity measures—and changes at the micro-level, which can be seen in the rising incidence of women-headed households and the restructuring of women's traditional household roles to accommodate the need for additional family income. Concurrently, many of the international health initiatives depend on women as key implementors of primary health care and child survival interventions, and thus may lead to an increased demand on women's time.

The studies in this volume collectively address the questions of how women manage their work and child care responsibilities and whether specific types or patterns of women's work have negative impacts on child welfare. The multifaceted nature of women's work and child welfare and the benefits of using a variety of research approaches and methodologies are evident in this collection. The authors provide carefully drawn conclusions that identify a number of key relationships and criteria that need to be considered by both economic development and health programs. As a collection of case studies supported by reviews that provide analytical frameworks, *Women, Work, and Child Welfare in the Third World* is a significant contribution to the development literature. It raises critical questions, discusses various approaches and provides findings that undoubtedly will motivate and guide others to follow.

Scott B. Halstead
Rockefeller Foundation

1

Introduction

Joanne Leslie and Mayra Buvinic´

Two fields of social action that have been given increasing attention in the last decade in much of the developing world are the survival and healthy development of children, and the social and economic roles of women. Researchers, policy makers, and program planners in both fields have been concerned about the relationship between women's work and child welfare, although frequently from differing points of view. The primary focus of those in the women in development field has been on ways to enhance women's economic opportunities; this focus has led to a tendency either to deemphasize women's child care responsibilities, or to assume that substitute child caretakers would provide equally good care. In a similarly one-sided fashion, those concerned with child survival and development, usually professionals from education and public health, have tended to view women primarily as an instrument to produce healthy children, ignoring or minimizing the opportunity costs of women's time, and the genuine need in most low-income households for mothers to earn income during the same years that they are bearing and raising children.

Uninformed by an appreciation of women's multiple roles, a main policy inference from research on child health and nutrition has been that reduced malnutrition rates and increased child welfare, result from keeping poor women at home rather than promoting their participation in the marketplace. Uninformed by a child welfare orientation, a main inference from women-in-development literature has been that women's incorporation into the workforce offers only benefits and no costs to women and children.

It is only quite recently that bridges have been built and a fruitful dialogue has begun between the women in development and child welfare fields (Myers and Indriso 1987; Leslie, Lycette, and Buvinic' 1988). A genuine collaboration between those working for the survival and healthy development of children and those working to support the social and economic roles of women should produce policy and program recommendations that will improve both the status of women and the welfare of children in developing countries. Initial collaboration has already enriched research in both fields, as is evident from the studies included in this volume.

A Brief History

A precursor to interest in the relationship between women's work and child welfare was an interest in the relationship between women's work and fertility. More than two decades ago, first in industrialized countries and then in developing economies, demographers and economists began to look at the relationship between women's labor force participation and fertility in order to understand population and labor supply trends. In fact, studies on the relationship between women's labor force participation and fertility represent some of the earliest attempts to integrate a gender perspective into economic development research and policy.

The central hypothesis of the research carried out in industrialized economies, which was then transferred to developing ones, was that there was an inverse relationship between female labor force participation and fertility behavior. This hypothesis was based on an assumed incompatibility between women's work in the marketplace and women's reproductive and childbearing functions at home. Extensive empirical research with large data sets demonstrated, however, that the relationship between these two variables was much more complex than originally anticipated. In industrialized countries it was generally found that increased female labor force participation was positively correlated with lower birth rates when women in low income groups were excluded (Oppenheimer 1970). In developing countries, however, the relationship between female labor force participation and fertility varied dramatically depending on, among other things, rural-urban residence, education, and participation in modern or traditional sectors of the economy; the empirical evidence in developing countries often contradicted the original predictions (Piepmeier and Adkins 1973). One principal factor that could explain these opposite empirical findings was the relative lack of conflict in developing countries between women's roles as workers and mothers (Standing 1978). In fact, some authors argued quite forcefully that the notion of incompatibility between labor force participation and reproductive and child care tasks was derived from an ethnocentric Western model that did not apply to traditional and/or rural-based economies where women's work and child care were compatible activities (Ware 1975).

Researchers within the women in development framework, along with more traditional demographers and economists, have continued to undertake empirical studies in order to clarify the relationship between women's market work and fertility patterns, as well as the broader relationship between women's status — measured by women's education and labor force participation — and fertility behavior (Cochrane 1978). These studies have benefitted from the knowledge gained in the women in development field and, at the same time, have shed light on the complex nature of women's work in developing economies, particularly of work that takes place outside the modern marketplace (see, for instance, Dixon 1975; Birdsall 1976; and Youssef 1974).

The new household economics, based on the model of the household as a productive unit, has also provided valuable insights and analytical tools in the growing effort to understand the relationship between women's economic and reproductive roles (Schultz 1973). One important contribution of the new household economics has been the explicit consideration of the economic value of goods and services produced and consumed within the family. This has led to a greater recognition of the value of women's economic contribution, since women are the primary producers of goods and services within the home, and to a greater appreciation of the opportunity cost of women's time. Another central feature of the new household economics is the model of the household as a rational decision-making unit, which is presumed to lead to an optimal allocation of time by different household members among different domestic and income-generating tasks. While valid questions have been raised about the appropriateness of treating the household as a single decision-making unit (Dwyer and Bruce 1988), an important contribution of the model of the rational household has been to provide a framework within which to examine the tradeoffs between time spent on child care, time spent in the labor force, and other uses of women's time (Birdsall 1980; DaVanzo and Lee 1983).

The original hypothesis of conflict between women's work and childbearing roles, which had positive implications both for increasing women's economic status and reducing population growth in developing countries, took a more negative turn when transferred to the field of public health and child development. A corollary to the hypothesis of the inverse work-fertility relationship is the hypothesis that women's labor force participation will be negatively related to child welfare. It is assumed that women's labor force participation is directly related to a reduction in time spent in breastfeeding and child care, which, in turn, has negative consequences for child welfare (Nerlove 1974; Monckeberg 1977; Popkin 1978).

As the studies in this volume indicate, the hypothesized inverse relationship between women's market work and child welfare in developing countries is as fraught with similar complexities and inconsistencies as the earlier postulated inverse work-fertility relationship. Until recently, however, the assumption of a negative relationship between women's market work and child welfare went largely unquestioned in the literature in part because the research did not benefit from collaborative inputs from women in development and child health and development perspectives. It is probable that, as the positive policy implications for women's economic advancement and reduced birth rates nurtured the development of a gender dimension in population studies, contrary or negative policy implications regarding women's economic participation and child welfare built a gulf that, until recently, prevented collaboration between those concerned with women in development and those concerned with child welfare.

Recent Trends

An interest in the relationship between women's work and child welfare is particularly relevant given several recent trends in developing countries. One is women's increased participation and visibility in the market economy. Another is the continuing high levels of child mortality, morbidity, and malnutrition in many developing countries. A third is the recent promotion of child survival technologies, which rely heavily on women as agents in their dissemination. The following sections briefly review these trends to provide a context in which to consider the findings from the studies in this volume.

Trends in Women's Work

The majority of women of reproductive age, in industrialized and developing countries alike, face the need at some point in their lives to combine economically productive work with nurturing their children. The burden of these dual responsibilities, however, falls most inevitably and heavily on low-income women in the Third World. While the true economic contribution made by women in the developing world may not have increased in the post-colonial period, the pattern of women's work has changed substantially. Increased urbanization, industrialization, and migration have caused greater numbers of women to seek income-generating work away from home. The proportion of women officially recorded as being part of the paid labor force in developing countries increased from 28 percent in 1950 to 32 percent in 1985 (Sivard 1985). At the same time, more women have become the primary economic support of themselves and their children. Estimates of the proportion of households headed by women range from almost half in Botswana, to a third in Jamaica, to a minimum of 10 percent in most Arab Middle Eastern countries (Youssef and Hetler 1984).

The worldwide economic recession of the past few years and the severe food production crisis throughout much of sub-Saharan Africa has intensified the burden that poor women in the developing world have to contribute to, if not to assume the sole responsibility for, the economic welfare of their households (Gozo and Aboagye 1985; Savane 1985). Few low-income women have the option of devoting themselves exclusively to nurturing their children, even during the first year after childbirth. At the same time, child care responsibilities during the reproductive years are increasingly being recognized as a major reason for the high proportion of women in informal-sector jobs, many of which are low paying and insecure (Lycette and White 1988).

The changing nature of women's work in less-developed countries — more women working away from home and more women earning a cash income — and the resultant increased recognition of the importance of women's economically productive roles, is one factor that has led to a desire to understand better how women combine their productive and maternal roles and to what extent, or under what circumstances, the one may interfere with or constrain the other.

Trends in Child Survival and Development

Overall, the chances of survival of children in the Third World have improved considerably in the past 20 years. The infant mortality rate (IMR) in countries that the World Bank defines as "middle-income" declined from an average of 104 per 1000 births in 1965 to 68 in 1985, and child death rates over the same period declined from 17 to 8 deaths per 1000 children aged 1 to 4 years (World Bank 1987). Even in the lowest-income countries, the average IMR fell from 150 to 112 and the average child death rate from 27 to 19. In spite of these substantial declines, however, infant and child mortality rates remain distressingly high, particularly in Sub-Saharan Africa. There is also a growing concern that certain trends, such as the increasing prevalence of female-headed households, and more recently, the economic recession and structural adjustments to it, could be reversing the trend towards improvements in child survival (Cornia, Jolly, and Stewart 1987).

One of the earliest issues that focused interest on the relationship between women's work and child welfare was the belief that changing patterns of work among women were a major cause of declining rates of breastfeeding, which in turn were having a negative effect on child survival and nutritional status (Jelliffe 1962; Wray 1978). Recent evidence suggests, however, that changes in breastfeeding patterns have been less dramatic than originally thought, particularly among rural populations. The main change seems to have been a reduction in duration of breastfeeding in urban areas (Popkin, Bilsborrow, and Akin 1982; Millman 1986). In addition, most studies have found that the need to work, or factors related to work, have been cited by a surprisingly small proportion of women as their reason for not initiating breastfeeding, for introducing supplementary bottles, or for terminating breastfeeding (Van Esterik and Greiner 1981). Nonetheless, concern about the influence of maternal work patterns on breastfeeding behavior continues and is one of the reasons that it seemed essential in this volume to carefully review the actual empirical evidence concerning women's work as a determinant of infant feeding patterns (see particularly Chapters 2, 4, 5, and 6).

Another issue that has gained increasing attention in recent years — one that suggests the possibility of both negative and positive effects of women's work on child health and nutritional status — is the importance of a protein-and energy-dense diet to ensure adequate nutrition among weaning-age children (Gibbons and Griffiths 1984). Children in this age group have particularly high nutritional needs, due to the combined effects of rapid growth and a high prevalence of infectious diseases. Because they are also unable to consume large amounts of food at one time, weaning-age children need frequent, nutrient-dense meals to prevent malnutrition. Mothers who are not working or who work at home may be better able to assure frequent meals and to monitor intrahousehold food distribution to ensure that weaning-age children receive an adequate share. On the other hand, mothers who are working may be better able to produce or purchase the more expensive oils, legumes, and animal source proteins needed to provide energy- and protein-dense diets for their weaning-aged children. The findings from Guatemala reported by Engle in Chapter 8 are particularly interesting in regard to weaning-age children. While she found some evidence of a negative effect of maternal work on nutritional status among children less than a year old, she found that, during the second year of life, children of women who worked were less malnourished than children of women who did not work, which she attributed in part to their mothers being better able to buy higher-quality, age-appropriate foods.

Women's Role in Child Survival Interventions

The recent emphasis within the international health community on increasing child survival through the use of selective primary health care interventions relies heavily on women as agents in introducing new health technologies and practices. UNICEF's 1986 State of the World's Children states, "whether we are talking about breastfeeding or weaning, oral rehydration therapy or immunization, regular growth checking or frequent handwashing, it is obvious that the mother stands at the center of the child survival revolution" (UNICEF 1986).

Of the four central components of the child survival approach to selective primary health care, only one, breastfeeding, focuses on a traditional practice. Breastfeeding was felt to warrant promotion, however, precisely due to the concern discussed earlier that substantial numbers of mothers were breastfeeding less — to the detriment of their children's nutritional status and health. Unfortunately, in the last ten years considerably more effort has gone into establishing the undeniable benefits to both mothers and children of appropriate breastfeeding (both directly and indirectly through its effect on increasing birth intervals) and to documenting regional and urban/rural differences in rates of change in infant feeding practices than into understanding women's reasons for choosing a particular pattern for feeding their infants or assessing the costs and benefits of different infant feeding patterns, given different family and economic structures.

The other three main components of the child survival strategy — oral rehydration therapy, immunizations, and growth monitoring (including improved weaning practices) — all demand that women understand and accept new knowledge about their children's health and nutrition and that they incorporate new activities into their schedules. As with breastfeeding, the attention of researchers has been directed more to establishing the health and nutrition benefits to children of these new technologies than to assessing their costs, particularly costs to mothers and households. Each of these technologies is potentially life saving, and, properly implemented, can certainly be health and nutrition promoting. Making them available as widely as possible increases the range of options available to households in developing countries to produce child health and nutrition, and that is desirable. However, utilization of these child survival technologies also requires the input of time and money on the part of someone responsible for the target child, usually the child's mother.

The monetary costs of the technologies are generally modest, but they are not inconsequential, particularly for the poorest families. Such costs may include ingredients for home-prepared oral rehydration salts (ORS) and special weaning foods, transportation costs to get to the location where immunizations are being given or growth monitoring is being carried out, or payment for packaged ORS, immunizations, growth charts, or community-prepared weaning foods.

From the user perspective, the time costs of the child survival technologies may be even more significant than the monetary costs (Leslie 1989). Averaged out in terms of minutes per day, neither ORT, immunizations, nor growth monitoring would add much to a mother's work day.

However, the time costs are not distributed evenly, but are bunched. When a child needs ORT, someone must be in attendance almost constantly. In order to take a child to be weighed or to be immunized, a mother may have to forego as much as an entire day of work, depending on the distance to be traveled and the number of other children involved. In contrast to the potentially disruptive but occasional time costs of ORT, immunizations, and growth monitoring, the preparation and feeding of appropriate weaning foods is a daily activity. Initial supplemental foods usually cannot be the same foods eaten by the rest of the family, weaning-age children should eat more frequently than older children and adults, and avoiding bacterial contamination requires preparation of small amounts at a time and careful cleaning of all utensils used. All of these mean that improving current weaning practices requires a substantial increase in the amount of time mothers and others in the household devote to child feeding. The effects of women's work on adoption of child survival technologies, in terms of competing demands on women's time, level and control over household income, or some other linkage warrant serious study.

This Volume

This book represents one of the first efforts to bring together in a single volume the work of a growing number of researchers who are interested in simultaneously studying women's roles and child welfare in the Third World. The volume is based on a symposium organized at the May 1986 Annual Meeting of the American Association for the Advancement of Science, although several papers not presented at the original symposium have been included and all of the papers have been substantially updated and revised. The predominance of research from Latin America, which characterized the original symposium, continues in this collection. However, the inclusion of the two cross-country review chapters, as well as one country study each from Asia and from Africa, make it clear that the issue of the relationship between women's work and child welfare raises similar challenges to understanding and policy throughout the Third World.

The studies included in this volume illustrate not only the multifaceted nature of women's work and child welfare (as will be discussed in greater detail), but also the benefits of using a variety of research techniques to explore the complex relationships between them. "Women's Work and Child Nutrition in the Third World" (Chapter 2) and "Women's Work and Social Support for Child Care in the Third World" (Chapter 3) demonstrate that, when carefully analyzed and considered as a whole, a great deal can be learned from research and project evaluations that may not have been specifically designed to focus on the relationship between women's work and child welfare. These two overview chapters are included because they present interesting preliminary findings concerning the relationship between women's work and two key aspects of child welfare — child nutrition and child care — and provide a framework and point of departure for reading the country-specific studies (chapters 4-11).

The country studies can all be loosely categorized as multidisciplinary in that, to a greater or lesser extent, they draw on concepts and methods from several different academic disciplines, including economics, anthropology, and the health sciences. However, the main methodological approach taken differs considerably among the eight chapters. "The Effects of Women's Work on Breastfeeding in the Philippines 1973-1983" (Chapter 4), "Women's Market Work, Infant Feeding Practices, and Infant Nutrition Among Low-Income Women in Santiago, Chile" (Chapter 6), and "Effects of New Export Crops in Smallholder Agriculture on Division of Labor and Child Nutritional Status in Guatemala" (Chapter 9) are primarily microeconomic studies in which mathematical models of the relationship among the variables are tested and the results presented quantitatively. At the other end of the continuum, "Women's Community Service and Child Welfare in Urban Peru" (Chapter 11) presents the findings of an ethnographic study in a predominantly descriptive, nonquantitative style. The remaining four studies report data from health or nutrition field surveys, but each is strengthened by reference to specific social science concepts and analytical frameworks. "Breastfeeding and Maternal Employment in Urban Honduras" (Chapter 5) and "Women's Agricultural Work, Child Care, and Infant Diarrhea in Rural Kenya" (Chapter 10) both include findings from ethnographic studies that were carried out to provide information that would complement the results of the survey data. "Maternal Employment, Differentiation, and Child Welfare in Panama" (Chapter 7) uses the sociological concept of differentiation to explore specific linkages in the relationship between women's work and child welfare. "Child care Strategies of Working and Nonworking Women in Rural and Urban Guatemala" (Chapter 8) draws on theories of child development, and in so doing underlines the importance of taking the age of the child into consideration when looking at the effects of women's work on child welfare.

Key Concepts

At the core of each study included in this volume is the question of whether women's work, particularly recent increases or changes in women's labor force participation, may have a detrimental effect on the welfare of children in the Third World. The findings vary considerably depending on the specific characteristics of women's work in the study population, the particular measure(s) of child welfare used, and the theoretical and methodological approach taken. In fact, one of the conclusions that emerges most clearly from examining the studies presented in this volume is the importance of disaggregating both the concepts of women's work and of child welfare so that research results can be interpreted more meaningfully. Key characteristics of women's work — such as type of work, location of work, time spent working, income earned, and work-related benefits — as well as key aspects of child welfare — such as morbidity, nutritional status, cognitive development, dietary intake, and caregiver — need to be defined and measured separately. Although none of the studies in this volume include all of the important variables associated with women's work or child welfare, each makes a serious attempt to disaggregate both concepts, to investigate specific linkages, and to reach conclusions that go beyond the simplistic assertion that women's work has negative or positive consequences for child welfare. Some of the more interesting findings are summarized below.

Women's Work

In industrialized and developing countries alike, women's work differs in fundamental ways from men's work (Humphries 1988). Women's work includes production for the market, production for home consumption, and other domestic responsibilities. Market work standardly includes formal and informal sector income-generating activities as well as unpaid labor in the firm or the farm. Home production, as it is usually defined, encompasses activities that can be shifted to the market economy (e.g., food processing) but excludes child care. However, a broader definition of women's domestic work would certainly include child care, as well as care of other family members. Most researchers have categorized women's social activities as leisure, but social activities in many settings should more properly be considered as another component of women's work. Such activities are frequently part of a complex system of reciprocal exchange of services, including but not limited to child care (see Chapter 3). As Anderson's study from Peru (Chapter 11) also makes clear, women's unpaid community work can sometimes pose significant short-term risks to child welfare, particularly since such work has similar time costs to those of market work but without the benefit of income.

Women's participation in market production has time, income, and status effects, among others, that are important determinants of child care strategies and child welfare outcomes. As female wage rates increase, women's costs to allocate time to both home production and child care increase, but, on the other hand, the household can purchase additional goods (food, health care, etc.) while holding constant the time women spend in market work. This trade-off between time and income is explicitly considered in the study from Santiago, Chile, by Vial, Muchnik, and Mardones (Chapter 6), which investigates the effect of maternal work during an infant's first six months on both infant feeding practices and weight gain. The authors report significantly better weight gain among infants of working than nonworking mothers and conclude that, in this population, the negative effects of earlier termination of breastfeeding are outweighed by the benefits of higher incomes among working mothers, which allow increased expenditures for food and better access to health care.

An increase in women's income can increase women's status within the home and may lead to shifts in allocation of household resources among expenditures or among household members. The study by von Braun of the introduction of nontraditional export crops in highland Guatemala (Chapter 9) focuses on a situation in which women's work shifted from income-generating work in the informal sector to unpaid farm work. Von Braun concludes that if total household income increases, but at the expense of women's control over income, the expected nutritional benefits to children turn out to be significantly less than anticipated.

Child Welfare

In its broadest definition, child welfare encompasses a continuum of desirable outcomes ranging from mere survival to access to the necessary resources and opportunities for all children to develop to their full potential. Because child mortality, morbidity, and malnutrition remain widespread problems in most developing countries, and because other aspects of child welfare are difficult to achieve if good health and nutrition are lacking, studies on child welfare in the Third World have tended to focus on child health and nutrition outcomes, or on factors that are presumed to be direct determinants of child health and nutrition, such as breastfeeding, dietary intake, or child care. With the one exception of Anderson's study in Peru (Chapter 11), which presents some limited data on child development, the studies included in this collection all focus on child health and nutrition and their direct determinants.

The three studies that focus on the relationship between women's work and infant feeding practices all improve on the dichotomous categorization of children as breastfed or not breastfed that has characterized much of the earlier research (for a more detailed discussion of this problem, see Chapter 2). Popkin, Akin, Flieger, and Wong, in their longitudinal study of breastfeeding in the Philippines (Chapter 4), calculate the probability of an infant being breastfed at different ages and discover that most of the increases or decreases in breastfeeding probabilities over the decade from 1973 to 1983 that had a significant impact on duration took place during the second year of the infant's life, when they could be expected to have only small health or demographic effects. Both O'Gara, in her study of urban Honduran mothers (Chapter 5), and Vial, Muchnik, and Mardones, in their study of urban Chilean mothers (Chapter 6), report a similar pattern of an early shift from exclusive breastfeeding to mixed feeding (e.g., breast and bottle) among working and nonworking women alike, although there is some indication in the Chilean sample that working mothers shifted to exclusive bottle feeding if they could not take the baby to their work place. Another interesting finding from O'Gara's Honduran study is that employed women nurse less frequently, but for longer period than housewives, so that the total time spent nursing by working and nonworking women is virtually the same.

An intervening variable between maternal work and child health and nutrition that was examined in several of the studies in Part II is nonmaternal caregivers. In her study of urban and rural women in Guatemala, Engle (Chapter 8) found that the majority of rural working mothers and slightly more than half of urban working mothers still reported being responsible for child care for the whole day. Overall, working mothers reported receiving surprisingly little help with child care. However, when someone other than the mother did provide child care, Engle found that adult caretaking was positively related to child health and nutritional status, sibling caretaking was negatively related, and the effect on the child of the mother receiving no help with child care was somewhere in between.

In her study of urban and rural working mothers in Panama, Tucker (Chapter 7) examines quality of substitute child care, maternal differentiation (defined in terms of access to and ability to process information), and household differentiation (defined in terms of number of possessions and number of different economic activities) as intervening variables mediating the effect of maternal work on child health and nutrition. Tucker finds some evidence that substitute child care provided by relatives, particularly grandmothers, was associated with better child health and nutrition than child care provided by nonrelatives. In addition, she finds that measures of differentiation are important intervening variables, with maternal differentiation a key determinant of child growth, and household differentiation a key determinant of prevalence of parasitic infections among children.

Paolisso, Baksh, and Thomas, in a study of work patterns among Kenyan rural women with and without infants (Chapter 10), find that women with infants spend significantly less time on agricultural production and self care but similar amounts of time on social and leisure activities than do women without infants. Not surprisingly, the authors find that it is during the peak agricultural season that women's work and child care seem to be most incompatible. However, they also find that households deal with this incompatibility by having female siblings care for the infant in place of the mother. Most interesting is the finding that, in terms of incidence of diarrhea (which in this study measures child welfare), sibling care seems to be equally as effective as maternal care in promoting infant health.

Benefits of Collaboration

The collaboration between those concerned with the survival and healthy development of children and those concerned with the social and economic roles of women has already been fruitful in strengthening research on the relationship between women's work and child welfare. More importantly, it has begun to broaden the perspective of policymakers and program planners in both fields. The benefits of collaboration for those in the women in development field are myriad.

1. First and most importantly, it provides a more complete grasp of women's responsibilities and contributions in developing countries, which is essential for the design of balanced policies and interventions. As a result, it yields a new set of indicators to measure the impact of policy and project interventions on women, which can assess the success of policies and interventions simultaneously in increasing women's effectiveness as economic actors and as child care agents.

2. By identifying the use of alternative child care providers, it demystifies the notion of mothers as the only caretakers and, by assessing the time working women spend in child care, it counteracts the notion of working women as unlikely or unfit mothers. As a result, by challenging the notion of women as mothers only or as workers only, it provides a more accurate basis for understanding women's, as well as families', strategies for survival.

3. Through a focus on child care and promotion of child health and nutrition, it illuminates issues of how resources and benefits are allocated by gender and age, and how resources are transferred within households.

4. It draws attention to the fact that child care needs and/or child welfare can be important determinants of women's work choices.

5. It legitimizes supporting the development of women by strengthening their roles as mothers as well as workers.

For those concerned with the survival and healthy development of children, a main benefit of collaboration is to help them better understand one of their key target groups, mothers of preschool age children. More specifically:

1. It expands the range of strategies to be considered in promoting child health and nutrition to include policies and projects that enhance women's educational opportunities, women's economic opportunities, and women's status.
2. It suggests important additional criteria (e.g., indicators of effects on women) to be included in selecting among health and nutritional interventions, as well as to be used in assessing the impact of such interventions.
3. By focusing attention on women's multiple roles and responsibilities, it provides a more realistic appreciation of the constraints women face in adopting new health practices and in utilizing health services.
4. It suggests the possibility of building a broad base of support for strategies that enhance both women's economic opportunities and child welfare, such as interventions to improve the health and nutritional status of women, work-based or community-based child care, and increased access to family planning.
5. By increasing understanding of the variability in women's work patterns, it allows the design of studies that go beyond a simple categorization of mothers as employed or not employed and is able to clarify links between specific aspects of women's work and the welfare of their children. The results of those studies can then suggest ways by which policies and projects can reduce conflicts and increase compatibility between women's productive and reproductive roles.

References

Birdsall, Nancy.

1980."Measuring Time Use and Nonmarket Exchange." In *Third World Poverty: New Strategies for Measuring Development Progress*, pp. 157-174. Edited by William Paul McGreevey. Lexington, MA: Lexington Books.

1976."Women and Population Studies." *Signs* 1: 699-712.

Cornia, Giovanni Andrea; Jolly, Richard; and Stewart, Francis.

1987.*Adjustment with a Human Face: Protecting the Vulnerable and Promoting Growth*. New York: Oxford University Press.

Cochrane, Susan Hill.

1978.*Fertility and Education: What Do We Really Know?* Baltimore: Johns Hopkins University Press.

DaVanzo, Julie and Lee, Donald Lye Poh.

1983."The Compatibility of Childcare with Market and Nonmarket Activities: Preliminary Evidence from Malaysia." In *Women and Poverty in the Third World*. Edited by Mayra Buvinic´, Margaret A. Lycette and William Paul McGreevey. Baltimore: The Johns Hopkins University Press.

Dixon, Ruth B.

1975.*Women's Rights and Fertility*. Reports on Population/Family Planning, No. 17. New York: Population Council.

Dwyer, Daisy and Bruce, Judith.

1988.*A Home Divided: Women and Income in the Third World*. Stanford, CA: Stanford University Press.

Gibbons, Gayle and Griffiths, Marcia.

1984.*Program Activities for Improving Weaning Practices*. Report prepared for UNICEF. Washington, DC: American Public Health Association.

Gozo, K.M. and Aboagye, A.A..

1985."Impact of the Recession in African Countries: Effects on the Poor." Paper prepared for the International Labor Organization. Processed.

Humphries, Jane.

1988."Women and Work." In *The New Palgrave: A Dictionary of Economics*. Edited by J. Eatwell, M. Milgate, and P. Newman. New York: Stockton Press.

Jelliffe, Derrick B.

1962."Culture, Social Change and Infant Feeding: Current Trends in Tropical Regions." *American Journal of Clinical Nutrition* 10 (January 1962): 19-45.

Leslie, Joanne.

1989."Women's Time: A Factor in the Use of Child Survival Techonologies." *Health Policy and Planning*, vol. 4, no. 1.

Leslie, Joanne; Lycette, Margaret; and Buvinic', Mayra.
1988."Weathering Economic Crises: The Crucial Role of Women in Health." In *Health, Nutrition, and Economic Crises: Aproaches to Policy in the Third World*, pp. 307-348. Edited by David E. Bell and Michael R. Reich. Dover, MA: Auburn House Publishing Company.

Lycette, Margaret and White, Karen.
1988."Acceso de la Mujer al Crédito en América Latina y el Caribe." In *La Mujer en el Sector Informal: Trabajo Femenino y Microempresa en América Latina*. Compiled by Marguerite Berger and Mayra Buvinic'. Quito, Ecuador: ILDIS.

Millman, Sara.
1986."Trends in Breastfeeding in a Dozen Developing Countries." *International Family Planning Perspectives* 12 (September 1986): 91-95.

Monckeberg, Fernando.
1977."Recovery of Severely Malnourished Infants: Effects of Early Senso-effective Stimulation." Paper presented at the International Conference on Behavioral Effects of Energy and Protein Deficits, Washington, DC, December, 1977.

Myers, Robert and Indriso, Cynthia.
1987."Women's Work and Child Care: Supporting the Integration of Women's Productive and Reproductive Roles in Resource-Poor Households in Developing Countries." Paper prepared for the Rockefeller Foundation/IDRC Workshop on Gender, Technology and Development, New York, February 26-27, 1987.

Nerlove, Sara B.
1974."Women's Workload and Infant Feeding Practices: A Relationship with Demographic Implications." *Ethnology* 13: 207-214.

Oppenheimer, Valerie Kincade.
1970.*The Female Labor Force in the United States*. Berkeley: University of California Institute of International Studies.

Piepmeier, K.B. and Adkins, T.S.
1973."The Status of Women and Fertility." *Journal of Biosocial Sciences* 5 (1973): 507-520.

Popkin, Barry M.
1978."Economic Determinants of Breast-feeding Behavior: The Case of Rural Households in Laguna, Philippines." In *Nutrition and Reproduction*, pp. 461-497. Edited by W.H. Mosley, New York: Plenum.

Popkin, Barry M.; Bilsborrow, Richard E.; and Akin, John S.
1982."Breast-feeding Patterns in Low-Income Countries." *Science* 218 (December 10, 1982): 1088-1093.

Savane, Marie-Angelique.
    1985."Femmes, Production et Crise Alimentaire en Afrique en Sud du Sahara." Paper prepared for the International Workshop on Women's Role in Food Self-sufficiency and Food Strategies, Paris, France, January 14-19, 1985.
Schultz, T.W.
    1973."The value of children." *Journal of Political Economy* 92 (2), part 2.
Sivard, Ruth Leger.
    1985.*Women: A World Survey.* Washington, DC: World Priorities.
Standing, Guy.
    1978."Migration, Labour Force Absorption and Morbidity: Women in Kingston, Jamaica." Population and Employment Working Paper No. 68, World Employment Programme.
UNICEF.
    1986.*State of the World's Children 1986.* New York: UNICEF.
Van Esterik, Penny and Greiner, Ted.
    1981."Breastfeeding and Women's Work: Constraints and Opportunities." *Studies in Family Planning* 12 (April 1981): 184-197.
Ware, Helen.
    1975."The Relevance of Changes in Women's Roles to Fertility Behavior: The African Evidence." Paper presented at Annual Meeting of the Population Association of America, Seattle, April 1975. Processed.
Wray, Joe D.
    1978."Maternal Nutrition, Breast-Feeding and Infant Survival." In *Nutrition and Human Reproduction,* pp. 197-229. Edited by W. Henry Mosley. New York: Plenum Press.
World Bank.
    1987.*World Development Report 1987.* Washington, DC: The World Bank.
Youssef, Nadia H.
    1974.*Women and Work in Developing Societies.* Population Monograph Series, No. 15. Berkeley: University of California Institute of International Studies.
Youssef, Nadia and Hetler, Carol B.
    1984."Rural Households Headed by Women: A Priority Concern for Development." Rural Employment Programme Research Working Paper. Geneva: International Labour Organization.

2

Women's Work and Child Nutrition in the Third World*

Joanne Leslie

The dialogue continues to grow between those concerned with promoting enhanced opportunities for women in the Third World and those concerned with child welfare (Leslie, Lycette and Buvinic´ 1988; Myers and Indriso 1987). One outcome of this dialogue is an increasing recognition of two factors: that health and nutrition needs are only a few among many that low income households attempt to meet within the constraints of limited resources; and that women's productive roles may be as important as their reproductive roles in ensuring child welfare. This chapter intends to contribute to the empirical foundations of the dialogue by carefully analyzing research findings on the relationship between women's market work and one important aspect of child welfare, child nutrition.

Although several review papers have already been written on the relationship between women's work and child nutrition (Engle 1980; Nieves 1981; Carloni 1984; Ware 1984; Huffman 1987), most have considered only a small subsample of the available literature. The trends in women's economic roles and in child survival and development described in the preceding chapter, combined with the availability of findings from a number of recent studies (several of which are published in this collec-

*Support for this paper was provided by the Carnegie Coroporation of New York and the Rockefeller Foundation. The assistance of Karen White in the preparation of this paper is also gratefully acknowledged. A version of this paper appeared first as an article in *World Development*, vol. 16, no. 11 (November 1988). *World Development* is published by Pergamon Journals, Ltd. Oxford, United Kingdom.

tion), make it an appropriate time for a thorough, critical review of what is known about the relationship between women's work and child nutrition.

This chapter has two objectives. The first is to provide guidelines for future research by identifying gaps, regional or otherwise, in the literature and by critiquing past studies in terms of methodology and of definition of key variables. The second objective is to disaggregate the existing research relating women's work to child nutrition in order to look for patterns of findings on which to base some preliminary, policy-relevant conclusions.

Review of Empirical Evidence

Empirical evidence concerning the relationship between women's work and child nutrition is available from a reasonably large number of studies. However, only a few such studies were designed specifically to examine women's work as a determinant of infant feeding practices or of child nutritional status. Most studies simply included women's employment status as one of several socioeconomic variables examined. The analysis in this chapter is based on twenty-eight studies from twenty countries, which examined the relationship between women's work and infant feeding practices (see Table 2.1), and twenty-five studies (three of which are also included in Table 2.1) from sixteen countries, which examined the relationship between women's work and child nutritional status, usually defined in terms of anthropometric growth measures (see Table 2.2).

One might expect that the number of studies and the range of countries covered would have led to a reasonable sense of confidence in drawing conclusions about a positive or negative relationship between women's work and child nutrition. In fact, no consistent pattern of a negative or a positive relationship was apparent, either between women's work and infant feeding practices or between women's work and child nutritional status. As Tables 2.3 and 2.4 show, in many cases no significant relationship, either positive or negative, was found between women's work and child nutrition.

An earlier review by the author and others of studies concerning the relationship between women's education and child health and nutrition provides an interesting contrast (Cochrane, Leslie and O'Hara 1982). As Figure 2.1 shows, the relationship between women's education and child nutritional status is complex, and not all of the hypothesized links are positive. Nonetheless, virtually all empirical studies have found a significant positive relationship, not only between maternal education and child nutrition, but also between maternal education and other measures of child welfare (Caldwell 1979; Cochrane, Leslie and O'Hara 1982; Ware 1984). As a result, a consensus has emerged that investment in education for girls is one important way to improve child survival and development in the Third World (see UNICEF 1985; Mahler 1986; World Bank 1988).

However, as the following discussion of the studies summarized in Tables 2.1 and 2.2 shows, the relationship between maternal work and child nutrition seems to be more complex, or at least less consistent, than the relationship between maternal education and child nutrition. It therefore does not lead to straightforward policy recommendations. The failure to find as consistent a relationship between women's work and child nutrition as has been found between women's education and child nutrition should, perhaps, come as no surprise. A woman's work status, unlike her educational status, is not fixed, but can and usually does vary over time. Furthermore, women's work status and child nutrition are both likely to be closely related to household income or wealth, making it difficult to establish the existence of a direct causal relationship between the two. A final complication is that both directions of causality are possible — a child's nutritional status may influence the mother's decision to work, as well as a mother's work affecting the nutritional status of her child (Carloni 1984).

Women's Work and Infant Feeding Practices

The findings from the first thirteen of the twenty-five studies summarized in Table 2.1 are of somewhat limited value due to serious methodological weaknesses in the study design and/or the data analysis. The majority of these studies were based on samples that were not chosen randomly; in addition, the only analysis of the data done in most cases was simple bivariate cross tabulations, often without any statistical test of significant differences being reported. The validity of many of the findings is even more limited due to the small sample size. Interestingly, however, the pattern of findings from these thirteen studies does not differ significantly from the pattern of findings from the more methodologically sophisticated studies. The thirteen bivariate studies show no consistent pattern of a negative or positive relationship between women's work and infant feeding practices. Four studies found no significant relationship between women's work status and infant feeding practices; four found less exclusive breastfeeding among employed than not employed mothers; another five, which looked only at employed women, found some significant variation in infant feeding among women in different occupational groups.

The results of the remaining fifteen studies (many of which are based on data from Asia) warrant more careful consideration because their design and data analysis were somewhat stronger. All had sample sizes over two hundred; many over one thousand. All but one had randomly chosen samples [Soekirman (1983) identified all women who met certain criteria (e.g., age of infant, length of employment) in a sample of factory workers and selected a comparable group of unemployed women]. In addition, all but one used multivariate analysis techniques (either exclusively or to supplement bivariate analyses) in order to control for other confounding factors in assessing the effect of maternal employment on infant feeding practices. The only exception was Knodel and Debavalya (1980), who used Multiple Classification Analysis in their study from Thailand to control for the effect of what they felt to be the most important confounding factors — region and education.

While the overall study design and data analysis were better in these fifteen studies, problems remain in interpreting their findings. It is particularly difficult to compare findings across studies, due to imprecision and inconsistency in defining both the main independent variable, women's work, and the dependent variable, infant feeding practices. As far as women's work is concerned, most studies simply categorized women as employed or not employed, although a few subdivided women as employed by such work-related factors as location of employment, occupation, or wage rate. Unfortunately, among women categorized as not employed, no study made a distinction between women who were unemployed due to their inability to find a job, and women who chose to be out of the wage labor force to take care of their children. An additional complication in interpreting results is that several studies grouped women working at home with nonworking women (Akin et al. 1985; Soekirman 1983; Winikoff et al. 1986a), apparently presuming that mother/child proximity was the main factor affecting infant feeding decisions rather than opportunity costs of women's time. In Knodel and Debavalya's study from Thailand (1980), women who engaged in market work but were not paid (i.e., worked on the family farm or for a family business) were considered as a separate group. In the other studies, however, it is not clear whether such non-wage-earning working women were categorized as employed or not employed.

Given that the two major effects of women's work on child nutrition are hypothesized to be the positive income effect and the negative time effect (see Figure 2.1), it is surprising that only two studies looked for differential effects of work on infant feeding practices by mother's wage rate (Popkin 1978; Butz, Habicht and DaVanzo 1981). Further, only one looked for differential effects by the number of hours per week the mother worked (Winikoff et al. 1986c).

As far as measures of infant feeding practices are concerned, seven of the studies simply compared breastfeeding to not breastfeeding, without distinguishing between exclusive breastfeeding and mixed (bottle and breast) feeding. However, given the reported duration of breastfeeding and the age ranges of the children, it seems likely that in most of the studies "breastfeeding" included both exclusive and mixed feeding. [Presumably because the average age of infants in his sample was only three months, Soekirman (1983) grouped the mixed and the exclusively bottlefed together, and compared them with exclusively breastfed infants.] The four studies by Winikoff and others primarily looked at duration of breastfeeding, but also specified age at which bottlefeeding was initiated. In O'Gara's study from Honduras, she used three infant feeding categories: breastfeeding, mixed feeding, and bottlefeeding (see Chapter 5). The most satisfying approach was by Akin et al. (1985) and by Vial, Muchnik and Mardones (see Chapter 6). In their studies, infants were not classified in just one infant feeding category, but rather were coded "yes" or "no" for each of three feeding variables: breastmilk, breastmilk substitutes, and supplementary food.

Whatever infant feeding measures were used, most of the studies categorized infants by type of feeding without disaggregating by age of infant. Mothers of older infants are both more likely to work and less likely to breastfeed. In addition, the nutritional significance of <u>exclusive</u> breastfeeding during the first three months of life (when it is a desirable practice) is quite different from its significance after the infant is six months old (when it is undesirable). For both of these reasons, the failure to disaggregate by age of infant may bias the results of some studies, and certainly makes all of them more difficult to interpret.

In spite of these ambiguities in the definition of the key variables, and data analysis weaknesses in a few of the studies, these fifteen studies make a significant contribution to our understanding of the relationship between women's work and infant feeding choices. While the findings are not completely consistent, certain patterns begin to emerge. In most studies, prevalence of breastfeeding is not found to differ significantly between employed and non-employed mothers. The most consistent effect of maternal employment on infant feeding practices is to cause mothers to shift earlier from exclusive breastfeeding to mixed feeding (Akin et al. 1985; O'Gara [Chapter 5]; Soekirman 1983; Vial, Muchnik and Mardones [Chapter 6]; Winikoff et al. 1986b and 1986c). There was also some evidence of earlier termination of breastfeeding among working women, although O'Gara in Honduras found that working women reported either significantly shorter or significantly longer durations of breastfeeding than nonworking women.

Four studies found location of work to be an important factor. Winikoff and her colleagues in Thailand (Winikoff et al. 1986b) and in Indonesia (Winikoff et al. 1986c) found a shorter duration of breastfeeding among women employed away from home than among those who worked at home or those who were not employed. However, Akin and his colleagues in Sri Lanka (Akin et al. 1981) and in Yemen (Akin et al. 1986) found that women who worked at home breastfed longer than either women who did not work or women who worked away from home. Data from the World Fertility Survey on socioeconomic differentials in breastfeeding also show a longer duration of breastfeeding for self-employed women than women who do not work in most countries, although women in other occupations show a shorter duration (Balkaran and Smith 1984). Of particular interest is one of O'Gara's findings from Honduras; she found that mothers who worked at home tended to view breastfeeding as a burden that took time needed for other tasks, while many mothers who worked away from home felt that time spent breastfeeding was a time to relax and recover from work.

The two studies that examined the relationship between wage rates and breastfeeding also report contradictory results; Butz et al. (1981) find a higher probability of breastfeeding among women with lower wage rates, while Popkin (1978) finds longer duration of breastfeeding among women with a higher wage rate. As far as type of occupation is concerned, two studies find that women farmers are more likely to breastfeed than either nonworking women or women working in other occupations (Butz et al. 1981; Knodel and Debavalya 1980).

Overall, Table 2.1 gives the strong impression that the simple fact of whether or not women are in the labor force is not a key determinant of infant feeding practices. In fact, most studies found remarkable similar patterns of infant feeding between employed and nonemployed women suggesting that local and temporal norms may be the main factor affecting infant feeding decisions of all women, regardless of employment status. Where employment is found to be a significant factor, its effect depends, among other things, on both the type and location of women's work. The single finding that seems widespread enough to warrant a generalization is that women who work while breastfeeding are likely to start mixed feeding earlier than women who are not working.

Women's Work and Child Nutritional Status

As with the studies discussed above concerning the relationship between women's work and infant feeding practices, nine of the twenty-five studies summarized in Table 2.2 concerning the relationship between women's work and child nutritional status are somewhat weak methodologically and of limited value. The poorest of these studies include five that were based on relatively small, nonrandomly selected samples. In each of these five, only simple bivariate analyses were done; in the case of the two studies from India (Grewal, Gopaldas and Gadre 1973; Shah, Walimbe and Dhole 1979), no statistical tests of significant differences were reported. Slightly stronger are Ballweg's 1972 study from Haiti, Haggerty's

1981 study from Haiti, Bittencourt and DiCicco's 1979 study from Brazil, and Wray and Aguirre's 1969 study from Colombia. All four had randomly selected samples, and the Brazil and Colombia studies had quite adequate sample sizes — 488 mother/child pairs in Brazil and 354 families with 721 children in Colombia. However, the only analyses were cross tabulations of mother's work status with child nutritional status, and in the case of the Ballweg study, no statistical test of significant differences was reported.

Similar to the bivariate studies examined in Table 2.1, these nine studies in Table 2.2 of the relationship between women's work and child nutritional status show a mixed pattern of findings. Most report some evidence of a negative relationship between mother's employment and child diet or growth. However, Haggerty's 1981 study from Haiti (one of the few of any of the studies reviewed that disaggregated by age of child) found children of mothers who were not employed to have somewhat better growth during the first year, but poorer growth during the second year. In addition, both Ballweg (1972) in rural Haiti, and Tripp (1981) in Ghana found that mothers who engaged in trading had children with better nutritional status than children of mothers who were farmers.

Because they are methodologically stronger, the findings from the remaining sixteen studies summarized in Table 2.2 can be used with greater confidence in drawing some tentative conclusions concerning the relationship between women's labor force participation and child nutritional status. Most of the analyses were based on adequately sized and appropriately selected samples, although several used purposive rather than random samples, and Kumar's 1977 study from India (which has many compensatory strengths) was based on only forty-eight households.

By making an effort to use an appropriate statistical technique to control for confounding variables, all of the researchers indicated recognition of the problem that mother's work status was likely to be correlated with other factors that might relate significantly to child nutritional status. All but one of the studies used multiple regression analysis to control statistically for other factors in the relationship between women's work and child nutritional status. Marchione's 1980 study from Jamaica used factor analysis to group variables that were highly correlated; the relationship between these "factors" and child nutritional status was then examined. Popkin and Solon's 1976 study from the Philippines used multiple regression analysis to control for the effect of confounding variables on the relationship between maternal employment and children's dietary intake. However, they used only a simple bivariate analysis (with no statistical tests) to examine the differences in prevalence of xerophthalmia by maternal work status and household income.

Although there is some imprecision and considerable variability in the definitions of the key variables — women's employment status and child nutritional status — overall these sixteen methodologically stronger studies present fewer definitional problems than the earlier studies relating women's work to infant feeding practices. All but one measure child nutritional status using accepted anthropometric or dietary measures related to recognized international standards. The only exception is Bailey's 1981 study from Jamaica, which uses aggregated data to report differences in rates of hospital admission for severe malnutrition (kwashiorkor, marasmus, and marasmic-kwashiorkor) across nine urban constituencies.

There is considerably more variation in the way women's employment status is defined. Five of the studies (Bailey 1981; Marchione 1980; Popkin and Solon 1976; Powell and Grantham-McGregor 1985; Zeitlin et al. 1978) simply categorized women as employed or not employed. Most of the others categorized women as employed or not employed and also examined the effect of one or more work-related variables on child nutritional status. The most frequently examined work-related variable was some measure of the proportion of time spent working. Adelman (1983) in Peru and Franklin (1979) in Colombia categorized women as working part-time or full-time. Popkin (1983) in the Philippines and Soekirman (1983, 1985) in Indonesia categorized women as working more or less than forty hours a week. Kumar (1977) in India categorized women as working more or less than 250 hours per year; Greiner and Latham (1981) in St. Vincent also categorized women by whether or not they worked year-round.

Another frequently examined work-related variable was whether women worked at or near home or away from home (Popkin 1980, 1983; Smith et al. 1983; Tucker [Chapter 7]; Vial, Muchnik and Mardones [Chapter 6]). In addition, both Soekirman (1983, 1985) in Indonesia and Vial, Muchnik and Mardones [Chapter 6] in Chile used a measure of distance to work. Only four studies — Adelman (1983); Engle, Pederson and Smidt (1986) and Engle [Chapter 8]; Kumar (1977); and Wolfe and Behrman (1982) — subcategorized working women by type of occupation.

Relatively few studies looked either at the effect of maternal income or the quality or type of the substitute child care, which are two key variables frequently hypothesized to be work-related. Only four studies (Kumar 1977; Soekirman 1983, 1985; Tucker [Chapter 7]; and Wolfe and Behrman 1982) analyzed child nutritional status in terms of mother's wage rate or income. And only three studies — (Engle, Pederson and Smidt 1986 and Engle [Chapter 8]; Tucker [Chapter 7]; Vial, Muchnik and Mardones [Chapter 6]) — looked at the effect of person or place providing child care.

The multitude of variables included in these sixteen studies, particularly relating to women's employment, provides a richness that is lacking in most of the studies relating women's work to infant feeding practices. At the same time, however, the multiple variables make it more difficult to discern clear patterns. The one study that found a simple negative relationship between mother's work and child nutritional status was Powell and Grantham-McGregor's 1985 study of 229 low-income urban households in Kingston, Jamaica. However, their finding of a negative relationship is somewhat contradicted by the findings of the three other studies from the West Indies. Marchione's 1980 study from Western Jamaica found no direct correlation between maternal employment and child nutritional status although his family cohesion factor, which included father's presence, mother's presence, father's support, mother's age and mother's employment loaded negatively, was found to be the most significant determinant of better child nutritional status. Data from St. Vincent (Greiner and Latham 1981) showed no significant relationship between maternal employment and child nutritional status, although it should be noted that only 38 percent (76/200) of mothers were employed and only 9 percent (18/200) reported having full-time, year-round jobs. Finally, in her study of hospital admissions for malnutrition in Kingston, Bailey (1981) reported a significant relationship between maternal *unemployment* and child malnutrition, just the opposite of Powell and Grantham-McGregor's finding.

A study perhaps most frequently cited as showing a negative effect of maternal employment on child nutritional status is the 1976 study by Popkin and Solon in two rural and two urban locations in Cebu Island, Philippines. Using multiple regression analysis on nutrient intake of 130 children, they found first that the independent effect of mothers' work on food expenditures was positive; that is, that mothers' wages increased weekly food expenditures by one to five percent. However, they also found that the children of working mothers had a significant decrease in vitamin A intake, although this was only true in the rural barrios. The reported decrease in vitamin A intake, furthermore, was only marginally significant. Among households in the two lower-income quartiles, they found more children with xerophthalmia when mothers were employed than when they were not; however, a lower proportion of children with xerophthalmia was found among working mothers in the upper two income quartiles. Contrary to the standard interpretation (but consistent with the authors' own conclusions), the results from Popkin and Solon (1976) do not show a clear negative effect of mothers' market work on the nutritional status of children, as measured either by dietary intake or prevalence of xerophthalmia.

Popkin's follow-up to the Cebu study, an analysis of data from 573 households from 34 rural barrios in Laguna (a province of the Philippines) demonstrates clearly both the complexity of the relationship between women's work and child nutritional status and the fact that somewhat different conclusions can be drawn from the same data depending on the analytic approach used. In a 1980 paper focusing on intrahousehold issues, Popkin reported that mother's labor force participation (1) had no significant effect on children's intake of energy and protein, (2) significantly reduced mothers' child care time (although total child care time was not reduced) as well as mothers' leisure time, and (3) had a significant negative effect on the weight-for-age and height-for-age of younger (0- to 35-month) children, although the results were not statistically significant for older preschool children. In a later analysis of the same data, Popkin (1983) chose to bypass the intrahousehold issues by using average child care time, dietary intake, and anthropometric status for all preschool children in a household as the dependent variables. In addition, the 1983 analysis emphasized an instrumental variables approach, which focused on the estimated effect of maternal labor force participation on child nutritional status through predicted child care time and dietary intake and avoided a direct estimation of the effect of mother's labor force participation on child nutritional status. Using a different definition of the dependent variables and a more rigorous analytic approach, the 1983 paper reported that the negative effect of mother's labor force participation on time she spent on child care was small and not statistically significant. Labor force participation primarily had a large and significant negative effect on her leisure time, as well as a significant positive effect on child- care time by siblings. In terms of children's dietary intake, the 1983 analysis found that mother's labor force participation had a significant positive effect on energy intake (an average increase of 145 kilocalories per day) and a positive but not significant effect on protein intake. When the combined effects of mother's labor force participation, working through changes in child care time and changes in dietary intake, on nutritional status were estimated, it was concluded that mother's labor force participation had no significant effect on child nutritional status.

Findings concerning differences in nutritional status of children of women who work part-time and women who work full-time are contradictory. Adelman (1983) in Peru found that, at the same level of income (and controlling for genetic factors), mothers who did not work or worked only part-time had taller children than those who worked full-time. A similar inference about possible positive effects of part-time versus full-time work might be drawn from Wolfe and Behrman's 1982 study from Nicaragua, where better nutritional status (by at least some anthropometric measures) was found among children whose mothers worked in the informal sector than among children whose mothers had formal-sector or domestic jobs. However, the opposite finding is reported by Franklin (1979) from Colombia. Franklin found a negative association of child nutritional status with part-time but not with full-time maternal employment. [This is similar to the finding from the Wray and Aguirre (1969) study from Colombia.] Franklin suggests that the negative effect of substitute child care may predominate in households where mothers work part-time, whereas the positive income effect may predominate in households where mothers work full-time. Unfortunately, Franklin had no direct income or child care data to test this hypothesis.

Soekirman (1983, 1985) looked directly at the income/time tradeoff in his study from Indonesia. He found that the negative effect of mother's employment on child nutritional status was only significant if mothers worked more than forty hours and earned less than the minimum wage; if mothers worked more than forty hours but were better paid, there was no significant effect. Several other studies also provided some direct evidence of the effect of maternal income on child nutritional status. Kumar (1977) reported from Kerala State in India that income from mother's work had a net positive effect on child nutritional status, and that increments in wage income were translated into improved nutrition more readily among wage-earning than non-wage-earning women. Tucker [Chapter 7] from Panama also reported a positive relationship between maternal income and child diet, as well as a positive relationship between maternal income activity at home and anthropometric measures of child nutritional status. However, Wolfe and Behrman (1982) found no significant effect of mother's predicted income on child nutritional status. Their finding may result in part from the fact that they assigned an imputed wage to non-wage-earning women and therefore were not examining the relationship between actual earned income and child nutritional status.

A final pattern that emerges from these studies is the possible importance of maternal presence at home during the first year of life and the effect of the quality of substitute child care on child nutritional status. Similar to the Haggerty (1981) study cited earlier, Engle's study from Guatemala (see Chapter 8 and also Engle, Pederson and Smidt 1986) found that maternal employment had a negative effect on nutritional status for infants and a positive effect for children during the second year of life. Engle and colleagues also found that children had better nutritional status if they were cared for by an adult care giver when the mother was working (as did Shah, Walimbe and Dhole 1979, and Bittencourt and DiCicco 1979). Vial, Muchnik and Mardones [Chapter 6] found no significant effect on weight gain of the child from being in a day care center or not; however, a very small fraction of the mothers used formal day care.

Discussion

The above review of empirical literature on the relationship between women's work and child nutrition was undertaken in part to determine what is already known with reasonable certainty that could be useful to policymakers, and in part to provide directions for future research. This section will present conclusions on each of these issues.

Implications for Policy

The central conclusion of this chapter can be stated as follows: a careful review of empirical research to date does not suggest that maternal employment should be expected to have a negative effect on child nutrition, measured either in terms of infant feeding practices or nutritional status. Therefore, policies that have the effect of limiting employment opportunities for women in developing countries (whether intentionally or unintentionally) cannot be justified on the grounds that child welfare will be enhanced by mothers remaining out of the paid labor force.

As Table 2.3 shows, few studies found a significant relationship between women's work status and extent of breastfeeding. Survey data, supported by ethnographic information where available, suggest strongly that the majority of working women want to breastfeed their infants, and in most cases, they succeed in doing so, at least during the critical first six to nine months. However, regardless of location or type of work, working mothers appear to introduce breastmilk substitutes relatively early, and in most but not all cases, earlier than nonworking mothers.

The studies that looked at the relationship between women's work and child nutritional status found more evidence of a significant association, and more cause for concern about a possible negative effect of women's work than did the studies that looked at women's work and infant feeding practices (see Table 2.4). A number of studies that compared the nutritional status of children of employed and non-employed mothers found a negative association between maternal employment and child nutritional status. However, none demonstrated a causal relationship. Most researchers apparently assumed that mother's work was the determinant and child nutritional status was the outcome, without examining the alternative explanation that concern about their child's nutritional status might have caused mothers to seek work.

Not only are the studies that found a negative association between maternal employment and child nutritional status open to more than one interpretation, there are also a number of studies that found a positive association between women's work and child nutrition. Several studies found better nutrient intake among children whose mothers worked, particularly among children of higher-income working mothers. In some cases, better nutrient intake was reflected in better child growth, although the effects were not consistent and not usually large. Two particularly interesting studies disaggregated results by age of child. Both found evidence of a negative association between maternal work and child nutritional status for infants and a positive association for weaning-age children.

The findings concerning most of the specific work-related variables such as location, amount of time worked or type of occupation, are quite inconsistent and do not lead to any easy generalizations. However, one factor that does emerge as possibly being important is age of substitute child caretaker. Few of the studies explicitly considered this issue, but those that did consistently found that children who were cared for by an adult when their mothers were working had better nutritional status than children cared for by another child.

Given widely differing patterns of female labor force participation, and of child care and feeding practices throughout the developing world, most policy recommendations concerning women's work and child nutrition will need to be based on country-specific research. However, while awaiting the results of these new studies, the following recommendations based on the empirical literature reviewed in this chapter, may contribute to the development of policies and programs to meet the needs of both mothers and children:

1. Health and nutrition communication/education activities should continue to encourage breastfeeding among working mothers, particularly emphasizing the need for frequent nursing during non-work hours to maintain milk production. At the same time, information on appropriate ingredients for and preparation of breastmilk substitutes also needs to be made widely available.

2. To the extent possible, efforts should be made to allow mothers to stay in close contact with or to closely supervise the care of their infants during the first year after birth, while also maintaining their ability to earn income. Possible strategies to achieve this would include paid maternity leave or cooperative maternity insurance for women in formal-sector jobs, and improved marketing of home based production or reciprocal exchange of child care for women in informal-sector jobs.

3. Efforts to raise women's incomes are of central importance to ensure that mothers will be able to obtain the nutritionally high quality foods necessary to prepare appropriate breastmilk substitutes and weaning foods. Equally important, higher incomes are necessary to ensure that women consume an adequate quantity and quality of food to meet

their own high energy and protein needs, particularly when they are experiencing the combined stresses of lactation and strenuous or long work hours.

Guidelines for Research

Given the lack of consistent findings from the research reviewed in this chapter, and the fact that few of the studies were specifically designed to investigate the relationship between women's work and child nutrition, it is clear that more and better research is needed. Perhaps the most important lesson for future research that emerges from this review is the importance of carefully defining and measuring the key variables.

Future research should pay particular attention to how women's work is measured. In most cases, a simple subdivision of women into the categories of employed and not employed will not be appropriate. Care should be taken to avoid using too exclusive a definition of work (for example, only women working for wages or only women in formal-sector jobs) and at the same time to avoid grouping together subsistence farmers, women who work at home, women with intermittent informal-sector work and women with regular formal-sector jobs.

In many cases, nonworking women will also need to be disaggregated, or at least their socioeconomic status vis à vis working women in the sample will need to be stated. Since it is quite likely that in some settings nonworking women will be better off than working women (usually due to the income of a partner or spouse), and that in other settings working women will be better-off, this point will need to be clarified in order for results to be interpreted meaningfully.

The two key links between women's work and child nutrition are usually hypothesized to be the time and income effects. Since not only are income and time hypothesized to work in opposite directions, but there is also some evidence that they interact (see Adelman 1983; Soekirman 1983, 1985), future research should look at how mother's work affects child nutrition through income and time. Another issue that should be carefully considered in any study of the relationship of women's work to child nutrition is the availability and quality of substitute child care.

It is clear that the range of findings in the research to date on the relationship between women's work and child nutrition reflect not only methodological and definitional weaknesses, but also the complexity of the relationship. Therefore, future research should not attempt to arrive at a simplistic conclusion that women's work has a positive or negative effect on child nutrition. Rather, it should aim, on the one hand, to identify linkages through which women's work affects infant feeding practices and child nutritional status and, on the other hand, to highlight factors that may mediate the relationship, such as access to and quality of substitute child care, prices of food (particularly food targeted to infants and weaning-age children) or nutrition and health knowledge.

References

Adelman, Carol.
1983."An Analysis of the Effect of Maternal Care and Other Factors Affecting the Growth of Poor Children in Lima, Peru." D.Sc. Thesis, Johns Hopkins University, School of Hygiene and Public Health.

Akin, John S.; Bilsborrow, Richard; Guilkey, David K.; and Popkin, Barry M.
1986."Breastfeeding Patterns and Determinants in the Near East: An Analysis for Four Countries." *Population Studies*, vol. 40, no. 2, pp. 247-262.

Akin, John S.; Griffin, Charles C.; Guilkey, David K.; and Popkin, Barry M.
1985."Determinants of Infant Feeding: A Household Production Approach." *Economic Development and Cultural Change*, vol. 34, no. 1, pp. 57-81.

Akin, John S.; Bilsborrow, Richard; Guilkey, David K.; Popkin, Barry M.; Benoit, Daniel; Cantrelle, Pierre; Garenne, Michele; and Levi, Pierre.
1981."The Determinants of Breastfeeding in Sri Lanka." *Demography* 18: 287-307.

Bailey, Wilma.
1981."Clinical Undernutrition in the Kingston/ St. Andrew Metropolitan Area: 1967-1976." *Social Science and Medicine* 15: 471-477.

Balkaran, Sudat and Smith, David P.
1984."Socio-economic Differentials in Breastfeeding." *WFS Comparative Studies (Cross National Summaries: Additional Tables*. Processed.

Ballweg, John A.
1972."Family Characteristics and Nutrition Problems of Pre-school Children in Fond Parisien, Haiti." *Environmental Child Health* 18: 230-243.

Bamisaiye, A. and Oyediran, M.A.
1983. "Breastfeeding Among Female Employees at a Major Health Institution in Lagos, Nigeria, "*Social Science and Medicine* 17 (1983): 1867-1871.

Bittencourt, Sonia and DiCicco, Emily.
1979."Child Care Needs of Low Income Women: Urban Brazil." Washington, DC: Overseas Education Fund of the League of Women Voters.

Brazil, Ministry of Education and Culture.
1980 "Breastfeeding." Sao Paulo: Ministry of Education and Culture. Processed.

Butz, William P.; Habicht, Jean-Pierre; and DaVanzo, Julie.
1981."Improving Infant Nutrition, Health, and Survival: Policy and Program Implications from the Malaysian Family Life Survey." Report prepared for the U.S. Agency for International Development. Santa Monica, California: The Rand Corporation.

Caldwell, J.C.
1979."Education as a Factor in Mortality Decline: An Examination of Nigerian Data." Paper prepared for the Meeting on Socioeconomic Determinants and Consequences of Mortality, Mexico City, June 19-25, 1979.

Carloni, Alice Stewart.
1984."The Impact of Maternal Employment and Income on the Nutritional Status of Children in Rural Areas of Developing Countries: What is Known, What is not Known and Where the Gaps Are." Report prepared for U.N. FAO, Administrative Committee on Coordination, Subcommittee on Nutrition. Processed.

Chen, S.T.
1978. "Infant Feeding Practices in Malaysia," *Medical Journal of Malaysia* 33 (December 1978): 120-123.

Cochrane, Susan; Leslie, Joanne; and O'Hara, Donald J.
1982."Parental Education and Child Health: Intracountry Evidence." *Health Policy and Education* 2: 213-250.

Di Domenico, Catherine M. and Asuni, Judith Burdin.
1979. "Breastfeeding Practices among Urban Women in Ibadan, Nigeria." In *Breastfeeding and Food Policy in a Hungry World*, pp. 51-57. Edited by Dana Raphael. New York: Academic Press.

Durongdej, Somchai; Kawsiri, Duangporn; and Chularojanamontri, Vichai.
1982. "Infant Feeding Study: I. Current Trend of Breast Feeding among Primaparae in Urban Bangkok and Factors Related," *Journal of Tropical Pediatrics* 28 (October 1982): 262-265

Engle, Patricia.
1980."The Intersecting Needs of Working Women and Their Young Children: A Report to the Ford Foundation." Report prepared for the Ford Foundation. Processed.

Engle, Patricia L.; Pederson, Mary; and Smidt, Robert K.
1986."The Effects of Maternal Work for Earnings on Children's Nutritional Status and School Enrollment in Rural and Urban Guatemala." Final Project Report to USAID/PPC.

Franklin, David L.
1979."Malnutrition and Poverty: the Role of Mother's Time and Abilities." Paper prepared for the Research Triangle Institute, Economics Department. Processed.

Greiner, Ted and Latham, Michael C.
    1981."Factors Associated with Nutritional Status among Young Children in St. Vincent." *Ecology of Food and Nutrition* 10: 135-141.
Grewal, Tina; Gopaldas, Tara; and Gadre, V.J.
    1973."Etiology of Malnutrition in Rural Indian Preschool Children (Madhya Pradesh)." *Environmental Child Health* 19: 265-270.
Haggerty, Patricia Ann.
    1981."Women's Work and Child Nutrition in Haiti." M.A. Thesis, Massachusetts Institute of Technology.
Huffman, Sandra L.
    1987."Women's Activities and Impacts on Child Nutrition." In *Food Policy: Integrating Supply, Distribution, and Consumption,* pp. 371-384. Edited by J. Price Gittinger, Joanne Leslie and Caroline Hoisington. Baltimore: Johns Hopkins University Press.
Ignacio, Ma; Socorro, E.; Ona, Lucia N.; and Azares, Flora A.
    1980. "Factors Related to Mother's Choice of Infant Feeding Method," *Philippine Journal of Nutrition* 33 (1980): 209-213.
Jain, Anrudh K. and Bongaarts, John.
    1981. "Breastfeeding: Patterns, Correlates, and Fertility Effects," *Studies in Family Planning* 12 (March 1981): 79-99.
Knodel, John and Debavalya, Nibhon.
    1980."Breastfeeding in Thailand: Trends and Differentials, 1969-1979." *Studies in Family Planning* 11: 355-377.
Kumar, Shubh K.
    1977."Role of the Household Economy in Determining Child Nutrition at Low Income Levels: A Case Study in Kerala." Occasional Paper no. 95. Ithaca, New York: Cornell University, Department of Agricultural Economics.
Leslie, Joanne; Lycette, Margaret; and Buvinic´, Mayra.
    1988."Weathering Economic Crises: The Crucial Role of Women in Health." In *Health, Nutrition, and Economic Crises: Approaches to Policy in the Third World,* pp. 307-348. Edited by David E. Bell and Michael R. Reich. Dover, Mass: Auburn House Publishing Company.
Lillig, Kimberly K. and Lackey, Carolyn J.
    1982. "Economic and Social Factors Influencing Women's Infant Feeding Decisions in a Rural Mexican Community," *Journal of Tropical Pediatrics* 28 (1982): 240-247
Mahler, Halfdan.
    1986."Of Mud and Alligators." *Health Policy and Planning* 1: 345-352.
Manderson, Lenore.
    1984. "These are Modern Times: Infant Feeding Practices in Peninsular Malaysia," *Social Science Medicine* 18 (1984): 47-57.

Marchione, Thomas J.
1980."Factors Associated with Malnutrition in the Children of Western Jamaica." In *Nutritional Anthropology: Contemporary Approaches to Diet and Culture*, pp. 223-273. Edited by Norge W. Jerome, Randy F. Kandel and Gretel H. Pelto. Pleasantville, New York: Redgrave Publishing Co.

Marshall, Leslie B.
1984. "Wage Employment and Infant Feeding: A Papua New Guinea Case," *Ecology of Food and Nutrition* 15 (1984): 179-190.

Marshall, Leslie B. and Marshall, Mac.
1979. "Breasts, Bottles and Babies: Historical Changes in Infant Feeding Practices in a Micronesian Village," *Ecology of Food and Nutrition* 8 (December 1979) : 241-249.

Moreno-Black, Geraldine.
1983. Dietary Status and Dietary Diversity of Native Highland Bolivian Children," *Ecology of Food and Nutrition* 13 (1983): 149-156

Myers, Robert and Indriso, Cynthia.
1987."Women's Work and Child Care: Supporting the Integration of Women's Productive and Reproductive Roles in Resource-Poor Households in Developing Countries." Paper prepared for the Rockefeller Foundation/IDRC Workshop on Gender, Technology, and Development, New York, February 26-27, 1987.

Nieves, Isabel.
1981."A Balancing Act: Strategies to Cope with Work and Motherhood in Developing Countries." Paper prepared for the ICRW Roundtable on the Interface between Poor Women's Nurturing Roles and Productive Responsibilities, Washington, DC, December 10, 1981.

Pathmanathan, I.
1978. "Breast Feeding — A Study of 8750 Malaysian Infants," *Medical Journal of Malaysia* 33 (December 1978): 113-119.

Popkin, Barry M.
1983."Rural Women, Work and Child Welfare in the Philippines." In *Women and Poverty in the Third World*, pp. 157-176. Edited by Mayra Buvinic, Margaret Lycette and William Paul McGreevey. Baltimore: Johns Hopkins University Press.

1980."Time Allocation of the Mother and Child Nutrition." *Ecology of Food and Nutrition* 9: 1-14.

1978."Economic Determinants of Breast-feeding Behavior: The Case of Rural Households in Laguna, Philippines." In *Nutrition and Human Reproduction*, pp. 461-497. Edited by W. Henry Mosely. New York: Plenum Press.

Popkin, Barry M. and Solon, Florentino S.
1976."Income, Time, the Working Mother and Child Nutriture." *Environmental Child Health*, 156-166.
Powell, Christine A. and Grantham-McGregor, Sally.
1985."The Ecology of Nutritional Status and Development in Young Children in Kingston, Jamaica." *American Journal of Clinical Nutrition* 41: 1322-1331.
Rawson, Ian G. and Valverde, Victor.
1976. "The Etiology of Malnutrition among Preschool Children in Rural Costa Rica," *Environmental Child Health* (February 1976): 12-17.
Shah, P.M.; Walimbe, S.R.; and Dhole, V.S.
1979."Wage-Earning Mothers, Mother-Substitutes and Care of the Young Children in Rural Maharashtra." *Indian Pediatrics* 16: 167-173.
Smith, Meredith F.; Paulsen, Steven K.; Fougere, William; and Ritchey, S.J.
1983."Socioeconomic, Education and Health Factors Influencing Growth of Rural Haitian Children." *Ecology of Food and Nutrition* 13: 99-108.
Soekirman.
1985."Women's Work and its Effect on Infants' Nutritional Status in Central Java, Indonesia." Paper presented at the 13th International Congress of Nutrition, Brighton, England, August 18-23, 1985.
1983."The Effect of Maternal Employment on Nutritional Status of Infants from Low-income Households in Central Java." Ph.D Thesis, Cornell University.
Tripp, Robert B.
1981."Farmers and Traders: Some Economic Determinants of Nutritional Status in Northern Ghana." *Journal of Tropical Pediatrics* 27: 15-22.
UNICEF.
1985.*State of the World's Children 1985*. New York: UNICEF.
Ware, Helen.
1984."Effects of Maternal Education, Women's Roles and Child Care on Child Mortality." In *Child Survival: Strategies for Research*, pp. 191-214 Edited by W. Henry Mosley and Lincoln C. Chen. New York: The Population Council.
Winikoff, B.; Latham, M.C.; Solimono, G.; Elliott, T.; Cerf, B.; Laukaran, V.H.; Van Esterik, P.; Post, J.E.; Smith, R.A.; Lee, L.W.; Agunda, K.O.; Kekovole, J.; Kigondu, J.; Scotney, N.; Kogi, W.; Njogu, W.; and Okello, M.
1986a."The Infant Feeding Study: Nairobi Site Report." Report prepared for the U.S. Agency for International Development, Office of Nutrition. Processed.

Winikoff, B.; Latham, M.C.; Solimano, G.; Cerf, B.; Laukaran, V.H.; Van Esterik, P.; Post, J.E.; Smith, R.A.; Lee, L.W.; Muangman, D.; Durongdej, S.; Svetsreni, T.; and Dejthai, T.
1986b."The Infant Feeding Study: Bangkok Site Report." Report prepared for the U.S. Agency for International Development, Office of Nutrition. Processed.

Winikoff, B.; Latham, M.C.; Solimano, G.; Castle, M.A.; Laukaran, V.H.; Van Esterik, P.; Post, J.E.; Smith, R.A.; Lee, L.W.; Trastotenojo, M.S.; Hariyono, F. Muis; Sumantri, A.; Budiori Kana, N.; and Wiratno, S.
1986c."The Infant Feeding Study: Semarang Site Report." Report prepared for the U.S. Agency for International Development, Office of Nutrition. Processed.

Winikoff, B.; Latham, M.C.; Solimano, G.; Castle, M.A.; Laukaran, V.H.; Van Esterik, P.; Post, J.E.; Smith, R.A.; Lee, L.W.; Trastotenojo, M.S.; Hariyono, F. Muis; Sumantri, A.; Budiori Kana, N.; and Wiratno, S.
1986d."The Infant Feeding Study: Semarang Site Report." Report prepared for the U.S. Agency for International Development, Office of Nutrition. Processed.

Wolfe, Barbara L. and Behrman, Jere R.
1982."Determinants of Child Mortality, Health and Nutrition in a Developing Country." *Journal of Development Economics* 11: 163-194.

World Bank.
1988.*Education in Sub-Saharan Africa: Policies for Adjustment, Revitalization and Expansion.* Washington, D.C.: The World Bank.

Wray, Joe D. and Aguirre, Alfredo.
1969."Protein-Calorie Malnutrition in Candelaria, Colombia: I. Prevalence: Social and Demographic Causal Factors." *Journal of Tropical Pediatrics* 15: 76-98.

Zeitlin, M.; Masangkay, Z.; Consolacion, M.; and Nass, M.
1978."Breast Feeding and Nutritional Status in Depressed Urban Areas of Greater Manila, Philippines." *Ecology of Food and Nutrition* 7: 103-113.

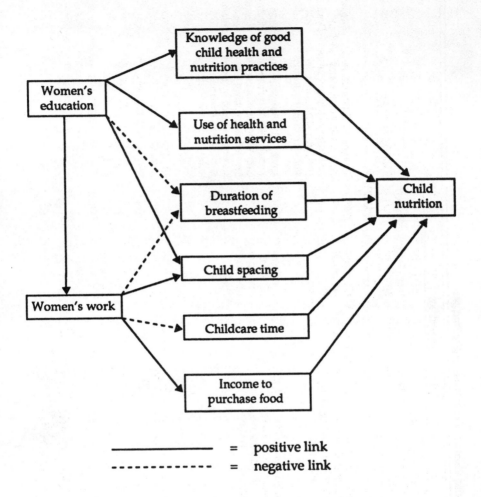

Figure 2.1
A Model of the Usual Hypotheses Concerning Linkages
between Women's Education, Women's Work and Child
Nutrition

Table 2.1   Summary of Studies Relating Women's Work to Infant Feeding Practices

Country	Sample			Methodology				Source
	Urban/ Rural	Size	Description	Measure of Women's Work[a]	Infant Feeding Measures[b]	Method of Analysis[c]	Reported Findings	
						BIVARIATE		
Nigeria, Lagos 1981	Urban	98	Mothers of children <2 yrs. who had ceased breastfeeding; 8% of female employees of large health clinic	AE: compared women at different salary levels	Extent and duration of BF	CT;NT	Duration of BF inversely related to salary level: 8 mos. for women with lowest salaries compared with 3.3 mos. for women with highest salaries.	Bamisaye and Oyediran 1983
Brazil, Sao Paulo ND	Urban	191	56 primiparous and 135 multiparous mothers selected from several maternities and followed for 8 mos.	E/NE[d]	Duration of BF; age at weaning or introduction of MF	CT;NT	Among 23 of 53 women who worked away from home after birth, work was presumed to have influenced infant feeding since weaning or change to mixed feeding occurred within one month of going to work.	Brazil Ministry of Education and Culture 1980
Malaysia (peninsular) ND	Urban	100	Mothers of children 6 mos. to 2 yrs. admitted to the Pediatric Unit of the University Hospital were interviewed	E/NE	Extent and duration of BF	Not shown	No significant difference in extent or duration of BF between E and NE women.	Chen 1978
Nigeria, Ibadan 1976	Urban	468	115 Yoruba women with children <6 yrs. working in the traditional (nonformal) sector and 284 working in the modern (formal) sector interviewed at their place of work	AE: compared women working in nonformal and formal sectors	Age at weaning	CT;NT	39% of women in formal sector weaned before 6 mos. compared with 26% of women in nonformal sector.	Di Domenico and Asuni 1979

Table 2.1 Continued
Summary of Studies Relating Women's Work to Infant feeding Practices

Country	Urban/Rural	Sample Size	Sample Description	Measure of Women's Work[a]	Infant Feeding Measures[b]	Method of Analysis[c]	Reported Findings	Source
				Methodology				
Thailand, Bangkok ND	Urban	586	Primiparous mothers from several randomly selected hospitals and clinics interviewed at time of discharge after childbirth	Compared women on the basis of occupation including housewives and agricultural workers	Type of feeding: BF, M or B	CT;CS	Type of feeding was significantly related to woman's occupation; highest percentage BF (50%) found among agricultural workers, next highest (45%) among construction workers and housewives.	Durongdej, Kawsiri and Chularojanamontri 1982
Philippines, Quezon City ND	Urban	319	Low-income mothers attending a nutrition class	E/NE[e]	Type of feeding: BF or B	CT;CS	Significantly less BF reported among E women (71%) compared with NE women (89%) 1980.	Ignacio et al. 1980
Mexico (southwest) Malinalco 1978	Rural	100	Random sample of mothers with child <2 yrs. drawn from civil birth records	E/NE[f]	Type of feeding: BF, MF, B, or B introduced after BF for 3 mos.	not shown	No significant difference in type of feeding between E and NE women.	Lillig and Lackey 1982
Malyasia (peninsular) 1978-79	Urban and rural	278	Malay, Chinese and Indian women interviewed at one MCH clinic in each of five states	E/NE	Age of child at weaning, introduction of B and introduction of SF	not shown	No significant difference in age of introduction of B between E and NE women.	Manderson 1984

Location, Year	N	Description	Comparison	Feeding measure	Method	Results	Source
Papua New Guinea, Port Moresby 1980-81	Urban	97	All nurses and aides in 11 public clinics and some wards of Port Moresby General Hospital who had children (260 children) and could find time to be interviewed at place of work	AE: compared women by length of postpartum absence from work	Type of feeding BF, MF or B	CT;CS	Almost no B was reported; MF was significantly more common among women who returned to work <6 mos. postpartum (40%) than among women who returned at 7-12 mos. (13%) or >12 mos. (8%).	Marshall 1984
Micronesia, Moen Island (Truk District) 1976	Rural	83	All women in village who had borne children while residing on Moen Island (375 children) were interview	E/NE	"Rare if any use of bottle" compared with "some regular use of bottle"	CT;CS	Significantly more E women (82%) reported some regular use of bottle than NE women (50%).	Marshall and Marshall 1979
Philippines, Cebu Island 1973	Urban and rural	321	Survey of households in 4 ecological zones: urban squatter, urban barrio, rural coastal and rural hinterland; only data on children <2 yrs. were analyzed	E/NE: rural E women who worked at home, in same barrio or in different barrio were compared	Type of feeding: BF, MF or B	CT;UT	Significantly less BF among E women in urban barrios, rural coastal and rural hinterland; among rural E women main effect was more MF among women working in different barrio compared with in home or same barrio work.	Popkin and Solon 1976
Malaysia (peninsular) 1973-74	Urban and rural	5160	Random sample of Malay, Chinese and Indian women from urban areas of Kuala Lumpur, Ipoh and Petaling Jaya and rural areas of 5 states; data on 8755 live births during 4 yrs. preceding survey were analyzed	Compared women on the basis of occupation including housewives and agricultural workers	Extent of BF	CT;CS	BF was significantly related to occupation among rural and urban Chinese and Indian: highest prevalence of BF was found among medical and agricultural workers; BF lower among other E women than among housewives.	Pathmanathan 1978
Philippines, Manila (Pasig) 1975	Urban	72	All women in selected neighborhood with child 0-24 mos. (77 children) were interviewed	E/NE[f]	Type of feeding: BF, MF or B	CT;UT	No significant difference in type of feeding between E and NE women.	Paredes, Rabuco and Burgess 1977

Table 2.1 Continued
Summary of Studies Relating Women's Work to Infant feeding Practices

			Methodology					
		Sample						
Country	Urban/ Rural	Size	Description	Measure of Women's Work[a]	Infant Feeding Measures[b]	Method of Analysis[c]	Reported Findings	Source
					MULTIVARIATE			
Sri Lanka, 1971	Urban and rural	4308	National probability sample (World Fertility Survey): only data on children borne in most recent 4 yr. period were analyzed	E/NE: women who worked at home and away from home compared	Extent and duration of BF	MA	Women who worked at home were more likely to BF and reported longer duration than NE women or women who worked away from home.	Akin et al. 1981
Philippines, Bicol region, 1978	Urban and rural	618	Bicol Multipurpose Survey of 1903 households in 100 randomly chosen communities: only data on households having at least one child <24 mos. were analyzed	E/NE[f]	Type of feeding (BF and/or B and/or SF) at 3 month intervals from birth to 12 mos.	MA	No significant effect of employment on initiation of BF; higher probability of introducing B after 3 mos. among E women.	Akin et al. 1985
Egypt, Jordan, Tunisia, Yemen, 1976-77	Urban and rural	Ranged from 2262 in Yemen to 6424 in Egypt	National probability samples (World Fertility Survey): only data on children borne in most recent 4 yr. period were analyzed	E/NE: E women who worked at home and away from home compared	Extent and duration of BF	MA	No significant effect of employment on extent of BF; in Yemen women who worked at home reported longer duration of BF than NE women or those who worked away from home.	Akin et al. 1986
Malaysia (peninsular) 1976-77	Urban and rural	1262	Malaysian Family Life Survey: mother's retrospective life histories (5500 live births)	E/NE: E women were compared on basis of hourly wage and history of agricultural work in prior 2 yrs.	Extent and duration of BF	MA and MCA	Higher probability of BF among women with lower wages; higher probability of BF among women with recent history of agricultural work.	Butz, Habicht and DaVanzo 1981

Location/Year	Urban/rural	Sample size	Description	E/NE	Outcome	Method	Findings	Reference
Bangladesh, Colombia, Guyana, Jordan, Indonesia, Panama, Peru and Sri Lanka 1976	Urban and rural	Ranged from 1276 in Guyana to 4064 in Indonesia	National probability samples (World Fertility Survey): only data on married women with 2 or more children borne 3 to 15 yrs. prior to interview were analyzed.		Extent and duration of BF	MA	No significant differences in extent or duration of BF between E and NE women.[g]	Jain and Bongaarts 1981
Thailand 1969-79	Urban and rural	Ranged from 1026 for NS to 2891 for SOFT	Data from National Longitudinal Study of Social Economic and Demographic Change (LS), Survey of Fertility in Thailand (SOFT) and National Survey of Family Planning Practices, Fertility and Mortality (NS) were analyzed	E/NE: rural women were compared by whether or not they worked for wages, on a farm, or for the family; urban women were compared by whether or not they worked for wages, for the family, and by 6 occupations, which included housewife	Extent and duration of BF	MCA	Rural women who worked on the family farm or for the family reported longer duration of BF than NE women or women who worked away from home; among urban women there were no significant differences in BF by employment status.	Knodel and Debavalya 1980
Honduras 1982	Urban	912	Survey of representative sample of 5000 households in Tegucigalpa; data on mothers with infant <1 yr. at time of survey were analyzed (also included ethnographic study)	E/NE[h]: E women were divided into formal and non-formal sector workers; formal sector workers were compared on the basis of postpartum leave	Extent and duration of BF, and type of feeding: BF, MF or B	CT;CS and MA	No significant differences in extent or duration of BF between E and NE women; higher percentage of MF in early mos. among E than NE women; among E women in formal sector, length of postpartum leave was most significant determinant of duration of BF.	O'Gara 1989[k]

Table 2.1 Continued
Summary of Studies Relating Women's Work to Infant Feeding Practices

Country	Sample			Methodology			Reported Findings	Source
	Urban/ Rural	Size	Description	Measure of Women's Work[a]	Infant Feeding Measures[b]	Method of Analysis[c]		
Philippines, Laguna Province 1975	Rural	314	Random sample of 573 households; data on 324 children <3 yrs. were analyzed	E/NE: E women were compared on the basis of household wealth, their wage rate and compatibility of job with child care	Extent of BF during first 3 mos. and duration of BF	MA	Among E women from wealthier households, extent of BF during first 3 mos. was lower for those with higher wage rate; however, a higher wage rate was associated with significantly longer duration of BF among all E women.	Popkin 1978
Philippines 1973-1983	Urban and rural	3573 (1973) 5396 (1983)	Comparable National Demographic Surveys from 1973 and 1983; data on most recent birth from the 3 yr. period preceding the survey were analyzed	E/NE: E women working in modern, transitional, mixed and traditional occupations were compared	Extent and duration of BF	MA and CT	Extent of BF decreased for all occupational groups (including NE) from 1973 to 1983 except for a significant increase among E women in modern occupations; a significant increase in duration of BF from 1973 to 1983 was due to behavioral changes by working women.	Popkin et al. 1989[k]
Indonesia, Semarang 1981	Peri-urban	244	From sample of 4453 low wage female workers in 20 factories in Semarang, 122 women with an infant 0 to 6 mos. were studied for 3 mos. along with a comparable group of 122 NE mothers[j]	E/NE[i]	Type of feeding: BF or MF; also frequency of BF during day and at night	MA	Employment status of mother was the most significant determinant of type of feeding, with higher rates of MF among E women. Frequency of BF during day was lower among E women but no different from that of NE women at night.	Soekirman 1983

Location/Year	Setting	n	Study design	Comparison	Variables	Method	Findings	Reference
Chile, Santiago 1984-85	Urban	612	Prospective, longitudinal sample of women giving birth in Sotero del Rio hospital between 7/84 and 12/84 and followed for 6 mos. postpartum	E/NE: E women were compared on the basis of occupation, availability of maternity leave, distance to work and access to day care centers	Duration of BF; type of feeding: BF and/or B and/or SF	MA	Overall patterns of infant feeding were similar for E and NE women, but E women introduced B and SF earlier either as complements to or substitutes for BF; among E women, access to day care was significantly related to longer MF.	Vial et al. 1989[k]
Kenya, Nairobi 1982	Urban	980	Representative cluster sample excluding income neighborhoods; women with child born during 18 mos. preceding survey were interviewed (also included ethnographic study)	E/NE[f]: E women were compared on the basis of availability of maternity leave	Extent and duration of BF; age at introduction of B	MA and CT	No significant difference in extent or duration of BF between E and NE women; CT suggest higher initiation of BF but shorter duration among women with maternity leave compared to those without.	Winikoff et al. 1986a
Colombia, Bogota 1981	Urban	711	Representative cluster sample excluding income neighborhoods; women with at least one child <12 mos. were interviewed (also included ethnographic study)	E/NE	Extent and duration of BF; age at introduction of B	MA	No significant difference in extent of BF between E and NE women, however E women reported significantly shorter duration of BF.	Winikoff et al. 1986b
Thailand, Bangkok 1982	Urban	1422	Representative cluster sample of mothers with a living child born during the 12 mos. preceding interview (also included ethnographic study)	E/NE: E women who worked at and away from home were compared	Extent and duration of BF; age at introduction of B	MA and CT	No significant difference in extent of BF among women NE, E at home or E away from home; shorter duration of BF and earlier introduction of B among women E away from home than NE women or women E at home	Winikoff et al. 1986c

Table 2.1 Continued
Summary of Studies Relating Women's Work to Infant feeding Practices

Country	Sample			Methodology				Source
	Urban/ Rural	Size	Description	Measure of Women's Work[a]	Infant Feeding Measures[b]	Method of Analysis[c]	Reported Findings	
Indonesia, Semarang 1982	Urban and peri-urban	1358	Representative cluster sample of women with a child <24 mos. (also included ethnographic study)	E/NE: E women who worked at and away from home were compared; also on basis of hours worked and location of child while mother worked	Extent and duration of BF; age at introduction of B	MA and CT	No significant difference in extent of BF among NE women, women E at home and away from home; women E away from home had significantly shorter duration of BF than NE women or women E at home; all E women introduced B significantly earlier than NE women.	Winikoff, et al.

a   Symbols used for measure of women's work: AE - all employed; E/NE - compared employed and not employed

b   Symbols used for infant feeding measures: BF - breastfeeding; MF - mixed (bottle and breast) feeding; B - bottle feeding; SF - supplementary foods

c   Symbols used for method of analysis: CT - cross tabulation; UT - unspecified statistical test of significant differences; NT - no statistical test of significant differences reported; CS - chi-square tests of significant differences; MA - multivariate analysis; MCA - Multiple classification analysis

d   A total of 73 women were employed, but the relationship between work and infant feeding was analyzed only for the 53 who worked and were separated from the infant.

e   Only 14 women were categorized as employed; the 305 NE included 50 who were gainfully employed at home.

f   Employed was defined as employed outside the home; NE included mothers who worked at home.

g   For Sri Lanka this is the same data set as analyzed by Akin et al. 1981 above, who found a significant relationship between women's work and BF.

h   Only women who reported that they had earned income the day prior to the interview were classified as employed.

i   This study was undertaken as a substudy of the one analyzed in Winikoff et al. 1986d.

j   MF includes infants who received only bottle feeding as well as those who received both bottle and breast feeding.

k   Appears as a chapter in this volume.

Table 2.2 Summary of Studies Relating Women's Work to Child Nutritional Status

Country	Urban/Rural	Sample Size	Description	Measure of Women's Work[a]	Infant Feeding Measures[b]	Method of Analysis[c]	Reported Findings	Source
						BIVARIATE		
Haiti, Fond Parisien 1970	Rural	114	Stratified random sample of 409 children 6 mos. to 5 yrs. selected to give equal numbers in each of 4 nutrition status categories	AE: women were classified by occupation	WA	CT;NT	Children of women who were cultivators had lower WA than children of women with other occupations, most of whom were street vendors.	Ballweg 1972
Brazil, Salvador 1974	Urban	488	Random sample of women from second largest low-income neighborhood of the city; only data on children <7 were analyzed	E/NE: children of E mothers were compared on the basis of amount and time of day mother was absent and who provided child care	WA	CT;CS	Children of E women had significantly lower WA; children left alone or in care of sibling had significantly lower WA; no difference in WA by amount or time of day mother was absent.	Bittencourt and DiCicco 1979
India, Madhya Pradesh ND	Rural	89	Sub-study of Project Poshak; children 6 to 36 mos. selected from one tribal and one non-tribal district	E/NE	WA and clinical signs of malnutrition	CT;UT	Living in nuclear rather than joint family and having an E mother appeared to put children at high risk of low WA	Grewal, Gopaldas and Gadre 1973

Table 2.2 Continued
Summary of Studies Relating Women's Work to Child Nutritional Status

Country	Urban/ Rural	Sample Size	Sample Description	Measure of Women's Work[a]	Infant Feeding Measures[b]	Method of Analysis[c]	Reported Findings	Source
Haiti, Cite Simone 1980	Urban	188	Random sample from two neighborhoods; only data on children 0 to 23 mos. with anthropometric measures were analyzed	E/NE: E women were classified as merchants or other and were also compared by whether they worked at home or away and number of days/week	WA, HA and WH	CT;CS	At 0 to 11 mos. children of merchants had significantly poorer growth than NE or other, but at 12 to 23 mo. children of both merchants and NE had significantly poorer growth than other; children of mothers who worked at home had best growth at 11 mos. but poorest growth at 23 mos.	Haggerty 1981
Bolivia, La Paz ND	Urban	117	Sample of boys 7 to 11 screened for iron status from a random selection of clubs distributing food to needy children; most mothers were present at interviews	E/NE[d]: E women were ranked by occupation (domestic to professional)	D; dietary diversity and quality	CA	A negative but not significant correlation was found between both mother's employment and rank of occupation and diversity and quality of child's diet.	Moreno-Black 1983
Costa Rica, Concepcion de San Ramon ND	Rural	81	Ethnographic survey of entire district; all 250 children <6 yrs. were weighed and measured; 40 "normal" and 41 "deficient" households were compared	E/NE[d]	WA; households were classified as normal or deficient based on number of cases and severity of malnutrition among children <6 yrs.	CT;CS	Significantly lower child nutritional status in households with E mothers.	Rawson and Valverde 1976

Location	Setting	n	Study description	Variable classification	Outcome	Type	Findings	Reference
India, Maharashtra ND	Rural	108	9 of 79 villages in the Kasa Model Integrated MCH Nutrition Project were selected; within villages every 10th family was selected; children <6 yrs. were weighed regularly	E/NE: children of E mothers were classified by age of child care provider	WA	CT;NT	43% of children of NE mothers had low WA compared with 87% of children of E mothers; there was a strong positive relationship between the nutritional status of the child and the age of the provider of child care.	Shah, et al. 1979
Ghana, Winkoba 1975-77	Rural	113	An ethnographic study of compounds in one kinship based section of the community; anthropometric measures were made on 187 children 4 to 6 mos.	Women were classified by whether or not they worked in agriculture and whether or not they were traders.	WA	CT;CS	Trading activity of the mother was the most significant (positive) variable associated with WA.	Tripp 1981
Colombia, Candelaria 1963	Rural	354	Random sample of households with children <6 yrs (721 children)	E/NE: E women were classified by whether they worked part or full time	WA	CT;NT	More children of E women had low WA; women who worked part-time had more children with low WA than women who worked full time.	Wray and Aguirre 1969

MULTIVARIATE

Location	Setting	n	Study description	Variable classification	Outcome	Type	Findings	Reference
Peru, Lima 1967-76	Urban	217	Sample of mothers of children hospitalized for malnutrition plus their siblings (408 children); data collected nearest to child's 5th birthday were used	Women were categorized as housewives, domestics or professionals; also by whether they worked part-or full time	Height at 5 yrs.	MA	Children of NE women or women who worked part-time were significantly taller than children of women who worked full time. To produce same child height at age 5, household with full time E mother needed almost double the income of household with part time or NE mother.	Adelman 1983

Table 2.2 Continued
Summary of Studies Relating Women's Work to Child Nutritional Status

Country	Urban/Rural	Sample Size	Description	Measure of Women's Work[a]	Infant Feeding Measures[b]	Method of Analysis[c]	Reported Findings	Source
Jamaica, Kingston 1967-76	Urban	761	All hospital admissions for malnutrition over 10 yr. period for which complete clinical and SE data were available	E/NE	Number of hospital admissions for malnutrition per year and by constituency	MA	Unemployment of mothers was the most important variable in accounting for spatial and temporal variation in hospital cases of malnutrition.	Bailey 1981
Guatemala 1969-77	Urban and rural	1284	Sub-sample of mothers with children <7 yrs. in rural sample (962 children) and <3 yrs. in urban sample (322 children) from whom anthropometric data were adequate	E/NE: women were classified into four occupational groups; adult or sibling providers of substitute childcare were distinguished	WA and HA of 0 - 3 year olds for urban sample, and 0 - 4 year olds for rural sample	MA	No significant relationship between child nutrition and maternal work in rural sample; in urban sample 0-1 year olds of E mothers had significantly lower WA and 1-2 year olds of E mothers had significantly higher WA; in general WA children cared for by adults was better.	Engle, et al. 1986; Engle 1989[e]
Colombia, Cali ND	Urban	171	Sample of low-income households with at least one malnourished preschool child (274 preschool children)	E/NE: women were classified by whether or not they were sole earner and whether they worked part or full time	WA	MA	No significant relationship between maternal work variables and WA of children.	Franklin 1979

Location/Year	Setting	N	Sample	Variables	Outcome	MA/FA	Findings	Reference
St. Vincent 1975	Urban	200	Children aged 1 to 2 yrs. from low income households of two towns participating in community health program	E/NE: E women were classified by whether they worked year round or not	WA and WH	MA	No significant relationship between maternal work variables and child growth.	Greiner and Latham 1981
India, Kerala 1974	Rural	48	From a stratified random sample of 120 households in 3 districts, data on low-income households with a child 6 to 36 mos. were analyzed	E/NE: E women were classified by type of work, wage rate and amount of time worked during year	WA	MA	No significant differences in WA of children of NE women and women in household industry, but women who worked in fields had children with significantly lower WA; income from mothers' work had significant positive effect on WA.	Kumar 1977
Jamaica, Parish of St. James 1973	Urban and rural	164	Random sample of census districts; data from all households with child <1 yr. were analyzed	E/NE	WA and HA	FA	Maternal employment by itself was not significantly related to child growth; the "family cohesion factor", of which maternal employment was a negative component, related positively to WA.	Marchione 1980
Philippines, Laguna Province 1975	Rural	573	Random sample of households from 34 barrios; dietary data from only a sub-sample of 99 households with pre-school children (1-71 mos.) were analyzed	E/NE: E women were classified by amount of time worked per week and whether job was judged compatible with child care. Time spent on child care by other family members was also measured	D, WA and HA (Popkin 1983 uses means for all preschool children in household)	MA	Among children of E women, maternal child care time was reduced but energy intake was higher. Overall there appeared to be no significant effect on child growth although Popkin 1980 reported poorer growth among 1-35 mos. children of E women. No effect was found of work-related variables.	Popkin 1980; Popkin 1983

Table 2.2 Continued
Summary of Studies Relating Women's Work to Child Nutritional Status

Country	Sample		Methodology				Reported Findings	Source
	Urban/ Rural	Size	Description	Measure of Women's Work[a]	Infant Feeding Measures[b]	Method of Analysis[c]		
Philippines, Cebu Island 1973	Urban and rural	626	Sample of households with children 1 to 16 yrs. (1715 children) from 4 different ecological settings; dietary data from 24 hour recall on sub-sample of 130 children	E/NE	D and prevalence of xerophthalmia	MA for D; CT;NT for xerophthalmia	No significant effect of maternal work on energy or protein intake, but in one of two rural locations Vit. A intake of children of E mothers was significantly lower; in low income households children of E women had more xerophthalmia and in higher income households, less.	Popkin and Solon 1976
Jamaica, Kingston 1979	Urban	229	All households from two typical poor urban neighborhoods with one or more children <4 yrs. (309 children)	E/NE	WA, HA and WH	MA	Significantly poorer growth among children of E women	Powell and Grantham-McGregor 1985
Haiti 1978	Urban and rural	160	Mothers who attended Mothercraft Center or health clinic with one or more children <5 yrs; data for child closest to 18 mos. were analyzed	Mothers were classified by number of occupations and number of days spent working away from home	WA, HA and WH	MA	No significant relationship between maternal work variables and child growth	Smith et al. 1983

Location	Setting	N	Sample	Classification	Measures		Results	Reference
Indonesia, Central Java 1981	Peri-urban	244	From a sample of 4453 low wage female workers in 20 factories in Semarang, 122 women with an infant 0 to 6 mos. were studied for 3 mos. along with a comparable group of 122 NE women	E/NE[d]: E women were classified by wage rate, amount of of time worked per week and distance to to work	WA	MA	Children of E women had significantly lower WA; children of E women who worked >45 hrs./week had significantly lower WA than women who worked <45 hrs. if mother earned less than the minimum wage, but if women earned more than minimum wage, no significant difference was found.	Soekirman 1983; Soekirman 1985
Panama, Chiriqui Province 1983-84	Peri-urban	178	Random sample of children 3 to 5 years from vaccination records at health clinics	E/NE: women were classified as working away from home or not and as having income activity at home or not; provider of substitute child care and maternal income were also analyzed	WA, HA, WH, and biochemical measures	MA	Overall children of E women had significantly better diets. Children of women E away from home had significantly greater dietary diversity; children of E women at home had significantly better WH and hg. and serum carotene; higher maternal income and more hours worked per week were both significantly positively related to child's diet.	Tucker 1989[e]
Chile, Santiago 1984-85	Urban	612	Prospective, longitudinal sample of women giving birth in Sotero del Rio hospital between 7/84 and 12/84 and followed for 6 mos. postpartum	E/NE: E women were classified by whether they worked at home or away, whether they had maternity leave, distance to work, whether they used day care and whether they took child to work	Monthly weight gain from birth to 6 mos.	MA	Significantly greater weight gain for children of E women; no significant effect of maternal work variables on weight gain.	Vial et al. 1989[e]

Table 2.2 Continued
Summary of Studies Relating Women's Work to Child Nutritional Status

Country	Urban/ Rural	Sample Size	Description	Measure of Women's Work[a]	Infant Feeding Measures[b]	Method of Analysis[c]	Reported Findings	Source
				Methodology				
Nicaragua 1977-78	Urban and rural	1281	Stratified random sample of women with child <5 yrs; analysis done separately for central metropolis, other urban, and rural	Women were categorized as working in the informal or formal sector (including domestics); predicted earnings for all women (including those only doing non-paid home production) were estimated	Standardized weight, height and arm circumference	MA	Children of women who worked in the informal sector in the urban sample had significantly better growth; no significant relationship between predicted earning and child growth was found.	Wolfe and Berhman 1982
Philippines, Manila ND	Urban	525	Cluster sample of children 5 to 48 mos. from 10 severely depressed neighborhoods of greater Manila	E/NE	WA, HA and WH	MA	No significant difference in growth of children between E and NE mothers.	Zeitlin et al. 1078

a   Symbols used for measures of women's work: AE - all employed; E/NE - compared employed and not employed

b   Symbols used for measures of child nutritional status: WA - percent of median weight for age; HA - percent of median height for age; WH - percent of median weight for height (or length); D - dietary intake (in most cases based on a 24 hour dietary recall).

c   Symbols used for method of analysis: CT - cross tabulation; UT - unspecified statistical test of significant differences; NT - no statistical test of significant differences; CS - Chi-square test of significant differences; MA - multivariate analysis; CA - correlation analysis

d   E women were defined as women working outside the home; NE may have included women who worked at home.

e   Appears as a chapter in this volume.

TABLE 2.3 Pattern of Findings from Studies Relating Women's Work to Infant Feeding[a]

Measure of Women's Work	Infant Feeding Measures						Total Studies[c]
	Extent of Breastfeeding		Duration of Breastfeeding		Type of Feeding[b]		
	Sig	(total)[d]	Sig	(total)	Sig	(total)	
Compared employed and not employed[e]	1	(12)	5	(9)	10	(13)	23
Compared women who worked at home and away from home	1	(4)	5	(5)	2	(2)	5
Compared women in different occupations	3	(4)	1	(2)	1	(2)	7
Compared women with different income/wage levels	2	(3)	2	(2)	---	---	3
Compared women on basis of availability of maternity leave or length of time postpartum before returning to work	1	(1)	2	(2)	1	(2)	4

a Based on the 28 studies summarized in Table 1.

b This measure usually divided children into some or all of the following categories: exclusively breastfed; exclusively bottlefed; mixed breast and bottle; breast plus supplementary foods; bottle plus supplementary foods; mixed plus supplementary foods.

c The total number of studies in each row is not necessarily equal to the sum of the numbers in parentheses because some studies reported more than one infant feeding measure; similarly some studies reported more than one measure of women's work.

d Number in parentheses is total number of studies that reported the measure; number outside parentheses is studies that reported a significant relationship.

e Several of these studies combined women who worked at home with women who were not employed.

TABLE 2.4 Pattern of Findings from Studies Relating Women's Work to Child Nutritional Status[a]

| | Measures of Child Nutritional Status | | | |
| | Clinical or Anthropometric Status[b] | Dietary Intake | Biochemical Measures | Total Studies[c] |
Measure of Women's Work	Sig (total)[d]	Sig (total)	Sig (total)	
Compared women who were employed and not employed[e]	11 (17)	2 (4)	4 (4)	19
Compared women who worked at home and away from home	1 (2)	1 (1)	—	3
Compared women in different occupations	6 (7)	0 (1)	—	8
Compared women based on amount of time worked	3 (9)	1 (1)	—	10
Compared different providers of child care	3 (3)	—	—	3
Compared women with different wage/income levels	2 (3)	1 (1)		4

a Based on the 25 studies summarized in Table 2.

b Most of these studies used percent of median weight for age and/or height for height; a few used absolute height or weight.

c The total number of studies in each row is not necessarily equal to the sum of the numbers in parentheses because some studies reported more than one measure of child nutritional status; similarly some studies reported more than one measure of women's work.

d Number in parentheses is total number of studies that reported the measure; number outside parentheses is studies that reported a significant relationship.

e Several of these studies combined women who worked at home with women who were not employed.

3

Women's Work and Social Support For Child Care in the Third World*

Susan Joekes

The great majority of women in developing countries are "working" in the sense of being economically productive in market-related or subsistence activities and devoting many hours daily to hard labor of some kind. At the same time, marriage and bearing children (in greater or lesser numbers) are virtually universal among women in developing countries. Consequently, a large fraction of working women are mothers (many of young children) who are doing economically productive work as well as child care and "domestic production," however narrowly defined.

In view of this situation, the main, surprising finding of this survey of the literature is that empirical information is scarce and scattered concerning how young children are cared for in Third World countries while their mother is employed. There is no coherent body of research to be assessed, such as is examined in the review of female employment and child nutrition by Leslie in Chapter 2. The topic has not been considered in depth within any of the relevant social science or biomedical disciplines.[1] Accordingly, this chapter should not be considered an exhaustive review, but rather an attempt to provide background information on the topic from a variety of sources and within a systematic framework.

The objectives of this chapter are to set out what is known about the means used for child care by working women in developing countries,

*Support for this paper was provided by the Carnegie Corporation of New York and The Ford Foundation. The paper draws on an earlier survey of social support systems in developed and developing countries prepared by Judith A. Graeff.

with regard to their household circumstances and occupational status, and to make suggestions for research and policy. Three levels of services are considered. First, child care provided by other members of the mother's household. Second, what might be called "informal" services, where child care is one type of support provided to each other by members of a residential or kin group on a reciprocal basis, usually without financial compensation. This kind of provision is embedded in, and is a product of, the existence of a social support network beyond the domestic unit. Finally, there is "institutional" child care provided for a fee by public or private agents. The distinctions between these categories are not absolute; they serve as ways of organizing disparate material rather than as a conceptual tool. The rationale for bringing together information on child care in this chapter is that it is one of the least studied of the intervening variables that determine the relationship between women's status and activities in developing countries and the health and welfare of their children.

MAIN PREMISES

Children's health and welfare are affected by the level of education of women and the nature of their work in a variety of sometimes contradictory ways. For example, education tends to improve women's knowledge of health and nutrition practices, as well as use of health and nutrition services. But education also tends to reduce duration of breastfeeding, frequently to the disadvantage of infants. Similarly, paid employment for women improves the ability of families to purchase food and promotes better child spacing, but it may also reduce the amount of time mothers spend caring for their children. However, the nature of the precise relationship between maternal and non-maternal child care and child welfare has never been examined directly in a comprehensive way. Few if any of the studies of the effect of female employment on child nutrition reviewed in the preceding chapter by Leslie explicitly consider the possible role of child care in the relationship. Accordingly, the hypothesis that children of women in paid employment receive less care (in some sense) than children of unemployed women is essentially unproven. In describing the variety of child care arrangements women currently make in developing countries, and the circumstances under which they make them, this review represents an initial attempt to sort out the issues involved.

The major premise underlying the hypothesis that women's work negatively affects child care is that women, as mothers, do in fact carry out care of their own children. This is only partially true. While it seems to be universally the case that women bear the responsibility of making care arrangements for their children (Anker and Hein 1985; Buvinic´ et al. 1983;

Myers and Indriso 1987; Schmink 1982; and Beneria and Roldan 1987), this does not mean that mothers themselves are the only persons actually carrying out the task. One wide ranging review paper, based on ethnographic data, purports to show that the great majority (80%) of young children are **not** cared for principally by their mother (Weisner and Gallimore 1977). It is not clear whether the situation arises because their mothers are working or because of more general, cultural reasons.

Child care can be defined as the process of attending to a child's basic needs of shelter, protection, food, clothing, and health (although it can also be more broadly understood as including a child's emotional welfare and cognitive and moral development (Myers and Indriso 1987; [Engle, Chapter 8]). Any or all of these functions can be delegated to the person charged with care, insofar as they arise on a continuous or periodic basis.[2] While reliable information on child care arrangements is sparse, information on the methods and satisfactoriness of various child care arrangements with respect to specific elements of the child care function is almost nonexistent. It is not obvious that child care by persons other than the mother is necessarily inferior or detrimental to a child's welfare. Therefore it is not possible, at this point, to make a balanced assessment of the impact of different methods of child care on any of these particular factors. This chapter necessarily — in view of the state of the literature — falls short of evaluating, for example, the relationship between child care services and young child feeding practices and critical health care interventions.

The study of social organization, of which child care is a part, is most central to sociology of all the social science disciplines. On the other hand, "work," referring to productive activities and the allocation of human labor time, is quintessentially an "economic" issue. The care of children is seen within this discipline as something that is mutually exclusive with "work," i.e. that there is a conflict (specific to women) between the demands of employment or income generation and child rearing (see e.g. Becker 1981).

Most — it could almost be said by definition all — low-income women with children in developing countries do economically productive work. The bulk of their working hours are directed towards activities that either directly or indirectly generate income for their household in cash or in kind or that minimize cash consumption outlays (i.e. by purchase of commodities, such as food, that need further processing before consumption, rather than in final form). Not all, however, are conventionally acknowledged as being in "formal" employment, either earning a wage or salary as a contracted employee on a casual or permanent basis, or devoting a certain number of hours each week to own account work in self-employment or to working unpaid for a family farm or other enterprise.[3] The

share of women recorded as in formal employment in this sense varies
between regions of the developing world, ranging from 9 percent in the
Middle East and North Africa, 25 percent in Latin America, 35 percent in
South Asia, 50 percent in Sub-Saharan Africa and 53 percent in the Far
East (Sivard 1985).[4] There are also considerable variations among countries in each region. Similar comparative regional data on age- and maternal status-specific labor force participation are unfortunately not available.

The formal labor force participation rate for women is an inadequate
indicator of the number of women "working." It does, however, contain at
its core that group of women who, if they are mothers of young children,
are in certain need of regular child care services. These are women who
work for fixed hours as contractual employees in the public or private
sector in a centralized workplace (and in developing countries, working
hours tend to be longer than in developed countries, with 48 hours per
week as the norm [Anker and Hein 1985]). However, not all mothers in
the labor force find their work activities incompatible with caring for their
children. While location of the workplace may be indicative, it is not
definitive. Paid work away from home may not be incompatible with
child care, whereas home-based activity may be. Wage labor in field
agriculture may or may not preclude the presence of infants or young
children; some types of domestically-based work (for example, in plastic
goods assembly or metal sorting piecework) may be disrupted by or
dangerous to young children (Beneria and Roldan 1987).

Domestic outworkers, while members of the labor force in principle,
often escape official record in practice. Domestic production can be no less
heavy and demanding of concentrated labor effort than wage labor, and
equally incompatible in some cases with supervision or active care of
young children. It may also be the case that other women in the domestic
unit, who are not in any kind of paid employment, also seek child care
services.

For all these reasons, it would be wrong to limit the subject of this
chapter to consideration of child care services used by women in formal
employment alone. The literature is often so imprecise in the definitions of
female employment, that to limit the review only to studies that give a
coherent description of women's work alongside their child care arrangements would be to reduce the material almost to zero.

CURRENT USE OF CHILD CARE SERVICES

There are no national-level surveys or other systematic data available
on methods of child care in any developing country. Only rarely is child
care a focus of inquiry, and information on the subject tends to appear pe-

ripherally to other concerns. Moreover, such direct evidence as there is, mostly relates to very small population samples. Often the data are not sorted with respect to a child's age, an important shortcoming since the adequacy of a child care method depends on a child's needs and capacities. For these reasons, comparison between different studies is difficult, and an overall assessment not yet possible.

Another complication, with implications for analytical purposes, is that single time-point observations of child care arrangements say nothing about the multiplicity of arrangements that a woman may undertake over time to ensure child care. More than one method may be routinely — or erratically — used over the course of a day, week or year (Myers and Indriso 1987). Rural women's need for and/or use of child care services may vary widely over the agricultural cycle. Children's need for care because of increased incidence of diseases in the community may be greatest at that point in the cycle when demands on women's agricultural labor time are greatest and they are least able to meet that need themselves or find adequate substitute care (Myers and Indriso 1987; [Paolisso, Baksh and Thomas, Chapter 10]). Rural surveys will miss the seasonality aspect in child care, as in other matters, if such peaks are overlooked.

Despite these shortcomings, scattered references provide some guidelines as to the array of child care arrangements that exist and occasionally indicate the prevalence of different types among certain selected samples of women. Findings in the literature are reported in the following sections.

Nonexistent Child Care

First, it must be noted that child care arrangements used in developing countries include, to a significant degree, the situation where children are unattended while the mother is otherwise occupied. While the existence of children increases women's need to work to provide income, the absence of acceptable child care services seriously constrains their ability to take work. Quite apart from the particular limitations of potential alternatives, substitute child care services are often completely unavailable to the mother. There are three possible outcomes. The absence of child care services may prevent the mother from taking employment; if economic necessity impels her to do so, it may force her to take extremely low paid work in the home or in other ways compatible with caring for her children; or finally it can mean that the child is unattended while she works.

A comparative survey of low-income women in six developing countries found that the presence of young children (and absence of substitute child care) was the reason most frequently cited by the women for not taking work (OEF 1979). It is not possible, however, in these data to separate out the women who did not wish to do paid work from those who wanted to take employment but were constrained by child care responsibilities.[5]

For the women who did not wish work, they presumably remained unemployed because there were other providers of income to their household. In most cases, but certainly not all, this would be an employed male partner, the father of the children. For women without another income-earning adult in the household, the absence of child care is a major constraint. These women are forced to provide for their unattended children's food needs and safety as best they can while they work. For example, it is common practice during peak agricultural periods in Zambia for women to feed their children a large meal in the morning and to leave them alone in the village while working all day in the fields (BAM Zambia 1981). Women from indigenous tribes in Colombia follow the same strategy when they are called to cultivate community farmlands (Buvinic' 1980). Reporting on the Philippines, Popkin (1980) gives no figures for unattended children in a study of women's time allocation, but states that the "number [of unattended children] may be substantial, particularly for female-headed households." The lack of other children and the ostracism of family causes severe child care problems for poor (unwed) teenage mothers in Mexico City, especially since it is difficult for them to qualify for government run services (Acevedo et al. 1986). Young women having their first child are the most vulnerable to problems in child care. They have no older children of their own to help; their economic position is weak so they cannot pay for child care; and social support networks are likely to be least developed at that point in their lives. The consequence can be an inescapable trade-off between severe poverty if the mother does not work and an unattended child (or children) if she does.

A survey of working single parents in Korea with children under 18 years revealed that while they were working 70 percent had no one to take care of their children (Kim 1986). Unfortunately, these data are not broken down by age and the proportion of young children uncared for cannot be determined. However, another study found that 17 percent of mothers of preschool children in urban areas in Korea routinely left their children unattended (OEF 1979). This is the highest level of unattended children reported in the comparative six country survey of low-income women cited earlier. In urban Brazil and urban Peru the proportion of women leaving children unattended is also significant, at five and eight percent respectively. In rural areas the share of children unattended is negligible or zero (op. cit.).[6]

In material terms, inadequate child care services have an important impact in constraining women's ability to generate income. The situation forces women into a compromise position, taking on work that has some financial return and is not fully incompatible with caring for their own children. It ensures a short-term solution only at the cost of reduced household income. For many low-income women, it is the only viable option.

The assumption of child care responsibilities by women is a prime determinant of the wage differential by sex that exists throughout developing (and developed) countries (Sivard 1985; Anker and Hein 1985). Much paid work is carried out by women in the home, ranging from work on own account or in family enterprises (for which the actual or computed wage may be quite high) to "domestic outwork" for payment by the piece. The presence of young children is what usually guides women to this type of work (Beneria and Roldan 1987). Piece work in simple industrial fabrication or assembly on commission (a type of productive activity found in all developing countries) is the worst type of employment opportunity. Its prevalence can only be guessed at, but it is substantial, especially in urban areas (op. cit. and Singh and Kelles-Viitanen 1987). Domestic outwork is comparable with working hours in regular production establishments (op. cit.). Of all remunerated activities it seems to be paid the least (Baud 1987; Beneria and Roldan 1987). Home-based work, done by women constrained by child care responsibilities, sets the floor level wage in the labor market; it depresses female wages throughout the occupational hierarchy by lowering women's wage bargaining position at each level.

Domestic outwork can have ill effects on children apart from lowering the level of attention the mother is able to provide. The types of outwork done are varied and include work with hazardous materials, such as metals and glass. Children's health and safety is sometimes threatened (Beneria and Roldan 1987). Women, faced with having their children close to their work and exposed to hazards, often keep their children outside the house or excluded in another room. Children are essentially uncared for in this situation, perhaps for hours at a time, though they would be counted in surveys as under the mother's supervision. Such a situation may explain the alarming number of children who "get lost" in low-income urban areas, as noted by Anderson in Chapter 11.

Child Care Within the Household

Child care alternatives include three categories of potential caretakers: other members of the mother's own household; family, friends, and neighbors external to the domestic unit; and formal child care facilities provided on an institutional basis.

The availability of caretakers from within the household is a function of the size and composition of the household.[7] Extended or joint domestic groups, particularly those with extended female kin such as grandmothers and co-wives, provide a wide range of caretaking opportunities (Myers and Indriso 1987). A study in Bogota, Colombia, found a relationship between household structure and caretaking patterns: mothers living in extended households relied on other female relatives; mothers living with men depended on friends, neighbors, and maids; and mothers in female-headed households relied on sibling care for the children (Rosenberg 1984; Myers and Indriso 1987). In El Salvador, formation of one fairly common type of household consisting of consanguineous adults, mostly female, and their children is hypothesized to be a function of child care needs. The presence of more than one cooperating adult female allows for shared care of more than one set of siblings; it provides a setting in which women can carry out both productive and reproductive roles with minimal conflict and enhances the economic stability of the domestic unit (Nieves 1979).

The majority of low-income women in the six country comparative study cited earlier met their child care needs within the household (OEF 1979). Mothers cared for their own children themselves if they worked in the home or were able to take their children with them to their place of employment. When they did paid work where it was not possible to have children present, or even on occasions when no external paid work was concerned, other household members took over the care of the children in most cases. Grandmothers, other female relatives, and other siblings were the preferred substitutes for the mother (op. cit.). Adult male household members reportedly play a minimal role, though pre-adolescent male siblings may take on some child care (OEF 1979; Weisner and Gallimore 1977). The authors of the six country comparative study observe that in Peru, "child care seems to drop out of a man's set of acceptable activities the moment he establishes a household of his own, fathers his first child, and — undoubtedly the most crucial factor — acquires rights to the labor of a woman in managing the household and rearing the child" (OEF 1979).

Child care seems to be more or less exclusively a female activity in Peru. However, there has been very little effort to check this proposition in empirical surveys in other locations. An exception is a survey of child care arrangements made by women in paid employment in Ghana, which found no instances of any male caretaker substituting for the mother (Date-Bah 1987). In the rare cases where the father's input into domestic production is observed within a time allocation study, direct child care is reported to take up only one hour or less each week, compared to 9-12 hours by mothers (Popkin 1980). There are, however, anecdotal reports that unemployed men in Jamaica will more readily mind the children than do housework (Powell 1987).

For Ghanaian women in paid employment, the single most common child caretaker for their children was the maternal grandmother, accounting for 36 percent of cases (Date-Bah 1987). Of other close family members the woman's sister and mother-in-law were the next most frequently involved (covering 14 and 9 percent of cases respectively) (op. cit.). It is not specified whether these kin were co-resident with the mother and children. Data from various other Third World countries also show that a working mother often depends on her own mother or mother-in-law for child care during working hours (Anker and Hein 1985).

In Jamaica, the younger a woman, the more likely she is to use her mother to help raise her children (Durant-Gonzalez 1976). In Korea, single mothers reportedly used their mothers as child caretakers less frequently than single fathers (Kim 1986). Single fathers are seen as more needy and less skillful in child rearing than single mothers and so are more successful in engaging relatives' help.

The OEF six country study does not specify family caretakers, but "extended family" members (excluding siblings) are noted as the most frequent substitute caretaker in all cases (OEF 1979). The place of residence of such family members is not given, however, and some will not be members of the mother's household.

Care of children by older siblings is a common form of child care in developing countries. It ranks as the most important type of nonmaternal child care in urban areas of the Dominican Republic, and the second most important source in Sri Lanka (urban and rural), urban Brazil, rural Dominican Republic and Peru (urban and rural) (OEF 1979). Its importance is significantly less in Korea (op. cit.), perhaps reflecting the high levels of school enrollments in that country. In Guatemala, siblings are a major contributor of child care, especially in the rural areas (Engle, [Chapter 8]). An ethnographic review of 186 societies determined that the principal nonmaternal companion of an infant is an older child in 25 percent of cases, and the principal companion for young children is a child or children of his own age or older in 57 percent of cases (Weisner and Gallimore 1977; age cut-offs are not specified).

In poor households in most countries, children must make a productive contribution to the household at an early age. Girls are especially called upon — as cause or symptom of lower female school enrollment rates at all ages in most developing countries — and their primary contribution is indirect: by devoting labor time to care for younger children, the mother is partially relieved of the task and is able to carry out more productive work herself (Popkin 1978; Myers and Indriso 1987). Girls are often kept out of school expressly to care for younger siblings (Nieves 1981; Safilios-Rothschild 1980; Engle et al. 1985). In rural Nepal, the presence in the household of female children between the ages of 10-14 years increases subsistence agriculture by women, by relieving their child care constraint (Acharya and Bennett 1982).

Another remarkable study pointed to the youthfulness of the child caretakers, scarcely past the age of needing care themselves. Shah et al.

(1979) found that 47 percent of the children from a rural area near Bombay were cared for primarily by older siblings, many of whom were between six and eight years old. This study is unusual also in investigating the differential impact of child care methods on a specific aspect of child welfare. The study reports that the incidence of severe malnutrition was 55.5 percent when children were cared for by siblings aged six to eight years old, compared to 21 percent under the care of a grandmother and 8.5 percent under the mothers care. The absolute level of these findings must be treated with caution, however, because there was no control for socioeconomic factors. Families that had to resort to small children as caretakers were most likely among the poorest in the sample. Still, the finding is striking and potentially highly significant for policy.

Child Care from Outside the Household: Social Support Services

In some of the evidence cited in the previous section, the sources are ambiguous about the location of the close-kin substitute child caretaker. It is often not stated whether a woman's mother is a member of her household or lives elsewhere. This is an example of the lack of distinction between types of child care noted above. In this section we attempt to present information about care of children by non-coresidential kin, friends, or neighbors.

First, the practice of fostering deserves attention. It is on the borderline between family and social support services. It refers to the practice of sending children away to live in another household within (but sometimes outside) the kinship network. Where a young child is concerned, fostering should be seen as a child care method; but as the child grows to an age where he or she can be economically productive and make a labor contribution to the household, fostering becomes something else. The contractual nature of the arrangement affects the degree to which the child is integrated into the foster family. Some are treated as indentured servants even though they are often young children themselves; while others, over the years, virtually become part of the family, and end up marrying through the intervention of their employer. If the fostering period extends over several years, it can be seen as a self-contained exchange; the young child may be taken in expectation that the social and material obligation thus created between the parties will be discharged by the child's own concurrent or subsequent labor contributions to the foster family.

Fostering is widespread in Sub-Saharan Africa (Frank 1985). Other types of child adoption, even with both parents living and capable of child support, is common in many parts of the world (e.g. Papua-New Guinea, Barlow 1984). It is not uncommon for barren women to adopt or rear a child (e.g. Jamaica, Durant-Gonzales 1976), especially in societies where child bearing is seen as a woman's primary role in life. In the Dominican Republic, nearly one-fifth of a sample of women factory workers had sent one or more of their children to live with relatives in the rural areas (Joekes 1987a). Ten percent of urban women in paid employment surveyed in Ghana had sent their child for fostering in a separate household (Date-Bah 1987). In 75 percent of the cases the children were sent to their grandmother frequently when they were very young — less than 18 months. The lengths of time children were sent away vary from less than six months to more than five years. Women in senior occupations did not use the practice of fostering. All the women employees who resorted to fostering were in low-level occupations. They utilized fostering as a solution to their child care problem in the city, adopting a traditional practice to facilitate participation in the modern sector labor force (Date-Bah 1987).

Insofar as a reciprocal obligation in fostering is acknowledged by the parties concerned, e.g., the child's own labor contribution is understood to be compensation to the foster family, fostering is an instance of a social support service, beyond the arena of familial exchanges. Social support services are generated within "social networks," the web of social ties that surrounds an individual by way of contact and relationships with family members outside the domestic unit. Networks are generally formed between domestic units that have a common standard of living, are physically close, and can provide some material, employment, social, and moral support, especially in times of emergency (Mellencamp 1983). Although the existence of a supporting social network is particularly apparent when an individual is in crisis, and much research has focused on such situations, networks are utilized on a regular basis for the services they provide (Mellencamp 1983). Generally, support from a social network is in the form of labor services (e.g., laundry, child care), advice or moral support, loans or gifts, logistical aid, or acting as an intermediary. Reciprocation is important in these relationships, and can occur in a variety of ways: payment (in kind or financially) or through labor contributions.

The few surveys that have been done of child care methods in developing countries all point to the importance of social networks as a source of child care for low-income women. Anderson (see Chapter 11) reports that about 60 percent of women in a low income area of Lima get help with child care from neighbors, some of whom are kin. The use of informal social support networks of kin and non-kin is reported as an important resource for child care among other services (Nieves 1979; Lomnitz 1979). On the other hand, the Overseas Education Fund reports an apparently low rate of utilization of neighbors and friends by mothers in six developing countries; the highest proportion of mothers is 11 percent in rural areas in the Dominican Republic (OEF 1979). But the categorization of care given is not clear; many of those "extended family" members who are the prime source of nonmaternal child caretakers may not live in the mother's household (and should be considered part of the social network instead).

Small, poor, and especially female-headed households, must have recourse to extra-household help with child care for women to maximize their income. Poverty precludes use of formal, institutional, or fee paying child care services, and it therefore relies on informal social support. However, it has also been suggested that small households in the early stage of family formation (female-headed households in particular) are the least able to develop or participate in social networks. Being poor both in resources and in numbers, i.e., in potential contributions of labor time, they have least to offer to a system built up on the basis of reciprocity of support (OEF 1979). A time element is built into expectations of exchanges under the reciprocity obligation: families that may be in need of help currently will be served by a network even if a return contribution is not expected until some time in the future. But if the expectation is low that the household will be able to reciprocate, even with a delay, this reduces their likelihood of belonging to a supportive network.

Institutional Child Care Facilities

In most developing countries, some commercial or communally-provided child care services have been established. Formal child care and pre-school services are those provided by governments, international funding agencies, religious and other charities, and employers. Many countries have passed legislation mandating that establishments with over a certain number of female employees of childbearing age must provide child care facilities. Many countries also provide nursing breaks, formal maternity leave policies, and other considerations for mothers of infants (APHA 1984).

Most studies report a low rate of utilization of formal facilities. In the six country OEF study, child care centers are the only type of formal facility reported. They are used, exceptionally, by 20 percent of mothers of preschool children in rural areas in Korea, but by none in any other country in the sample (OEF 1979). No formal facilities are used by low-income women in Anderson's study of urban Peru [Chapter 11]. Only 10 percent of employed women in urban areas in Ghana use a nursery or other formal facility for daily child care (Date-Bah 1987).

While it is an important first step to legislate services and considerations for child care, these preliminary efforts have had little impact on alleviating child care needs of poor working women in the Third World. First, most government legislation only applies to large establishments in the formal sector and therefore does not affect the majority of poor women who engage in informal sector work or live in rural areas. In addition, most governments do not enforce these laws, and establishments can circumvent child-care regulations by dismissing women when they marry and by keeping the number of female employees under the number that would require provision of nurseries (Anker and Hein 1985); cases of contracting out for child care services and not seeing that adequate services are provided have been reported in Brazil (Bittencourt 1979). As a consequence, in Brazil, while there are approximately 150,000 businesses in Sao Paulo alone, only 33 have nurseries. An American-owned factory in Rio de Janeiro that employs 1600 women and 1000 men has a nursery for 31 children. Only 20 children attend. One private nursery has contracts with 86 establishments in Rio that employ a total of 12,000 women. In eight years of operation, the nursery has cared for five children (op. cit.).

In Sri Lanka, the government requires nurseries in the rubber, tea, and coconut plantations, which employ about half the working women in the country. Utilization of these services had been low until UNICEF sponsored improvements in the centers around 1980. In this case, as in others, mothers had no inherent bias against institutional facilities — and conversely, no absolute preference for other types of child care — but made their current child care arrangements with regard to the availability and satisfactoriness of alternative services (OEF 1979).

In countries such as Cyprus and Cuba, where the government is strongly committed to providing child care services for young children, institutional child care facilities are a real option for most working women (Anker and Hein 1985). Elsewhere, facilities are not only scarce but often unsatisfactory to the mother. Facilities vary a great deal in quality, cost, and type of service provided. Some emphasize the educational, psychosocial, and nutritional needs of the child, while others mostly provide custodial care for children of working mothers during working hours (WHO 1981; Myers and Indriso 1987). Many pre-schools, in emphasizing child development needs, have limited hours not coinciding with parents' work schedules. Furthermore, they tend to be staffed by trained educational personnel at a high teacher/student ratio, and so charge fees too high for low-income mothers (Tyobeka 1985; Acevedo et al. 1986).

On the other hand, facilities operating primarily to accommodate both the schedules of working mothers and their ability to pay often do not maintain quality care programs and their facilities are not clean and safe enough for mothers to see them as viable alternatives to informal child care arrangements. Location of the facility can also contribute to underutilization. In an effort to service as many children as possible, a day-care facility is often centrally located, too far from homes of working mothers (Bittencourt 1979).

Some innovative and more satisfactory formal services do exist at a different level. Small neighborhood-based services work better to meet the needs of parents and children. In poor neighborhoods in urban Brazil, "spontaneous creches" are common. Older women in the community take in children of working neighbors. The mothers pay a small fee and contribute milk, cereal, sugar, soap, etc. to the creche. This arrangement allows for convenient, low cost, and appropriate care for the children of urban poor women (op. cit.). Another example, again from Brazil, is a combined local and governmental effort, where a national social welfare agency provides for child care centers in Brazil. The agency runs its own day-care centers and also subsidizes existing centers, mostly in low-income communities. The centers it runs itself are intended to complement local resources. Thus, when forming a unit in a neighborhood, it uses local buildings and equipment, and taps into neighborhood social networks and child care patterns already operating. It provides two meals a day to the children and nutrition information to parents. In 1979, the agency ran over 2000 centers nationwide with a total enrollment of about 100,000 (op. cit.).

Finally, a minority of working women are in a position to contract an individual caretaker for their children. The highest proportions of mothers employing a maid in the OEF six country study of low-income women was six percent in urban Brazil and two percent in urban Malaysia (OEF 1979). Fewer than one percent of women in a low-income part of the city in Lima, Peru, have a domestic servant to help with child care (Anderson, [Chapter 11]). The Latin American results are rather surprising in view of the very large proportion of women in paid employment in that region who work in the domestic service sector as maids (e.g., 28 percent of female nonagricultural workers in Peru were in domestic services in 1972 [Anker and Hein 1985]). Presumably only higher-income women, who fall outside the scope of most surveys reviewed here, use maids for child care, whether or not they are themselves in wage employment; or maids may be mostly directed to do housework rather than delegate for the mother in child care (OEF 1979). A sample of all working women in Ghana, which was not limited to poor women, found that 24 percent of women arranged for daily child care by employing a maid, of whom some (an unspecified proportion) are unpaid. The position of unpaid maids is not explained in the study, but it seems likely that in many cases they comprise the foster children who repay their board and lodging by child care, among other services, as noted above (cf. Frank 1985).

SOCIAL AND ECONOMIC FACTORS

This section discusses how the economic and social parameters that might affect the need for and provision of child care appear to be undergoing change. The purpose is not to give an authoritative review of what is known but to lay out possible lines of influence on child care in a coherent fashion.

Some authors (e.g., Anker and Hein 1985) agree quite strongly that the child care services situation is likely to worsen in developing countries, heightening the conflict between reproductive and productive roles for poor women in future. They suggest that the demand for nonmaternal child care will increase while current services may not only fail to expand but actually be reduced. Moreover, it is clear that the current level of provision is itself inadequate to present needs, if the large share of unattended children in many developing countries is taken as an indicator of child care failure.

Female employment patterns

The productive activities of women cover a spectrum of employment types from domestic outwork or household subsistence agriculture to regular full-time contractual employment in a centralized workplace such as an office or factory. There is a corresponding variation in the compatibility of employment with simultaneous child care (though, as noted above, even where there is no apparent incompatibility, concurrent productive work and child care may be problematic and unsatisfactory to both mother and child). Despite the limitations of official national statistics of female employment, it seems to be the case that the distribution of working women along this spectrum of work types has been moving towards the more formalized end. The proportions of women both in the official labor force and in contractual employment positions have been rising in the Third World.

Between 1950 and 1985 the female labor force participation rate in developing countries as a whole rose from 37 to 42 percent and women's share of the total labor force increased from 28 to 32 percent (Joekes 1987b). Within the labor force, women are entering into more formal employment relationships. In all eight developing countries in Asia and Latin America where reliable data are available, the share of the female labor force registered as employees as opposed to self-employed or unpaid family workers increased between 1970 and 1980, in some cases, e.g., Korea and Singapore, very markedly (Hopkins 1983). Data are not readily available on the equivalent changes for mothers of young children in developing countries: it is possible that the changes in participation and employment status have been concentrated among younger and older women who either have no children or whose children are grown.

For the Dominican Republic, however, there is evidence to the contrary. The rise in the female labor force participation rate, which by 1980 had reached 37.5 percent overall — double the level of twenty years before — has been a generalized phenomenon across all age groups (Joekes

1987a). One subgroup of the female workforce is of particular interest. Female employees in factories in the export manufacturing sector constitute between one-third and two-fifths of all women working in industry. They are young, with an average age in the mid-twenties, and the majority of them have children, of whom many must be of an age to require child care services (op. cit.). These women workers are certainly not able to take their children to work with them; thus they bring a new and significant increase in demand for child care within that country. This case represents, in perhaps extreme form, a trend that may be embedded in the general statistics and points toward increases in the demand for child care services with changes in the nature of women's employment in developing countries.

Urbanization and Migration

The literature suggests that, in general, greater child care difficulties have existed in developing countries for women in towns and cities than in rural areas.[8] Various reasons for this can be suggested: possibly smaller household size and lesser presence of extended family in the urban locality for recent migrants from the rural areas; differential sets of job opportunities for women, slanted in towns towards more formalized jobs; a greater need for women to take paid employment in towns, reflecting the lesser opportunity for home-based subsistence production there than in rural areas; and higher school enrollment rates in towns for children who would otherwise provide sibling care.

Some of these factors are further discussed below, especially as they relate to household size and composition. The points to be made here are that urban populations are growing faster than rural in all developing countries and that there are some peculiarities of the social organization of rural-to-urban migrant populations that are relevant to child care.

In all regions of the developing world, the urban population has been growing faster than the total population (e.g., by 4.5 percent compared to 2.0 percent annually in low-income countries; and by 3.9 percent compared to 2.4 percent in middle-income countries according to the World Bank classification between 1973-1983 (World Bank 1985)). Accordingly, the share of urban populations (cities over 500,000 persons) has been rising: between 1960 and 1980 from 31 to 55 percent of total population in low-income countries and from 35 to 48 percent in middle-income countries (op. cit.).

A substantial part of the growth of urban populations is attributable to population movement out of rural areas. There is some indication that the rate of rural-to-urban migration may have slowed down in recent years along with reduced rates of national income growth (Kahnert 1987), but the demographic momentum is such that urban populations will continue to grow relatively fast in developing countries.

The normal pattern in rural-to-urban migration is for some, not all, members of an extended or nuclear family group to migrate to the city. Those considered to have the best chance of finding work will move first, and some or all (or none) of the group will later join that person in the urban area (see e.g. Stark and Lauby 1987). For a greater or shorter length of time, the original rural family network will be geographically dispersed, with a high likelihood that mothers of young children will be separated from kin, especially older kin, who might otherwise have been available for child care. This is a negative spin-off of migration for mothers of young children. A woman's need for child care help may thus be an incentive for speedy reconstitution of the family group in the city, but it may not have enough weight to sway the household's strategic behavior. Observations from Uganda show that it is not unusual for town dwellers who are struggling to establish themselves to conceal their address and place of work even from close family members to minimize the burden of providing accommodation, food, and jobs for needy relatives migrating from the countryside (Obbo 1980).

Changes in Household Forms and Composition

Household size and composition are relevant to child care because they determine, first, the availability of child caretakers close at hand to substitute for the mother and, second, the pressures on the mother to generate income and to have to seek child care services while she is working.

The issues here are the possibility that households may be declining in size and becoming less extended in composition. Falling fertility, as experienced in most developing countries, leads to reduced family size through limitation of the number of children born to a conjugal couple and reduced completed fertility among individual women. Urbanization, migration, and other social changes may be associated with a tendency towards nuclear rather than extended or joint family forms. The emergence of female-headed households, in particular (sometimes referred to as an "incomplete" family form), has major implications for child care needs. Smaller family-size means that fewer older children are available to take care of younger siblings. Simpler household composition implies a lower availability of substitute adult caretakers, combined with a likely increased — in the case of female-headed households, often an absolute — requirement on the mother to take paid work. Moreover, as noted above, smaller households may be even more resource-poor than appears, insofar as they have a lesser chance of belonging to a useful social network, and so have relatively weak access to social support services.

It is much easier to speculate about the likelihood of such changes than to supply evidence in support of them. There are methodological problems in that no standard household typology has been developed; and empirical data is seriously lacking. Studies may report cross sectional observations of the spatial distribution of different household forms, perhaps showing a higher incidence of nuclear households in urban rather than in rural areas. There are, however, no readily available time series data, nor any comprehensive studies relating, say, household forms to level of national income within regions of the Third World.

The statistical picture is equally unclear with regard to the incidence and trend of female-headed households in developing countries. A study completed ten years ago estimated that between one quarter and one third of households in the Third World were female-headed, the level varying from a low of 10 percent to a high of 48 percent of households in 78 developing countries (Buvinic' et al. 1978). No other up to date assessment has been made. There is no current estimate of the numbers and types of households headed by women and no in-depth, longitudinal view of their genesis and circumstances. The emergence of female-headed households is thought to be related to seasonal and international labor migration (which has been spreading and is mostly sex-selective), economic contractions that increase male unemployment and induce men to abandon their families, and to chronic male unemployment in areas like the Caribbean, where women's individual economic prospects are more stable (albeit at lower average earnings).

Whether or not their numbers are increasing, female-headed households are a major demographic feature in most developing countries. Though some female heads of household may receive income transfers, e.g. from a male migrant, in Latin America and the Caribbean and Africa (though not Asia), female-headed households have relatively low incomes (Population Council and ICRW 1987). Therefore, female heads of households generally have no alternative but to seek paid employment. The relatively low incomes they obtain are a reflection of low wages for women in the labor market and the low grade jobs that women obtain. It may be also that, to a disproportionate extent, female household heads are constrained by the presence of young children and absence of substitute household caretakers to take very low paid, home-based work.

Increasing Provision of Education for Girls
There is a clear trend throughout the world for increases in educational provision for girls in developing countries, though in some countries the level of female enrollments remains low, especially at secondary school level (World Bank 1985). Since it is an important goal of government and international aid agency policy to continue with these improve-

ments, the overall level of female educational provision for girls is likely to continue its upward trend. This development has, however, a negative impact on child care possibilities for women in paid employment. First, it reduces the availability of sibling child care and may increase the numbers of unattended younger children: if this is deleterious to them, this amounts to shifting the costs of increased school attendance onto the youngest cohorts of children. Second, in West Africa, the establishment of more rural schools for girls is associated with a reduction in fostering of rural girls in urban families, which was done so that they might continue their education (Date-Bah 1987). At the same time they became extra resource persons within the household to care for the younger children of the foster mother. Increases in female education also seem likely to reduce the supply of women workers to the domestic service sector, as noted in Ghana and Peru (Anker and Hein 1985). While these changes may eventually help to improve the general position of women in the labor market, they may impact negatively both on young children and on working mothers in the short-term.

All these points, taken together, tend to confirm the hypothesis presented at the beginning of this section, that child care services may well become more needed and at the same time more difficult to obtain for mothers of young children in developing countries. It becomes more pressing, in consequence, to reach a better understanding of the characteristics of current methods of child care, particularly as they affect the welfare of children.

RESEARCH AND POLICY IMPLICATIONS

The literature relating to child care in the Third World is generally very deficient in information and analysis of the different child care methods used under different circumstances. There has been virtually no careful study of the characteristics of different methods as they relate to child welfare, and therefore the role of child care as an intervening variable in the relationship between women's work and child welfare is at this stage almost completely indeterminate.

The one exception to this is the graphic result reported by Shah et al. (1979): there is a strong association between one type of non-maternal child care, namely use of a young child, often a sibling, to care for an even younger child, and malnutrition in the tended child. The result might not, however, stand if the data were adjusted to take account of household income and other factors, which is not done in the source document. Testing of this as a hypothesis in other situations is an obvious and important subject for research.

Research on the relationship between child care and child welfare has to overcome several methodological difficulties. First, each of the three variables involved in the women's work — child care — child welfare relationship is complex. This chapter has attempted to indicate some of the relevant dimensions of the first two of those variables. Any further work will have to rest on the development of a plausible conceptual scheme specifying hypothetical relationships between particular aspects of the variables. Empirical studies will similarly have to decompose the different aspects of each factor and make multidimensional observations of each variable.

Furthermore, attempts to evaluate the impact of different child care arrangements on child welfare will be undermined if no account is taken of the past history and possible complexity of child care arrangements for individual children. Current child care arrangements are not the appropriate measure of the potential explanatory variable if "child welfare" is measured in terms of nutritional status, cognitive abilities, etc., for these measures are the outcome of accumulated past influences. A history of multiple, co-existing child care arrangements for individual children makes rigorous, comparative assessment of the effects of different methods highly problematical.

Another relevant consideration is the child's age. Child care needs vary critically according to the age of the child. Research needs to be done specifying those needs and disaggregating the findings and analysis by the child's age. Despite the obvious importance of this procedure, it is used in scarcely any of the existing studies on the topic.

Policy implications are difficult to derive at this point, given the slightness of the empirical findings noted in this chapter. However, should an association between child malnutrition and the use of young child caretakers be confirmed, it would be of major significance to policy, and point very strongly to the need for promotion of child care services to broaden women's options for nonmaternal child care beyond use of siblings. Other social policy considerations, such as educational objectives, point in the same direction. Analysis of the range of likely factors affecting demand for and supply of child care services reinforces this conclusion.

The most appropriate type of child care service to promote should, properly speaking, await further research into the impact of different types on child welfare.[9] However, the matter is too urgent and important to await such investigations, and the types of neighborhood-based child care facilities used in Brazil offer, at low cost, a service satisfactory to the mothers — the best judge of their children's welfare that could be taken as a model elsewhere.

Notes

1. The particular expertise and resources at the International Center for Research on Women may have contributed to a bias towards the social sciences at the expense of the biomedical sciences in the literatures surveyed for this paper. This is unlikely to have affected the balance of information retrieved.

2. Nurturing and stimulation are also part of child care, fulfilling basic psycho-social and educational needs, but these are not explored in this paper.

3. These are women who fit the statistical definition of "employed" members of the labor force. For discussion of the limitations of statistical definitions with respect to women's work see Anker 1983 and Beneria 1981.

4. Turkey, Israel, and Cyprus are not included in the Middle East figure.

5. In most societies, a woman's worth and hence her self image continues to be defined by her role as a mother. Mothers may choose to give priority to the time-consuming task of child care and not seek paid work if their economic circumstances permit.

6. The point made previously about multiple child care methods may be relevant here. Although the source document is not explicit on the point, the surveys seem to record the primary method of child care only. It is possible, therefore, that other children spend a minor part of their time unattended.

7. Household here signifies a co-residential domestic unit of persons whose labor time allocation decisions are to some extent jointly determined.

8. Increased poverty and landlessness in rural areas, particularly in Africa and parts of Asia, make it imperative for more women to take paid employment, increasing their need for child care services. The urban-rural disparity therefore may not persist in future.

9. Myers and Indriso (1987) and OEF (1979) offer descriptions of child care projects undertaken by aid agencies and governments in a number of locations in the Third World.

References

Acevedo, Maria Louisa; Aguilar, Jose Inigo; Brunt, Luz Maria; and Molinan, Maria Sara.
1986. "Child Care in Mexico City." In *Learning About Women and Urban Services in Latin America and the Caribbean,* pp. 273-276. Edited by Marianne Schmink, Judith Bruce and Marilyn Kahn. New York: The Population Council, Inc.

Acharya, Meena and Bennett, Lynn.
1982. "Women and the Subsistence Sector: Economic Participation and Household Decision-Making in Nepal." World Bank Staff Working Paper No. 526. Washington, DC: The World Bank.

APHA/Clearinghouse on Infant Feeding and Maternal Nutrition.
1984. "Government Legislation and Policies to Support Mothers and Breastfeeding, Improve Maternal and Infant Nutrition and Implement a Code of Marketing of Breastmilk Substitutes." Report No. 3. Washington, DC: American Public Health Association.

Anker, Richard.
1983. "Female Labour Force Participation in Developing Countries: A Critique of Current Definitions and Data Collection Methods." *International Labour Review,* vol. 122 no. 6, pp. 709-723.

Anker, Richard and Hein, Catherine.
1985. *Sex Inequalities in Urban Employment in the Third World.* New York: St. Martin's Press.

BAM Zambia.
1981. "Some Observations on Households Run by Women Alone." Zambia. Photocopy.

Barlow, Kathleen.
1984. "The Social Context of Infant Feeding in the Murik Lakes of Papua New Guinea." *Ecology of Food and Nutrition* 15 (1984): 61-72.

Baud, Isa.
1987. "Industrial Subcontracting: the Effects of the Putting Out System on Poor Working Women in India." In *Invisible Hands: Women in Home-based Production.* Edited by Andrea M. Singh and Anita Kelles-Viitanen. New Delhi, Newbury Park and London: Sage Publications.

Becker, G.
1981. *A Treatise on the Family.* Cambridge, MA: Harvard University Press.

Beneria, L.
1981. "Conceptualizing the Labour Force: The Underestimation of Women's Activities." *Journal of Development Studies,* vol. 17, no. 32, pp. 10-27.

Beneria, L. and Roldan, M.
  1987. *The Crossroads of Class and Gender*. Chicago and London: Chicago University Press.
Bittencourt, Sonia.
  1979. "Child Care Needs of Low Income Women: Urban Brazil." Washington, DC: OEF International. Photocopy.
Buvinic´, Mayra
  1980. "CBIRD Revisited: An In-depth Evaluation of the Effects of a Development Program Grant on SCF's Program in Colombia and Honduras." DC: ICRW.
Buvinic´, Mayra; Lycette, Margaret; and McGreevey, William, eds.
  1983. *Women and Poverty in the Third World*. Baltimore: Johns Hopkins University Press.
Buvinic´, Mayra; Youssef, Nadia; and Von Elm, Barbara.
  1978. "Women-headed Households: the Ignored Factor in Development Planning." Washington, DC: ICRW. Photocopy.
Date-Bah, Eugenia.
  1987. "Sex Segregation and Discrimination in Accra-Tema: Causes and Consequences." In *Sex Inequalities in Urban Employment in the Third World*. Edited by Richard Anker and Catherine Hein. New York: St. Martin's Press.
Durant-Gonzalez, Victoria.
  1976. "Role and Status of Rural Jamaican Women: Higglering and Mothering." Dissertation submitted to University of California, Berkeley.
Engle, Patricia; Pederson, Mary; and Smidt, Robert.
  1985. "The Effects of Maternal Employment on Children's Nutritional Status and School Participation in Rural and Urbanizing Guatemala." Report prepared for U.S. Agency for International Development.
Frank, O.
  1985. "La Mortalite des Enfants et L'Autosuffisance Economique des Femmes dans le Mileu Patriarcal Africain." Paper prepared for the International Workshop on Women's Role in Food Self-Sufficiency and Food Strategies, Paris.
Hopkins, Michael.
  1983. "Employment Trends in Developing Countries, 1960-80 and Beyond." *International Labour Review*, vo. 122, no. 4 (July/August 1983) pp. 461-478.

Joekes, Susan.
  1987a. "Employment in Industrial Free Zones in the Dominican Republic: A Report with Recommendations for Improved Worker Services." Prepared for USAID/Dominican Republic. Washington, DC: ICRW. Photocopy.
  1987b. *Women in the World Economy.* New York: Oxford University Press, for United Nations/INSTRAW.

Kahnert, Friedrich.
  1987. "Improving Urban Employment and Labor Productivity." World Bank Discussion Paper No. 10. Washington, DC: The World Bank.

Kim, Jung-Ja.
  1986. "A Study of the Support System for Single-Parent Families." In *Women's Studies Forum*, pp. 5-49. Seoul: Korea Women's Development Institute.

Lomnitz, Larissa.
  1979. "Organización social y estrategias de sobrevivencia en los estratos marginales urbanos de América Latina." Proyecto CEPAL/ PNUMA, Santiago, 19 al 23 de noviembre. Mexico City: Universidad Nacional Autónoma de Mexico.

Mellencamp, Amy.
  1983. "Survival Strategies of the Poor: A Review of the Latin American Literature." Washington, DC: ICRW. Photocopy.

Myers, R. and Indriso, C.
  1987. "Women's Work and Childcare." Paper prepared for Rockefeller Foundation workshop, *Issues Related to Gender, Technology and Development*, February 26-27, 1987.

Nieves, Isabel.
  1981. "A Balancing Act: Strategies to Cope with Work and Motherhood in Developing Countries." Paper presented at the ICRW Policy Round Table, "The Interface between Poor Women's Nurturing Roles and Productive Responsibilities," December 10, 1981. Washington, DC: ICRW. photocopy.
  1979. "Household Arrangements and Multiple Jobs in San Salvador." In *Signs: Journal of Women in Culture and Society* 5 (1979): 134-142.

Obbo, Christine.
  1980. *African Women: Their Struggle for Economic Independence.* London: Zed Press.

OEF (Overseas Education Fund).
  1979. "Child Care Needs of Low Income Mothers in Less Developed Countries." Washington, DC: OEF International.

Popkin, Barry M.

1980. "Time Allocation of the Mother and Child Nutrition." *Ecology of Food and Nutrition* 9 (1980): 1-14.

1978. "Economic Determinants of Breast-feeding Behavior: The Case of Rural Households in Laguna, Philippines." In *Nutrition and Human Reproduction*. Edited by W. Henry Mosely. New York: Plenum Press.

Population Council and International Center for Research on Women (ICRW). 1987. "Family Formation, Poverty, and the Emergence of Female Headship in Latin America, the Caribbean, and Africa." Proposal of joint program of research. New York.

Powell, Dorian L.

1987. Personal communication. Kingston, Jamaica: University of the West Indies, School of Social Sciences.

Rosenberg, T.J.

1984. "Employment and Family Formation among Working Class Women in Bogotá, Colombia." *Journal of Comparative Family Studies,* vol. 14 no. 3, pp. 333-345.

Safilios-Rothschild, Constantina.

1980. "The Role of the Family: A Neglected Aspect of Poverty." In *Implementing Programs of Rural Development,* World Bank Staff Working Paper No. 403. Washington, DC: The World Bank.

Schmink, Marianne.

1982. "Women in the Urban Economy in Latin America." Women, Low-income Households and Urban Services Working Papers, No. 1., New York: Population Council.

Shah, P.M.; Walimbe, S.R.; and Dhole, V.S.

1979. "Wage-earning Mothers, Mother Substitutes and Care of the Young Children in Rural Maharashtra." *Indian Pediatrics* 16 (1979): 167-173.

Singh, Andrea M. and Kelles-Viitanen, Anita.

1987. *Invisible Hands: Women in Home-based Production.* New Delhi, Newbury Park and London: Sage Publications.

Sivard, Ruth.

1985. *Women: A World Survey.* Washington, DC: World Priorities.

Stark, O. and Lauby, J.

1987. "Female Labor, Mobility, Skill Acquisition and Choice of Labor Markets: Theory and Evidence from the Philippines." Report DRD284. Washington, DC: World Bank Development Research Department.

Tyobeka, Jennifer D.

1985. "Community Preschool Education in Swaziland." University of Swaziland Social Science Research Unit/UNICEF.

Weisner, Thomas S. and Gallimore, Ronald.
    1977. "My Brother's Keeper: Child and Sibling Caretaking." *Current Anthropology* 18 (June 1977): 169-190.
WHO.
    1981. "A Report on Alternative Approaches to Day Care for Children." Geneva: Maternal and Child Health Division of Family Health, World Health Organization.
World Bank.
    1985. *World Development Report 1985.* Washington, DC: The World Bank.

4

The Effects of Women's Work on Breastfeeding in the Philippines, 1973-1983

Barry M. Popkin, John S. Akin, Wilhelm Flieger
and Emelita L. Wong

Breastfeeding during the child's first year is one of the most important behaviors affecting infant health (Popkin et al. 1986). Breastfeeding is a time-intensive activity requiring the mother's activities to be compatible with infant care. Women who are away from the infant over long periods of time, or whose activities are physically stressful, may have great difficulty in successfully lactating, particularly beyond the infant's first few months of life when women may feel economic pressures to engage in income-earning activities.

The effects of women's work on breastfeeding are of considerable interest to development policymakers for two separate but related reasons. First, many Third World women have become increasingly involved in labor market activities, either through employment in the modern industrial and commercial sectors, or due to the commercialization of subsistence activities. These new employment possibilites may be less compatible with infant care than more traditional women's occupations. At present, however, only a few studies have actually documented changes in breastfeeding behavior as a consequence of changing levels and types of maternal market labor force participation (Pelto 1981; Popkin et al. 1983). Unfortunately, most of this research has focused narrowly on breastfeeding and its relationship to women's participation in the labor force. Studies that differentiate infant feeding patterns into exclusive and mixed-feeding, or that consider the age at which breastmilk substitutes and supplemental foods are introduced, have been rare (see Akin et al. 1985; Leslie, Chapter 2).

Second, it is believed that in many developing countries the extent and duration of breastfeeding is declining. More precise analysis of

breastfeeding patterns and trends shows that (1) urban women are generally less likely to initiate breastfeeding, and that they do so for shorter
durations than rural women; (2) women in the Caribbean, Latin America,
and large Asian and North African cities breastfeed less than Third World
women elsewhere; and (3) analyses of trends in breastfeeding behavior
over the past two decades are mixed, with increases found as often as
reductions (Ferry and Smith 1983; Millman 1986; Popkin et al. 1982; 1989).

This chapter reports the results of a study on the effects of women's
work on breastfeeding in the Philippines between 1973 and 1983. In particular, we describe the patterns of breastfeeding and then test the relative
effects of selected population characteristics and structural-behavioral
changes on trends in breastfeeding extent and duration. Concern here is
with variables at the macro level, and not with the specific behaviors
underlying the maternal work and child feeding relationships identified.

Changes in behavior that occur between cross-sectional surveys are
the result of changes in the characteristics of the population and changes
in the way individuals respond to identified variables. For example, those
who use the population characteristics approach attribute differentials in
breastfeeding to variations in parents' education, female market work
patterns, residence, and contraceptive practices (e.g. Akin et al. 1981, 1985;
Pelto 1981; Popkin et al. 1983). Almost all studies of this type use cross-
sectional data that tend to obscure time-related behavioral variations. To
date, only a few researchers have tried to alleviate this problem by using
longitudinal or time-series data (Butz and DaVanzo 1981; Haaga 1984;
Millman 1985).

The second approach focuses not on population characteristic correlates of breastfeeding behavior but on concomitant changes over time in
perceptions of appropriate roles and the actual behavior of women. These
changes alter the mother's position within the family or larger social
group and affect the household's decisions on strategies for providing
child care (Butz 1978; Gussler and Briesemeister 1980; Raphael 1976). This
second approach, which emphasizes changes in individual response to
causal factors, is referred to here as the "structural-behavioral" approach.

DATA

The data for this research were collected as part of the 1973 and 1983
National Demographic Surveys (NDS) of the Philippines, both of which
had nationally representative samples of ever-married women drawn by
multistage, stratified cluster sampling. Subsamples of 3,573 and 5,396
ever-married women and children from the 1973 and 1983 original samples,
respectively, were used in the analysis. The results are based on Filipinos
living in private households containing at least one ever-married woman,

at least 15 years, who had borne at least one child in three years preceding the surveys.

A few methodological compromises were made in order to obtain sufficiently large and comparable data sets from the two surveys. First, the reference period for births was extended to the three years before each of the two surveys, a procedure that no doubt introduces a number of recall errors into the data. A smaller sample could have been obtained from the data but would have yielded subsets too small for analysis.

Second, exclusion of other children born during the three-year period immediately preceding each survey was necessary because the 1973 NDS contains information only on the last child. Using this procedure captures about 80 percent of all births that occurred during these time periods. Inasmuch as the excluded children were born to women of relatively high fertility (short birth intervals) and, therefore, probably with shorter breastfeeding durations, it is assumed that their absence results in a small upward bias in the estimated probabilities of breastfeeding in both samples. The alternative approach of analyzing the most representative sample for each survey for the three-year periods immediately preceding them (the last birth between 1970-1973 and all births between 1980-1983) would overestimate any decline in breastfeeding extent and/or duration (cf. Page et al. 1980, 1982).

Third, explanatory variables were defined in a comparable manner. The variables selected for inclusion in our model are discussed in detail elsewhere (e.g. Akin et al. 1981; Butz and DaVanzo 1981; Page et al. 1982; Popkin et al. 1983). Variables available in both NDS surveys are similar to those available in the World Fertility Surveys.

Developing comparable women's work definitions required a focus on women working at the time of the survey (in 1973) or in the week preceding the survey (in 1983). Because of the restricted time periods, these variables considerably understate the proportion of women engaged in economic work. The derivation of the set of occupational variables eventually selected is discussed elsewhere (cf. United Nations 1981). It is important to note that these occupation variables capture to some degree the compatibility of women's work with infant care. Traditional occupations are most likely to be compatible with infant care followed in order by mixed, unskilled occupations, transitional occupations (clerical and sales), and professional occupations (e.g. DaVanzo and Lee 1983). Unfortunately, information on the location of the mother's work was collected only in the 1973 NDS and thus cannot be included in the analysis.

Unlike the 1983 file, that of 1973 has no indicator variable for children currently breastfed at the time of survey. To use the 1973 data for life table analysis, we make alternative assumptions on who are currently breastfed, namely 1) all children whose reported breastfeeding duration is greater than or equal to the computed ages; or 2) those children whose duration is equal to or at most two months greater than computed ages. (We treat other children whose duration is greater than age by more than two months as missing observation.) The mean estimates from 1973 are likely to be downwardly biased, but we find the median estimates to be the same under the above assumptions.

DESCRIPTIVE ANALYSES

Table 4.1 presents a number of selected demographic and socioeconomic indicators for the Philippines for the years 1973 and 1983. These indicators suggest that the country underwent a number of notable changes during the decade. The population not only became more urbanized, but also continued to concentrate in disproportionate numbers in the greater Manila area. Regional population figures show that migration from Visaya to Luzon and Mindanao continued throughout the period. Educational levels among ever-married females at least 15 years of age and their husbands rose substantially.

On the economic side, there was a rise in the median level of real income (at 1983 levels), and a doubling of the proportion of households with electricity. There was also considerable movement of men out of the traditional (agricultural) labor force and into the mixed or informal sector (i.e., the unskilled) rather than the modern sector. Interestingly, more women reported "none" for employment in 1983 than 1973, and among those employed there was a shift from the traditional and mixed sectors to the transitional and modern.

Changes in household composition were the opposite of what one might expect in a modernizing society. The proportion of extended households increased by three percent from 1973 to 1983, which is probably the result of rural-urban migration combined with the tendency of the immigrants to board with relatives or acquaintances. The average household size declined with slowly-falling birth rates in the country (mean parity declined by about half a child and contraceptive practice became more common).

TRENDS IN THE EXTENT OF BREASTFEEDING

Table 4.2 presents information on the proportion of mothers who ever breastfed classified by selected socioeconomic and demographic groups. The data indicate a 5.4 percent overall decline in the percentage of infants ever breastfed over the ten year period. The downward trend is more pronounced in urban than rural areas. A larger decline in breastfeeding also occurred among persons residing in Manila (9.4) and Mindanao (5.4) than among residents of other areas. Declines in breastfeeding also occurred among women with 4-9 years of formal education. Among the best educated women, there occurred an increase of about 7.4 percent in the proportion of breastfeeding in 1983 relative to 1973. Among women in modern occupations, the percent who ever breastfed increased by 10.0 percent over the period. Another striking finding presented in Table 4.2 is that the likelihood of ever breastfeeding decreased by 11.2 percent over the ten-year period for women in clerical and sales (transitional occupations).

TRENDS IN THE DURATION OF BREASTFEEDING

In addition to the proportion of infants ever breastfed, the multiple decrement life table procedure is used to examine whether the length of breastfeeding increased or decreased and at what age the infant ceased breastfeeding. Table 4.3 presents results on median duration of breastfeeding by selected socioeconomic and demographic groups. For infants ever breastfed, the changes in median durations differ considerably across subgroups. In the rural areas, the length of breastfeeding increased by 0.7 with most of the increase in duration occurring late in the first year (Figure 4.1). By five months of age, the proportion of rural infants breastfed in 1983 is already slightly higher than for infants of the same age in 1973. The slightly higher proportion (four percent) for 1983 rural infants continues until the twelfth month of age; afterward, the differences become larger, approximately 20 percent, and continue to increase for the older age groups.

By contrast, in the urban areas breastfeeding decreases by 2.6 months over the ten-year period (Table 4.3). However, the decrease in the length of breastfeeding in urban areas was due to decreases occurring primarily in the first year of life. By the fourth month, 8.8 percent fewer of the infants in the 1983 urban sample were breastfed than in the 1973 sample. By the age of seven months, 6.8 percent fewer infants were breastfed in 1983. At 14 months, however, a higher proportion was being breastfed in 1983 (Figure 4.1). From these findings it is clear that the decreased duration in urban areas for 1983 results from decreased breastfeeding of infants below the age of 11 months.

Also noteworthy in Table 4.3 is the large increase in duration of breastfeeding during the ten-year period for women with ten or more years of schooling. As shown in Table 4.4, these changes appear to be due to breastfeeding changes that occurred after the infant's fourth month. By contrast, in 1983 more infants of mothers in the highest education groups were breastfed at birth (Table 4.2), and at all later ages studied (Table 4.4), than were infants of mothers in the same education group in 1973. As the age of the infant increases, the gap between the percentages of breastfed infants observed for this education group in 1973 and 1983 increases.

Increases in the duration of breastfeeding between 1973 and 1983 also occurred for two other groups, the Visayans (2.8 months) and infants whose mothers had traditional occupations (5.5 months) (Table 4.3). In both cases, these increases occurred after the infant's first year (Table 4.4).

Decreases in the duration of breastfeeding were observed for other population groups. Residents of metropolitan Manila, and other urban areas, and wives of husbands in modern occupations all breastfed for shorter periods of time in 1983. However, the declines in the duration of breastfeeding for these groups were quite small, except for women with husbands in modern occupations (-3.2) and residents of Manila (-3.7) (Table 4.3). In all cases, the downward shifts in the duration of breastfeeding can be seen to be primarily the result of changes in the probability of breastfeeding occurring after the infant's first year. The data yield a somewhat surprising result with respect to patterns for women with modern occupations. While more infants in this group were breastfed at birth in 1983 than in 1973, the percentage being breastfed between four and 13 months of infant age was greater for the 1973 sample.

These descriptive relationships do not control for numerous confounding factors that may affect breastfeeding behavior. They only identify groups at a higher or lower level of risk of not breastfeeding. Multivariate analysis is needed to ascertain, while controlling for confounding factors, how much of the effect of changes in breastfeeding is due to changes in the population characteristics or structural behavioral variables.

MULTIVARIATE ANALYSIS[1]

Estimation Methods

In the multivariate analysis of breastfeeding trends, two dependent variables are of interest. The first is whether or not the mother chooses to breastfeed the child at all. Because of the dichotomous nature of the dependent variable, the logit method of estimation was used. The dependent variable was defined as $Y_i = 0$ if the ith mother breastfed the child and $Y_i = 1$ if the child was not breastfed. Thus, positive coefficients in the logit regression indicate increased probability of *not* breastfeeding.

The second dependent variable of interest is the duration of breastfeeding for those mothers who did breastfeed. For this study, we use a nonparametric, discrete time approach that allows the hazard to be nonproportional, thus the effects of the covariates on the risk of terminating breastfeeding are allowed to change through time.

To obtain the equation for actual estimation, we formulate the logistic function as a function of explanatory variables:

$$\log \left[\frac{q_j}{1 - q_j} \right] = \gamma_j + X_i \beta_j \tag{1}$$

where X_i are independent variables and β_j and γ_j unknown coefficients allowed to vary in different time segments. This variation in coefficients allows the estimated effects of the explanatory variables to differ for different durations of breastfeeding. Equation (1) can be solved for q_j and the expected duration of breastfeeding for a woman with any specified socioeconomic characteristics can be calculated (see Guilkey and Rindfuss [1986] for details).

Specification of the Model[2]

The goal of the analysis is the detection of the effects of changes in population *and* structural-behavioral characteristics on breastfeeding decisions. A first step in this process is to examine whether changes of the latter type have occurred. In the absence of any such changes in behavioral responses to causal factors, the coefficients in identical models estimated for 1973 and 1983 would be expected to be the same.

To distinguish between what we call unmeasured time effects and time effects that can be explained by shifts in either population characteristics or social structures, the model is first tested by introducing time-interaction terms. The following discussion will be in the context of the decision-not-to-breast-feed equation (1), which can easily be extended to allow for time effects. If we let $T = 1$ for each observation from the 1973 sample, and $T = 0$ for each observation from the 1983 sample, then

$$\log \left[\frac{P(Y_i = 1)}{P(Y_i = 0)} \right] = \alpha + \alpha^* T + X_i B + T X_i B^* \tag{2}$$

If $\alpha^* = \beta^* = 0$, then no behavioral difference exists in how the 1973 and 1983 samples of women respond to the same variables, and any difference in the probability of breastfeeding can be explained solely on the basis of changes in the observed values of the specified variables (differences in the population characteristics of the samples in 1973 and 1983 that are measured by X). α^* represents a purely exogenous effect of time not explained by the factors included in the model. If $\alpha^* \neq 0$, a shift in the probability of breastfeeding independent of the levels of the measured socioeconomic variables is indicated. Alternatively, a change in the effects of the socioeconomic variables themselves on the probability of breastfeeding between 1973 and 1983 is indicated when $\alpha^* \neq 0$. By noting which time interactions are statistically significant, the specific variables through which the structural-behavioral time changes operate can be identified. For example, if the variable "Manila residence" was the only one having a significant interaction effect, this effect would be the result of behavioral changes of Manila residents between 1973 and 1983. In short, if the coefficients of particular population characteristics differ significantly between 1973 and 1983 ($\beta^* \neq 0$), or if important unexplained time trends occur ($\alpha^* \neq 0$), then structural-behavioral changes (changes in the way individuals respond to causal factors) have occurred. An attempt to quantify all of the possible change mechanisms will be made in the simulations that follow.

Estimation Results

Logit results for the full model incorporating the pooled 1973 and 1983 samples appear in Table 4.5. The coefficients clearly indicate that almost all of the specified compositional factors have a significant effect on the decision to breastfeed and that many of them also affect decisions of breastfeeding duration.

A number of factors appear to increase significantly the likelihood of a mother deciding never to breastfeed her child. This likelihood not to breastfeed is increased for women who are older, have a high education (or have spouses with a high education), are urban residents (especially in Manila), reside in Mindanao, have a relatively high household income, or have electricity in their houses. These particular findings are consistent with those in the literature on the ever-never breastfeeding decision (cf. Popkin et al. 1983). Interestingly, many of these same factors are also significantly associated with likelihoods of different breastfeeding durations.

Determinants of breastfeeding duration include a woman's age, residence in Manila or Mindanao, household income and presence of electricity, woman's and husband's education levels, and woman's occupational status. While these results are consistent with the findings of others, they differ from earlier studies in their identification of several significant determinants, such as husband-related factors.

As indicated earlier, our model is able to capture a number of unique structural-behavioral change effects on breastfeeding behavior. Our results suggest that, over the time period measured, large and significant changes in breastfeeding duration occurred that are not explained by the causal variables included in the model. The statistically significant interactions between time and residence in Manila, residence in Mindanao, and occupations of the mothers, indicate a change over time in the impacts of each of these three factors on behavior. The time-interaction related to mothers' occupation is particularly interesting. Women who worked in modern sector occupations in 1983 were more likely never to breastfeed or to do so for only short periods (zero to two and three to five months) than comparable women ten years earlier. By contrast, women with traditional occupations in 1983 did not seem to exhibit any differences in their breastfeeding patterns from women in the same occupations in 1973.

Simulation Results

To help interpret the coefficients shown in Table 4.5, the probability that a woman with a certain set of characteristics will ever breastfeed, and her mean duration of breastfeeding if she does, is calculated. The "mean durations of breastfeeding" (Table 4.6) summarize the entire set of results on the probability of stopping breastfeeding during each interval listed in Table 4.5. They make it possible to examine the impacts of changes in the characteristics of the population (changes in the values of the variables in the model) separately from structural-behavioral changes (changes in the behavioral relationships that relate to the variables) on breastfeeding behavior between 1973 and 1983.

Row A presents the predicted probability of ever breastfeeding and the predicted mean duration of breastfeeding for a mother of average characteristics in 1973.[3] The last two rows (D1 and D2) present the average predicted likelihood and duration of breastfeeding in 1983, and the changes from 1973 to 1983. The comparison reveals an overall decline of about 3 percent in the extent of ever breastfeeding, and a feeding duration increase of about two months (for those ever breastfeeding) between 1973 and 1983. In the B and C sections of the table, these aggregate changes are decomposed into "population characteristic change" and "structural-behavioral change" effects.

Rows B1 to B3 present the "population characteristic change" effects. They show that most of the decline in the extent of ever breastfeeding can be explained by the variables of the model (2.8 percent of the 3.1 percent decline), thereby suggesting that the major part of the change is the result of the different characteristics of the mothers in the two samples rather than the result of behavioral changes between 1973 and 1983. For example, rows 3a to 3i contain estimates of some of the more important results of changes in sample characteristics. Increases in the education of mothers and their spouses, followed by electricity becoming available, changes in the occupations of women, and change to residence in Manila appear to be the more important characteristic factors affecting the extent of breastfeeding. The effect of "population characteristic" changes is to decrease the mean duration of breastfeeding by 0.86 months. Increased education of women and household electrification are associated with the largest predicted reductions in the length of breastfeeding, followed by increases in father's education, movement to residence in Manila, and increased household income.[4]

The "structural-behavioral" effects on the other hand, had a minor effect in reducing the extent of breastfeeding (-0.004), yet a large positive effect in increasing breastfeeding duration (+2.85 months). These results suggest that the actual response patterns to specific causal factors between 1973 and 1983 changed to some extent, and that this change had a large impact on decisions to increase the duration. For a mother for whom residence in Manila and each of the maternal occupation variables had the same values in 1973 and 1983, shorter breastfeeding durations would be expected in 1983 than in 1973. It should be noted that the larger predicted increase in mean breastfeeding duration is due mainly to the "time alone" effect (+3.29 months). This "time alone" variable measures a residual change in behavior between the two time periods that cannot be adequately explained by the specific variables in the model.

SUMMARY

The results of this chapter focus on two issues related to women's work and breastfeeding trends in the Philippines. The first relates to the identification of target groups — groups at higher risk of never breastfeeding or of decreasing the duration of breastfeeding. The second relates to identification of the factors associated with these changes in breastfeeding behavior.

Between 1973 and 1983, the extent of ever breastfeeding decreased by approximately five percent (88.9 to 83.5). Residents of Manila and Mindanao and women with clerical and sales transitional occupations showed the greatest declines in breastfeeding over the period; women with high education levels or professional occupations were actually more likely to breastfeed in 1983 than were similar groups in 1973.

On the average, the median age of the infant at which breastfeeding ceased remained constant from 1973 to 1983. Relatively large increases in the duration of lactation occurred between 1973 and 1983 and for Visayan residents, women with 10 or more years of education, and women with traditional occupations. The increase for these subgroups occurred because they were more likely to breastfeed their infants past the first year of life in 1983 than were similar groups in 1973.

Most increases or decreases in breastfeeding probabilities that had large impacts on the estimated duration of breastfeeding took place during the second year of the infant's life. The notable exception to this pattern is that infants whose mothers were residents of rural areas were more likely to be breastfed at five months of age in 1983 than were similar group members in 1973. In general, the longer duration of breastfeeding into the second year is expected to have only small health and demographic effects. In contrast, in urban areas the decreased duration of breastfeeding in 1983 resulted from reduced breastfeeding during the first year of life.

The findings provide evidence that changes in "population characteristics" and "structural-behavioral" relationships caused changes in breastfeeding behavior in the Philippines from 1973 to 1983. The behavioral change effects increased breastfeeding duration, an increase large enough not only to offset all contrasting effects of population characteristic changes between 1973 and 1983 but to increase mean duration by over two months. The specific factors modeled in this process were residence in Mindanao, residence in Manila, and mother's nontraditional occupations.

The changes associated with Mindanao residence were probably related to widescale social unrest and disruption. During the late 1970s and early 1980s, Mindanao was the site of both extensive fighting between the Philippine military and Muslim separatist movements and significant leftist guerrilla activities. Women living in Mindanao and exposed to this large-scale social unrest probably changed their behaviors with respect to even such fundamental activities as infant feeding.

Manila's rapid growth alone cannot explain the changes in behavior associated with residence there. If it could, the time interaction term would be insignificant. It is logical to suggest that the observed differences caused by Manila residence must result from changes in the behavior of mothers related to broader social changes that occurred in Manila and that were not explained by other explanatory variables. These changes in Manila may have been related to effects of the mass media, food markets, the health sector, transportation or other important unmeasured factors associated with residence in a large metropolitan area.

The location and type of work most women engage in has changed rapidly in the last decade. During the 1970s, the size of the modern service, governmental, and industrial sectors grew. At the same time, the nature of work in each of these occupations changed, as the size of the establishments grew and informal work rules became more formalized. The fact that women engaged in formal occupations tended to breastfeed for shorter durations in 1983 than in 1973 is not surprising.

The residual change not explained by any of the variables may be because of changes in attitudes, in decision-making processes, or in other relationships not well measured by the variables specified in our model. In his analyses of infant mortality trends, Preston (1985) concluded that socioeconomic variables alone do not adequately capture the significant determinants of infant mortality trends. He hypothesized that a major reason is the inability of socioeconomic variables to capture the determinants of breastfeeding and weaning practices.

The population characteristics effects, on the other hand, indicate reductions in extent of breastfeeding as a result of changes in characteristics of the Philippine population between 1973 to 1983. Most of the changes in the characteristics of the women sampled between 1973 and 1983 are of the type that would normally be associated with economic growth and modernization. The combined influence of these changes was a negative effect on the extent of breastfeeding. In particular, improved education, availability of electricity, increased income, and residence in Manila tended to reduce breastfeeding choices and durations.

Acknowledgments

This paper summarizes and extends two separate, published papers by Guilkey et al. (1988) and Popkin et al. (1989). We wish to thank the government of the Philippines, particularly the National Census and Statistics Office and its Director, Dr. Marcelo M. Orense, the Office of Population Studies who collected and prepared the NDS data, the University of the Philippines' Population Institute, and the Research Institute of Mindanao Culture, Xavier University. We thank Family Health International, in particular Barbara Janowitz, Kathy Kennedy, Shyam Thapa, and Nancy E. Williamson for helpful methodological and substantive suggestions and assistance in funding this research. We are also grateful to Ross Laboratories, in particular Tom McCollough, for analysis support. The Carolina Population Center provided logistical and computer support and we thank David Fugate, Lynn Igoe, Mandy Lyerly, and Margaret Mauney for assistance with this research.

Parts of this chapter (Figure 4.1, part of Table 4.2 and portions of related discussion) also appear in an article "Breastfeeding Trends in the Philippines," *American Journal of Public Health.*, (1989), vol. 79: 32-35.

Notes

1. Elsewhere we discuss the model and results in more depth (Guilkey et al. 1988).

2. Initially we tested the effects of alternate specifications of women's work on the extent and duration decisions. The variables related to mother's work, "ever-never work" and "mother's occupation" were statistically significant, with effects of occupation being more often found significant than those of the work-no work variable. The occupational variables probably capture some of both "work-no work" and "compatibility of work with child care" effects. Unfortunately, the data do not include a direct measure of one of the most appropriate work-related variables, the proximity of the mother's work to her home, or of any other proxy for the compatibility of the mother's work with child care (cf. Popkin and Solon 1976; Van Esterik and Greiner 1981). Our approach is similar to that of Davanzo and Habicht 1986.

3. In a related study, we examine in detail these patterns of breastfeeding duration (Popkin et al. 1989).

4. Note that the simulation results and life table results do not necessarily coincide because, for a nonlinear procedure such as the logit method, predictions of sample averages may not yield the sample average of the dependent variable. The simulations should be viewed as simulating the effects of changes in explanatory variables on a woman who starts out with average characteristics. Exactly the same changes in explanatory variables would have quantitatively different results if the hypothetical woman started out with different initial values for the explanatory variables.

References

Akin, John S.; Griffin, Charles C.; Guilkey, David K.; and Popkin, Barry M.
1985. Determinants of Infant Feeding: A Household Production Approach." *Economic Development and Cultural Change* 34: 57-81.

Akin, John S.; Bilsborrow, Richard E.; Guilkey, David K.; Popkin, Barry M.; Benoit, Daniel; Cantrelle, Pierre; Garenne, Michele; and Levi, Pierre.
1981. "The Determinants of Breast-Feeding in Sri Lanka." *Demography* 18: 287-307.

Butz, William P.
1978. "Economic Aspects of Breast-Feeding." In *Nutrition and Human Reproduction.* Edited by W. Henry Mosley. New York: Plenum.

Butz, William P., and DaVanzo, Julie.
1981. "Determinants of Breastfeeding and Weaning Patterns in Malaysia." Presented at the annual meeting of the Population Association of America, Washington, DC.

DaVanzo, Julie, and Habicht, Jean-Pierre.
1986. "Infant Mortality Decline in Malaysia, 1946-1975: The Role of Changes in Variables and Changes in the Structure of Relationships." *Demography* 23: 143-60.

DaVanzo, Julie, and Lee, Donald Lye Poh .
1983. "The Compatibility of Child Care with Market and Nonmarket Activities: Preliminary Evidence for Malaysia." In *Women and Poverty in the Third World.* Edited by Mayra Buvinic, Margaret A. Lycette, and William P. McGreevey. Baltimore: Johns Hopkins University Press.

Ferry, Benoit, and Smith, David P.
1983. Breast-Feeding Differentials." *World Fertility Survey Comparative Studies,* no. 23.

Guilkey, David K.; Popkin, B.; Flieger, W.; and Akin, J.S.
1988. "Changes in Breast-Feeding in the Philippines, 1973-1983." Chapel Hill, NC: Carolina Population Center. Draft Manuscript.

Guilkey, David K., and Rindfuss, Ronald R.
1986. "Logistic Regression Multivariate Life Tables: A Communicable Approach." *Sociological Methods and Research* 16:276-301.

Gussler, Judith D., and Briesemeister, Linda H.
1980. "The Insufficient Milk Syndrome: A Biocultural Explanation." *Medical Anthropology* 4: 145-174.

Haaga, John G.
1984. "Infant Feeding and Nutrition Policy in Malaysia." Rand Paper Series P-6995-RGI. Santa Monica, CA: The Rand Corporation.

Millman, Sara R.

1986. "Trends in Breastfeeding in a Dozen Developing Countries." *International Family Planning Perspectives* 12: 91-95.
1985.
"Breastfeeding and Contraception: Why the Inverse Association?" *Studies in Family Planning* 16: 61-75.
Page, Hilary J.; Lesthaege, Ron J., and Shah Iqbal H.
1982. "Ilustrative Analysis: Breast-Feeding in Pakistan." *World Fertility Study Scientific Report*, no. 17.
Page, Hilary J.; Ferry, Benoit; Shah, Iqbal H., and Lesthaeghe Ron J.
1980. "The Most Recent Births: Analytical Potential and Some Underlying Problems." Presented at the Seminar on the Analysis of Maternity Histories, International Union for the Scientific Study of Population, World Fertility Survey, and London School of Hygiene and Tropical Medicine, London.
Pelto, Gretel. H.
1981. "Perspectives on Infant Feeding: Decision-Making and Ecology." *Food and Nutrition Bulletin* 33: 16-29.
Popkin, Barry M.; Akin, John S.; Flieger, Wilhelm; and Wong, Emelita L.
1989. "Breastfeeding Trends in the Philippines." *American Journal of Public Health. 79:* 32-35
Popkin, Barry M.; Lasky, Tamar; Litvin, Judith; Spicer, Deborah, and Yamamoto, Monica E.
1986. *The Infant Feeding Triad: Infant, Mother, and Household.* Food and Nutrition in History and Anthropology. Vol. 5. Edited by John R. K. Robson. New York: Gordon & Breach Science Publishers.
Popkin, Barry M.; Bilsborrow, Richard E.; Akin, John S., and Yamamoto, Monica E. 1983. Breast-Feeding Determinnats in Low-Income Countries." *Medical Anthropology* 71: 1-31
Popkin, Barry M.; Bilsborrow Richard E.; and Akin, John, S.
1982. Breast-Feeding Patterns in Low-Income Countries." *Science* 218: 1088-1093.
Popkin, Barry M., and Solon, Florentino S.
1976. "Income, Time, the Working Mother and Child Nutriture." *Journal of Tropical Pediatrics and Environmental Child Health.* 22: 156-166
Preston, Samuel H.
1985. "Mortality and Development Revisited." In *Quantitative Studies of Mortality Decline in the Developing World.* Edited by Julie DaVanzo, Jean-Pierre Habicht, Kenneth H. Hill, and Samuel H. Preston. World Bank Staff Working Papers no. 683; Population and Development Series 8. Washington, D.C.
Raphael, Dana L.

1976. *The Tender Gift: Breastfeeding.* New York: Schocken.

United Nations, Department of International Economic and Social Affairs of the United Nations Secretariat, Population Division.

1981. *Occupational Classification Systems Constructed for Application in the United Nations Program of International Comparative Analysis of World Fertility Survey Data.* (ESA/P/WP.70) New York: Department of International Economic and Social Affairs.

Van Esterik, Penny, and Greiner, Ted.

1981. "Breastfeeding and Women's Work: Constraints and Opportunities." *Studies in Family Planning* 12: 184-197.

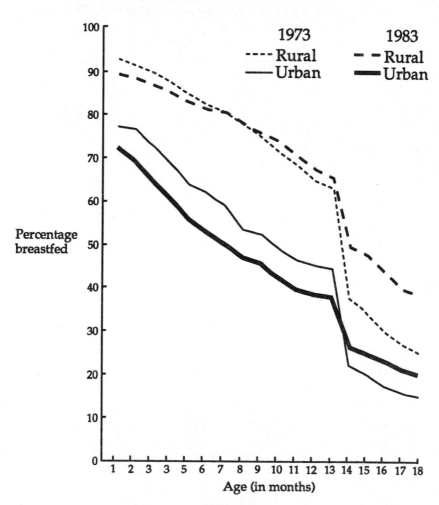

Figure 4.1
Percentage of urban and rural children breastfed
according to age in months, Philippines, 1973 and 1983.

Table 4.1   Socioeconomic and demographic characteristics of households with children born in the three years preceding each NDS survey[1]

Variables	1973 n = 3573	1983 n = 5396
Residence		
Metro Manila %	6.8	12.2
Other urban %	19.6	22.3
Rural %	73.6	65.5
Region		
Luzon including Manila %	50.3	55.2
Visayas %	25.7	20.8
Mindanao %	24.0	24.0
Migration Status		
Urban resident %	11.7	22.5
Urban migrant %	14.7	12.0
Mother's education Level		
None %	6.2	2.4
1-3 years %	13.6	8.2
4-6 years %	51.7	45.3
7-9 years %	18.4	11.5
10 and over %	10.2	32.5
Mean (years)	6.0	7.6
Father's education level		
None %	6.9	2.1
1-3 years %	14.5	11.5
4-6 years %	44.8	42.2
7-9 years %	12.8	9.3
10 and over %	20.9	34.9
Mean (years)	6.1	7.6
Father's Annual Cash Income[2]	6,570	8,100
(in median 1983 pesos)		
Low	1,642	4,500
Middle	6,570	8,100
High	13,140	16,500
Household has electricity (%)	23.7	49.0

Table 4.1 (continued)

Variables	1973 n = 3573	1983 n = 5396
Household Structure		
Mothers separated/widowed %	2.4	2.2
Extended family %	25.4	29.6
Male infants %	51.6	51.3
Mean household size (no.)	7.0	6.5
Parity of child (no.)	4.8	4.2
Mean age of mother at		
time of interview	30.5	29.3
Market Work		
Mother's occupation		
None %	75.3	78.5
Traditional %	8.8	4.2
Mixed %	10.8	9.7
Transitional %	1.3	2.0
Modern %	3.9	5.6
Working%	24.7	21.5
Mother's place of work		
None %	75.3	78.5
At home %	7.8	N.A.
Away from home %	17.0	N.A.
Father's occupation		
Traditional %	61.1	51.5
Mixed %	24.1	36.6
Transitional %	8.6	5.2
Modern %	6.3	6.7
Maternal Contraceptive Use		
Pill use %	7.0	5.9
Other clinical methods %		
(IUD, vasectomy, ligation)	2.4	7.5
Other traditional, less effective %	7.7	15.9
None %	83.0	70.8

1 Based on weighted statistics from the 1973 NDS and 1983 NDS.
2 For 1973 cut-offs used for low, middle, and high income groups are P1-1,000; P1,001-2,999; and P3,000 and over annual income, respectively. The 1983 corresponding figures for the income grouping are monthly values of P001-499; P500-999; and P1,000 and up.

Table 4.2   Incidence of breastfeeding among children aged 0 to 36 months
            at time of survey, Philippines, 1973 and 1983[1,2]
            (percentage ever breastfed, weighted life table results)

Characteristics	Incidence 1973	1983	Unadjusted Difference (1983 - 1973)
Total sample	88.9	83.5	-5.4
Area of Residence			
Urban	77.4	72.6	-4.8
Rural	93.0	89.3	-3.7
Migration Status			
Urban migrant	79.1	75.2	-3.9
Urban resident	75.4	72.3	-3.1
Region of Residence			
Manila	75.1	65.7	-9.4
Luzon	88.2	85.0	-3.2
Visayas	91.6	88.8	-2.8
Mindanao	91.0	85.6	-5.4
Mother's Education Level			
None	94.9	93.9	-1.0
1-3 years	92.4	91.0	-1.4
4-6 years	92.6	89.1	-3.5
7-9 years	86.7	82.2	-4.5
10 & over	66.2	73.6	7.4
Father's Education Level			
None	93.6	93.9	0.3
1-3 years	94.4	91.6	-2.8
4-6 years	92.5	88.9	-3.6
7-9 years	89.5	84.9	-4.6
10 & over	75.2	75.8	0.6
Mother's Work Status			
Works at home	79.4	N.A.	N.A.
Works away	89.3	N.A.	N.A.
No work	90.9	85.4	-5.5

Table 4.2 (continued)

Characteristics	Incidence 1973	1983	Unadjusted Difference (1983 - 1973)
Mother's Occupation			
Modern	53.0	63.0	10.0
Transitional	84.6	73.4	-11.2
Mixed	82.0	78.8	-3.2
Traditional	95.9	92.3	-3.6
Father's Occupation			
Modern	69.4	67.4	-2.0
Transitional	78.1	76.4	-1.7
Mixed	84.2	78.0	-6.2
Traditional	94.6	92.2	-2.4
Father's Income Level			
Low	93.9	91.3	-2.6
Middle	89.4	82.4	-7.0
High	75.1	69.7	-5.4

1 Information on the location of women's work is unavailable. Among all women engaged in market work, 76.7% breastfed their infants in 1983.

2 The adjusted differences for the total sample between 1973 and 1983 are -3.7, -3.4, -5.9, -1.6, -0.6, -4.3 and -2.7 when adjustment is done for area, migration status, region, mother's education, father's education, mother's occupation and father's occupation, respectively. The 1973 sample composition is used as reference population for the 1983 adjustment.

Table 4.3 Median duration of breastfeeding of children who were ever breastfed aged 0 to 36 months at time of survey, Philippines, 1973 and 1983.
(In months, based on weighted life table technique.)

Characteristics	1973	1983	Difference 1983 - 1973
Total Sample	12.4	12.5	0.1
Area of residence			
Urban	8.8	6.2	-2.6
Rural	12.5	13.2	0.7
Migration Status			
Urban migrant	9.2	8.9	-0.3
Urban resident	1.5	4.9	-3.6
Region of residence			
Manila	6.2	2.5	-3.7
Luzon	12.3	12.7	0.4
Visayas	12.6	15.4	2.8
Mindanao	12.5	12.2	-0.3
Mother's Education Level			
None	12.7	15.3	2.6
1-3 years	12.8	15.4	2.6
4-6 years	12.5	13.2	0.7
7-9 years	12.1	12.4	0.3
10 & over	3.8	6.5	2.7
Father's Education Level			
None	12.7	12.7	0.0
1-3 years	12.7	14.8	2.1
4-6 years	12.6	13.7	1.1
7-9 years	12.4	12.5	0.1
10 & Over	7.0	7.6	0.6
Mother's Work Status			
Works at home	12.4	N.A.	N.A.
Works away	12.0	N.A.	N.A.
No work	12.4	12.7	0.3

Table 4.3   (Continued)

Characteristics	1973	1983	Difference 1983 - 1973
Mother's Occupation			
Modern	1.7	1.8	0.1
Transitional[1]	12.2	4.9	-7.3
Mixed	12.1	9.1	-3.0
Traditional	12.9	18.4	5.5
No occupation	12.4	12.7	0.3
Working	12.2	6.9	-5.3
Father's Occupation			
Modern	6.2	3.0	-3.2
Transitional	9.1	9.6	0.5
Mixed	12.2	10.8	-1.4
Traditional	12.6	14.3	1.7
Father's Annual Income			
Low[2]	12.6	14.5	1.9
Middle	12.3	12.2	-0.1
High	6.8	4.5	-2.3

1   The limited number of cases necessitates caution in interpreting these results.
2   The weighted frequently distribution for 1983 is: low, 42.8%; middle, 42.0%; and high, 15.2%. For 1983, the weighted frequency distribution is: low, 48.8%; middle, 30.0%; and high, 21.2%. The differences in cut-off levels (pointed out in table 4.1, footnote 2), and frequency distribution explain the seemingly conflicting results in the trends for breastfeeding duration by income levels for 1973 and 1983.

Table 4.4 Probabilities of being breastfed at ages 4, 7 and 13 months, among children aged 0 to 36 months at time of survey, Philippines, 1973 and 1983 (based on weighted life table technique)[1]

	1973			1983		
	4 mos.	7 mos.	13 mos.	4 mos.	7 mos.	13 mos.
Total sample	77.3	69.2	31.0	71.9	65.6	40.3
Area of residence						
Urban	62.2	52.5	20.4	53.4	45.7	25.0
Rural	82.7	75.1	34.8	81.7	76.1	48.4
Migration status						
Urban migrant	62.5	53.6	21.4	61.0	53.2	30.9
Urban resident	62.1	51.6	19.3	49.6	40.9	21.6
Region of residence						
Manila	55.3	42.4	13.6	37.6	28.9	14.6
Luzon	75.6	67.9	29.2	75.4	70.4	43.5
Visayas	81.5	74.8	36.9	80.9	76.1	54.4
Mindanao	82.2	72.9	32.8	75.7	66.6	35.7
Mother's education level						
None	87.9	72.8	39.9	90.0	84.8	51.8
1-3 years	85.5	81.7	41.0	85.0	78.7	55.3
4-6 years	81.3	74.2	34.0	81.7	76.2	48.3
7-9 years	73.5	63.5	25.3	72.3	64.7	39.4
10 and over	47.3	35.0	6.7	53.7	46.4	25.7
Father's education level						
None	86.1	76.6	40.9	84.8	78.2	43.8
1-3 years	86.1	79.4	39.5	85.2	77.8	52.5
4-6 years	81.7	74.6	36.3	82.3	77.7	49.2
7-9 years	79.1	73.2	29.7	74.3	66.8	43.1
10 and over	58.4	46.9	13.2	56.9	49.1	26.9
Mother's work status						
Works at home	79.0	66.5	31.4	N.A.	N.A.	N.A.
Works away	68.4	61.9	28.1	N.A.	N.A.	N.A.
No work	79.2	71.1	31.6	76.5	70.3	43.5
With work	71.8	63.5	29.6	55.6	48.6	29.7

Table 4.4 (continued)

	1973			1983		
	4 mos.	7 mos.	13 mos.	4 mos.	7 mos.	13 mos.
Mother's occupation						
Modern	37.6	24.3	6.8	27.0	21.4	10.9
Transitional	70.2	63.5	22.1	49.4	43.6	28.9
Mixed	70.7	60.4	26.0	60.3	53.0	27.0
Traditional	88.0	83.7	43.5	86.2	77.0	62.1
Father's occupation						
Modern	53.5	39.9	11.1	39.1	31.7	16.6
Transitional	64.9	55.4	19.4	60.6	52.4	33.2
Mixed	71.0	62.7	25.7	64.0	57.6	35.2
Traditional	84.9	77.8	41.0	86.8	81.1	51.4
Income level						
Low	85.4	78.7	37.0	86.0	79.9	52.0
Middle	77.2	68.9	30.0	68.9	63.2	37.2
High	58.0	46.5	20.2	48.2	40.7	21.7

1 The ages of 4, 7 and 13 months represent ages following heap points (Page et al., 1982). Sample sizes for each subgrouping vary according to availability of information for that subgroup.

Table 4.5 Determinants of breastfeeding patterns in Philippines for last infant born in 36 months preceding survey date for pooled sample of 1973 and 1983

| | Never Breastfeed (0 = breastfed, 1 = not breastfed) | | Stop Breastfeeding During Interval (0 = continue to breastfeed through interval; 1 = stop breastfeeding in interval) | | | | | | | | | | | |
| | | | Months 0-2 | | Months 3-5 | | Months 6-8 | | Months 9-11 | | Months 12-14 | | Months 15-17 | |
	Coeff.	T-Value	Coeff.	T-Value	Coeff.	T-Value	Coeff.	T-Value	Coeff.	T-Value	Coeff.	T-Value	Coeff.	T-Value
Constant	-4.17	(-20.22)³	-5.16	(-15.89)³	-3.89	(-12.75)³	-2.08	(-7.17)³	-1.68	(-5.10)³	-0.31	(-1.22)	-0.80	(-1.67)¹
Mother's age	0.02	(3.13)³	0.02	(1.99)²	0.002	(0.17)	-0.05	(-3.94)³	-0.01	(-0.57)	-0.03	(-3.34)³	-0.34	(-1.94)¹
Male child	0.14	(2.16)²	0.11	(1.07)	0.00	(0.04)	0.04	(0.41)	-0.01	(-0.10)	-0.11	(-1.27)	0.16	(1.03)
Husband, modern	0.39	(2.69)³	-0.07	(-0.33)	0.27	(1.21)	0.33	(1.43)	0.20	(0.66)	-0.01	(-0.03)	0.63	(1.30)
Husband, transitional	0.57	(4.85)³	-0.19	(-0.98)	0.23	(1.27)	0.43	(2.48)²	0.30	(1.44)	-0.25	(-1.35)	0.60	(1.91)¹
Husband, mixed	0.47	(5.02)³	0.08	(0.55)	0.08	(0.54)	-0.06	(-0.42)	-0.06	(-0.37)	-0.28	(-2.39)²	-0.19	(-0.86)
Manila resident	0.42	(2.91)³	1.08	(5.03)³	1.12	(4.67)³	0.29	(0.90)	-0.72	(-1.17)	0.69	(1.91)¹	0.05	(0.06)
Mindanao resident	0.19	(2.14)²	0.05	(0.34)	0.41	(2.79)³	0.62	(4.47)³	0.52	(3.34)³	0.20	(1.52)	0.18	(0.81)
Has electricity	0.25	(2.93)³	0.60	(4.20)³	0.44	(3.26)³	0.51	(3.95)³	0.29	(1.92)¹	0.07	(0.59)	-0.45	(-2.02)²
Parity	0.05	(2.69)³	-0.01	(-0.39)	-0.01	(-0.45)	0.06	(2.23)²	-0.12	(-3.51)³	0.05	(2.03)²	0.01	(0.23)
Income, 1983 value	0.00	(2.66)³	0.00	(1.57)	0.00	(2.75)³	0.00	(0.96)	0.00	(0.30)	0.00	(1.19)	-0.00	(-0.74)
Husband's education	0.04	(3.22)³	0.06	(3.07)³	0.00	(0.12)	0.02	(1.09)	0.00	(0.13)	0.01	(0.68)	0.01	(0.34)
Wife's education	0.05	(4.11)³	0.07	(3.27)³	0.06	(3.27)³	0.01	(0.47)	0.00	(0.06)	0.05	(2.92)³	0.07	(2.09)²
Urban resident	0.37	(4.48)³	0.08	(0.61)	0.19	(1.47)	0.16	(1.29)	-0.29	(-1.98)²	0.07	(0.64)	-0.16	(-0.74)
Mother modern + transitional	0.17	(1.21)	0.47	(2.18)²	0.90	(4.00)³	0.69	(2.61)³	0.44	(1.21)	-1.23	(-3.14)³	-0.91	(-1.37)

Table 4.5 (Continued)

	Never Breastfeed (0 = not breastfed, 1 = breastfed)		Stop Breastfeeding During Interval (0 = continue to breastfeed through interval; 1 = stop breastfeeding in interval)										
			Months 0-2		Months 3-5		Months 6-8		Months 9-11		Months 12-14		Months 15-17	
	Coeff.	T-Value	Coeff.	T-Value	Coeff.	T-Value	Coeff.	T-Value	Coeff.	T-Value	Coeff.	T-Value	Coeff.	T-Value
Mother mixed	0.08	(0.61)	0.79	(4.01)[3]	0.57	(2.78)[3]	0.26	(1.19)	0.41	(1.68)[1]	0.19	(0.97)	0.12	(0.32)
Mother traditional	-0.03	(-0.11)	0.45	(1.03)	0.64	(1.76)[1]	-0.19	(-0.43)	-0.50	(-1.05)	-0.62	(-1.95)[1]	-0.26	(-0.51)
Time is 1973	-0.04	(-0.36)	0.90	(5.84)[3]	0.79	(5.09)[3]	0.68	(4.71)[3]	0.60	(3.80)[3]	1.03	(8.59)[3]	0.29	(1.34)
Manila, 1973	-0.28	(-1.35)	-1.13	(-3.72)[3]	-1.04	(-3.21)[3]	-0.45	(-1.10)	0.09	(0.13)	-0.43	(-0.99)	-0.34	(-0.33)
Mindanao, 1973	0.06	(0.36)	-0.13	(-0.51)	-0.47	(-1.93)[1]	-0.72	(-3.18)[3]	-0.34	(-1.37)	0.07	(0.32)	0.02	(0.06)
Mother, modern + transitional, 1973	0.39	(1.82)[1]	-0.61	(-1.80)[1]	-0.67	(-1.91)[1]	-0.30	(-0.74)	-0.98	(-1.52)	1.42	(2.64)[3]	-0.17	(-0.13)
Mother, mixed, 1973	0.19	(0.87)	-1.25	(-3.49)[3]	-0.04	(-0.14)	0.01	(0.03)	-0.83	(-2.12)[2]	0.05	(0.18)	-0.64	(-1.06)
Mother, traditional, 1973	-0.41	(-0.97)	-0.62	(-1.12)	-0.45	(-0.98)	0.23	(0.45)	-0.14	(-0.24)	0.43	(1.17)	0.03	(0.05)
Chi squared	673.3		1,440.2		1,612.5		1,823.6		1,407.3		3,937.1		799.7	

1. T-statistic significant at .10 level
2. T-statistic significant at .05 level
3. T-statistic significant at .01 level

Table 4.6 Simulation of population characteristics and structural-behavioral change effects on breastfeeding trends in the Philippines, 1973 to 1983.[1]

Variables	Likelihood of ever breast-feeding (1)	Mean duration of breastfeeding for women who ever breastfed (months) (2)
A. Predicted 1973 Behavior	0.902	12.54
B. Population Characteristics Effects		
1. Predicted 1983 level with only compositional effects	0.874	11.68
2. Net compositional effects	-0.028	-0.86
3. Decomposition of compositional effects:		
a. Mother's education level	-0.008	-0.30
b. Mother's occupation composition	-0.003	-0.02
c. Father's education	-0.006	-0.12
d. Father's occupation composition	-0.002	0.00
e. Household income	-0.002	-0.07
f. Has electricity	-0.006	-0.31
g. Parity	0.002	0.01
h. Resident of Manila	-0.003	-0.10
i. Resident of Mindanao	-0.001	-0.001
C. Structural-Behavioral Change Effects		
1. Predicted 1983 level with only structural-behavioral change effects	0.898	15.39
2. Net structural-behavioral change effects	-0.004	+2.85
3. Decomposition of structural-behavioral change effects:		
a. Time alone	-0.004	+3.29
b. Resident of Manila interacted with time	-0.002	-0.17
c. Mother's occupation composition interacted with time	0.000	-0.19
d. Resident of Mindanao interacted with time	0.001	-0.08
D. Total of Composition and Structural-Behavioral Change Effects		
1. Overall Predicted levels in 1983	0.871	14.55
2. Net change 1973 to 1983	-0.031	+2.01

1Column (1) based on logit results and column (2) on a nonparametric discrete time approach.

5

Breastfeeding and Maternal Employment in Urban Honduras

Chloe O'Gara

Is breastfeeding declining in the urban settings of developing countries because mothers are employed and thus unable to breastfeed? This question actually arises from two separate concerns: one, that in recent years fewer women breastfeed for shorter periods in developing country settings; the other, that mothers who are employed (earning income in the formal or nonformal sector, in or out of their homes) cannot or do not choose to breastfeed.[1] The research reported in this chapter shows that in Tegucigalpa, the capital city of Honduras, employed women breastfeed as successfully as nonemployed women.

The incidence or duration of breastfeeding has declined in recent years in some, but not all urban settings of developing countries (World Health Organization 1981; Millman 1986). A long-term perspective suggests that breastfeeding is a highly variable, culturally controlled, and learned behavior, with predictable health, nutrition, demographic, and economic outcomes (Fildes 1986). Breastfeeding practices have changed in many ways throughout history, and it is reasonable to anticipate that changes will continue to occur.

In recent decades, rapid changes in breastfeeding practices appear to have occurred in both developed and developing countries. This chapter will examine how women breastfeed in an urban area of one developing country (Tegucigalpa) focusing particularly on the challenges posed by employment. In the 1970s and early 1980s breastfeeding declined in Tegucigalpa, but recent data suggest that this trend has been reversed, and that duration of breastfeeding has increased.[2] (See Chapter 4 concerning a similar reversal of a decline among some working women in the Philippines.)

In the context of the debate over the changing roles of women and the implications of those changes for the rearing of children, concern about infant feeding has become a highly emotional topic. Women live these issues and conflicts every day in low income urban and periurban households of Tegucigalpa. The decisions they make are not simple, but most achieve a conscious balance and compromise between work and child-rearing responsibilities. One element of that balance concerns the manner in which they feed their infants. While very few employed women breastfeed exclusively for four to six months (as the World Health Organization recommends), the data from this study show that employed women do not terminate breastfeeding any earlier than unemployed women.

METHODOLOGY

Two studies of infant feeding practices were conducted in 1982 in Tegucigalpa. Study I was an ethnographic investigation of infant feeding practices in a purposive sample of 75 low income households over a nine month period (O'Gara and Kendall 1985). Results of this ethnographic study contributed to Study II, which was designed to test the generalizability of the ethnographic analysis to a larger representative sample (Martorell and O'Gara 1985). The ethnographic findings were not only the basis for design of a cross sectional survey, but also guided the plan for analysis and interpretation of survey data.

Study II was a cross sectional survey of 5,000 representative low income households in Tegucigalpa. In 927 of these homes there was an infant under one year of age at the time of the survey. In 912 of those households, mothers of infants were interviewed extensively and their infants were weighed and measured. The data that are analyzed here are for the 912 households and include:

- demographic profiles of households and mothers
- 24 hour recalls of infant feeding
- pregnancy, birth, and infant feeding histories
- anthropometric measures of infants
- maternal reports of infant morbidity and health care
- household income and employment

All quantitative data and statistical analyses referred to in this chapter are based on the cross sectional survey. Where ethnographic information or analyses are reported, that fact is noted.

Site

Tegucigalpa, where these studies were carried out, is situated in the central southwest highlands of Honduras in a shallow hilly basin of forested mountains. Growth of the city is rapid, currently estimated at almost 5 percent annually. Older neighborhoods are clustered in the center of a valley along a river. In these older central neighborhoods, buses and electricity are the norm, health services and markets are accessible, and most homes or rooms are rented. Newer neighborhoods, many of them originally land invasions, climb the hillsides around the center of the city. The existence or availability of roads, electricity, piped water, and other services varies from neighborhood to neighborhood.

Samples

The purposive longitudinal sample of 75 households, and the stratified cluster sample of 912 households with infants were demographically similar. Most of the descriptive information presented here is based on the survey data. In 1982, 81 percent of the households surveyed (from both old and new low income areas of the city), had electricity, and 40 percent had piped water. The birthrate was 27.8 per thousand; estimates of infant mortality ranged from 117 per thousand (extrapolated from the 1972 census) to 37 per thousand (based on 1982 city records).

Sixty percent of mothers interviewed were in-migrants to Tegucigalpa. They had lived in the city an average of 9 years. Almost 90 percent gave birth to their infants in hospital. Mean age of mothers was 25.13, and they had an average of 2.83 living children. Almost three quarters of these mothers said that the father of their infant resided with them. The average household numbered more than six people. About 95 percent of the co-residents were related by blood-ties to the conjugal pair.

PATTERNS OF EMPLOYMENT

Of the 912 mothers, 265 reported that they had earned income during the week prior to the interview. This indicator for "women's work" was chosen because an open-ended question about employment or expectations for employment resulted in more than three quarters of mothers responding that they generally worked or intended to work in the near future. Clearly this somewhat restrictive definition gives a lower boundary on the estimate of the proportion of mothers with infants who worked.

Of the employed women, 27 percent had no stable occupation, 39 percent worked at home, 22 percent worked in the nonformal sector outside their home, and 12 percent were employed in the formal sector. Each work classification encompasses several major activities as shown in

Table 5.1, as well as assorted other infrequently reported income generating activities.

As will be shown later, the type of work per se was not as important as the number of hours worked per day or week in determining women's satisfaction and choice of feeding methods. Among employed women, the number of hours worked per day and the number of days worked per week was related to the type of work in which they engaged. Thirty-three percent of women who worked in their homes reported spending more than eight hours per day on income generating activities. Similarly, 37 percent of women without stable occupations reported being employed more than eight hours on their last day of employment. Only 7 percent of women employed in the formal sector worked more than eight hours per day, and only 16 percent of women employed outside their home in the nonformal sector worked longer than eight hours.

Survey interviewers assessed the appearance of mothers and domiciles. Among employed mothers, condition of the women and their houses was related to income. The mothers who worked at home — the largest single group of employed women — and those without a stable occupation, worked longer hours for less pay. This was reflected in low interviewer ratings of their maintenance of themselves and their homes.

Eighty-four percent of employed women reported that they controlled decisions about household expenditures; 88 percent of nonemployed women reported control over these decisions. This difference was not statistically significant. A significant difference was found, however, in the amount of money over which employed and nonemployed women exert control. All respondents were asked how much disposable income from any source was available to them for weekly expenses. The results, by category of work, are shown in Table 5.2.

Nonemployed women as a group report scarcer resources than the poorest of employed women. Nonemployed women have less than half as much money to sustain their households than do women who work outside their homes in the formal or nonformal sector. The explanation of these data lies in the extremely small portion of their incomes that spouses were reported to contribute to household expenses. Less than half of the women interviewed were willing or able to report on spouses' income, but, unless the nonreporters were a distinctly different group, the pattern is very clear. Disposable income invariably included the mother's entire earned income, but not the total earnings of husbands or other members of the household. In the ethnographic study, most spouses and several maternal grandmothers and mature children made regular, but minimal, contributions to the household budget. This was supplemented by gifts of food, clothing, transport, or labor on which some mothers depended, but which they could not predict or insist upon. Milk powder was a favored gift among fathers of their children.

More than 80 percent of nonemployed, but only 63 percent of employed mothers reported that the fathers of their infants were co-resident with them. This difference and the ethnographic study suggest that need was a factor in some women's decision to work. However, in this urban population, most women also want and expect to work. Many of these women came to or stayed in the city because they wanted to earn income and enjoy the amenities that money can buy in a city. They viewed income generation as the route to bettering their lives and the lives of their children.

WOMEN'S WORK AND CHILD CARE

As a group, employed women reported more social and familial contacts outside of their immediate households than did nonemployed women, and more people helped employed mothers with the care of their children. Seventy-five percent of employed women, compared to less than 50 percent of nonemployed women, had help with child care. Sixty-five percent of employed mothers got regular help from their families, primarily their mothers or their sisters; only 45 percent of nonemployed mothers had similar assistance. Employed women's households were slightly larger, averaging 6.5 versus 6.1 people. Whether a broader network and more help with child care facilitates income generating activities, or whether employed women develop the support they need, cannot be determined from the survey data. However, the ethnography offers some insights.

In the ethnographic sample, women who perceived themselves as having choices — for example, to work or not to work, to live in the city or move to the country, to keep their children with them or foster the children to their own or their spouse's family, to breastfeed or not to breastfeed — were generally proactive in finding child care arrangements with which they were satisfied, and were active in maintaining those arrangements. These women tended to pay for child care or to explicitly reciprocate with services or goods. Many, but by no means all, of these women were employed and were aware that acceptable child care facilitated their income earning activities. These women persevered until they put themselves in a situation where they could achieve sustained child care arrangements. There is a clear association in the survey data as well as the ethnographic analysis between prolonged breastfeeding and satisfactory child care arrangements for six to twelve month old babies. In the ethnography and the survey, working mothers were a disproportionate percentage of women who terminated breastfeeding very early — in the first month — and those who continued to breastfeed through the first year of their child's life. The successful, prolonged breastfeeders did take time off from employment (usually 20-40 days) to rest, care for their babies, and establish lactation. They generally cultivated sustained support systems for child care and other assistance in their households. In the ethnography, household members referred to these women's breastfeeding as one reason why they need rest, relaxation, and assistance.

By contrast, working women who terminated breastfeeding early took very little time off from income generating activites, often as little as one or two weeks. Early weaners in the survey sample (those who introduced bottles early) reported having more help in the first weeks after giving birth, but less at later times. This pattern was also apparent in several of the families that participated in the ethnography. Relatives, neighbors, and fathers eager to assist a new mother see bottlefeeding as a tangible way to help. Weeks or months later, the baby is weaned and sick. The maternal energy and hours saved by "helpful" bottlefeeding in the first month after birth may have simply been traded for maternal days and weeks lost caring for a sick baby.

For five employed women in the ethnographic study, child care seemed to be one more obstacle that they could not surmount. These women, with one exception, were social and familial isolates. Several who were co-resident with a man were in physically abusive relationships. In more than one case, their current mates were not the fathers of their youngest children (the infant in one of these households died). These women tended to have unstable child care arrangements. They were often unhappy with the child care and distanced themselves socially and emotionally from the caretaker. They seldom expressed any notion of reciprocity about child care arrangements, whether paid or donated by family or neighbors. Three were earning very little money and sometimes living from hand to mouth. The economic realities of their lives sent them back to work within days or weeks after giving birth. These women were generally unable or unwilling to discuss their long term aspirations for themselves or their children. Several left their infants alone locked in their houses for hours at a time, or in the care of very young children. Invariably, other members of the community were aware and critical of these practices, but felt unable to intervene.

The ethnographic study revealed that women who worked in their homes were less likely to have their child or children cared for by another adult, and felt constant pressure to work, either on domestic chores or income generation. Feeding of infants was felt by many to be an interruption, which robbed time from tasks that were never finished. They believed that breastfed babies had to be fed more often, demanded more attention, and were more active (and thus more trouble) than bottlefed babies. Many of them saw bottlefeeding as a strategic approach to setting up a work routine to which they could adhere. More than half of the women who worked at home perceived themselves as having a hard time caring adequately for themselves and their infants. Mothers who worked long hours at home to earn income and were also responsible for all household maintenance, and those who were maintaining large households with several small children and no adults or older children during the day, were especially prone to these concerns. These observations raise serious doubts about the common assumption that work at home is the preferred arrangement for mothers and babies.

The women whose employment was not stable felt they had very limited options in terms of setting priorities and maintaining control of their lives and the lives of their infants. This was the group that spent hours to commute to jobs that paid little. (Tegucigalpa is a relatively compact city and very mobile. Women with fixed employment generally relocated to live close to their place of work.) Among those whose employment was unstable, decisions about feeding their children were based on accommodating jobs that materialized and disappeared from one week to the next. All these women — and numerous others who were not employed but hoped to work someday — worried that an infant who was not accustomed to a bottle in the first weeks of life would reject a bottle later. Therefore, they introduced bottles very early.

INFANT FEEDING PRACTICES

Breastfeeding Initiation and Duration

Health professionals and planners frequently cite employment as a constraint to breastfeeding because of logistical conflicts, the lactating woman's need for rest and calm, the difficulty of establishing and maintaining lactation with an employed woman's schedule, and the impact of breastfeeding on earning income. However, women in Tegucigalpa seldom mention income generation as the primary cause for terminating breastfeeding, which is consistent with the finding from the survey that incidence and duration of breastfeeding are as high among women who work as among women who do not work. The percentage of infants reported as having been breastfed in the 24 hours preceding the survey is very similar at all ages for employed and nonemployed women (see Figure 5.1).

Initiation of breastfeeding is almost universal: 96 percent of mothers begin breastfeeding their children. A greater percentage of employed than nonemployed mothers breastfeed (including exclusive and supplemented breastfeeding). The difference in rates between employed and unemployed mothers is not significant, but the trend is consistent: at all ages (with the exception of five months) a greater percentage of employed mothers breastfeed than do nonemployed mothers (see Table 5.3).

Employed mothers introduce supplements to breastmilk earlier than do nonemployed mothers, but do not stop breastfeeding. Early introduction of supplements is not predictive of early termination of breastfeeding for employed women, although for unemployed women the early introduction of supplements is associated with early cessation of breastfeeding.

Among employed women those at highest risk for early cessation of breastfeeding are those who earn low wages in the formal sector, work more than six hours per day five to six days per week, and have help with child care at home. Most of the variance in breastfeeding practices within the group of employed mothers is accounted for by short periods of postpartum leave — less than the traditional and legal forty days for most postpartum mothers. Multiple regression analyses show that for the population as a whole, early cessation of breastfeeding was primarily associated with the length of postpartum leave from work — including housework for women not generating income — and the number of hours worked per day ($R^2 = .25$, $P < .0001$).

In brief, for this population of low income women in Tegucigalpa, the dichotomous variable of employed versus nonemployed accounted for almost no variation in duration of breastfeeding. However, a greater number of hours worked daily during the forty days postpartum period and a shorter postpartum leave was as predictive of early termination of breastfeeding for housewives as it is for their employed sisters. The Honduran tradition of forty days postpartum respite from work seems to be an excellent prescription for successful lactation. For women at home, just as for their income earning sisters, there is no substitute for encouragement, support, and assistance. Declines in breastfeeding associated with urbanization may reflect changes in social and familial network support systems more than they reflect changes in employment patterns among women.

Patterns of Breastfeeding

Employed mothers reported more feeding of breastmilk substitutes (artificial milks) and supplements (other foods) than nonemployed mothers. Mean number of servings of semisolid foods per day for infants of employed mothers was 2.1, while for infants of nonemployed mothers it was 1.7 ($X^2 = 6.5$, $N = 894$, $p < .01$). Employed mothers did not introduce bottles significantly earlier than nonemployed mothers. In fact, 17 percent of nonemployed mothers gave their infants bottles on the first day postpartum, compared with 9 percent of employed mothers. Once bottlefeeding began, however, employed mothers gave their infants more milk in bottles and spent more of their income on milk powder. Infants of employed mothers were given an average of 3.8 bottles per day compared with 3.4 bottles for other infants. Weekly expenditures for milk powder averaged $7.13 for employed women and $6.67 for nonemployed women.[3]

The number of hours worked per day is negatively associated with the number of nursing sessions reported by employed mothers ($F=1.7$, $p<.01$). Although employed mothers nurse fewer times per day (2.4) than do unemployed mothers (3.1) and do not report more night feeding, employed mothers compensate for lowered frequency with longer nursing sessions. Mean number of minutes spent nursing per day by employed mothers was 25.2, compared with 24.7 minutes for nonemployed mothers. Rates of demand versus scheduled breastfeeding were found to be similar for the two groups.

The mothers' estimates of the time they spent breastfeeding — approximately 25 minutes per day — are also of interest for discussions of the opportunity costs of breastfeeding. These estimates and observations during the ethnographic study suggest that, once lactation is well established in the second or third month, time spent breastfeeding is comparable to time spent on bottle and milk powder procurement and preparation (when the mother herself performs these tasks).

Patterns of Bottlefeeding

Infants are typically fed on a schedule whether by a mother or a caretaker. Most breastfeeding "on demand," particularly for babies three months and older, is fit in between scheduled bottles. Women employed outside the home are the group most likely to breastfeed on demand without the interruption of scheduled bottles, although they do so only in the evening and on weekends.

Bottlefeeding in this population is done with a minimum of physical contact between baby and feeder, especially if the baby is over three months and can assist with holding the bottle. Propped bottles pose a health risk for young infants, and for infants of any age there may be psychological risks due to reduced tactile stimulation and social and emotional interaction.

Methods of bottlefeeding were distributed similarly among employed and nonemployed women. Only 27 percent of infants of employed mothers were routinely held while bottlefed; 30.5 percent were sometimes held, but usually left in bed with a bottle; 21.5 percent were always fed with a propped bottle in bed, while 21 percent of infants were expected to hold their own bottles. The percentage distribution among nonemployed women was approximately the same, although even more (27 percent) routinely left their babies with propped bottles. All women mentioned the convenience and freedom to work as a major advantage of bottles, and their practices suggest that they maximize the convenience. Most women cited the need to complete household chores rather than income generating activities as the significant work conflict with breastfeeding.

Nutrition and Health of Infants

Other analyses of these data (Martorell and O'Gara 1985) have shown that in this population breastfed infants enjoy better health and nutritional status than bottlefed infants, and that mixed fed infants occupy a middle ground between the two, especially in the first nine months of infant life (see Figure 5.2). Thus, it may be a matter of concern that infants of employed mothers are supplemented early. On the other hand, that concern is equally applicable to infants of nonemployed mothers; 80 percent of all infants in Tegucigalpa are given at least one bottle of milk daily by their second month birthday. Since employed and nonemployed mothers feed in similar ways, it is not surprising that the nutritional status of their infants is indistinguishable. Analyses examining type of employment, number of hours worked, and number of days worked showed that these variables were not predictive of infant nutritional status when age of infant and household income were controlled. The best predictors of infant nutritional status in this population are feeding patterns, and less than optimal feeding patterns are shared by employed and nonemployed women alike.

Reports of infant illness episodes do not differ significantly between the two maternal employment groups. The best predictor of infant morbidity is early introduction of supplements to breastmilk, regardless of a mother's employment status. Non-significant trends in the data for each trimester of infant age suggest that 3-12 months old children of employed mothers suffer more episodes of diarrhea. Increased risk of illness is concentrated in households where mothers report little assistance with child care or very young caretakers in charge of their infants while they work.

The more people who help employed women with child care, the better the nutritional status of the infant who is cared for (N=215, F=6.5, p<.001), when income and other variables are controlled. In the ethnography, employed mothers of older infants who had good support networks tended to breastfeed for long periods, were encouraged and assisted by their families, and were very careful in their choices about infant feeding, trying to maximize benefits for the infant while bringing in income for their households. They and other members of their households recognized the nutritional and health benefits of breastfeeding. Breastfeeding was very much a household endeavor, and the breastfeeding mother was generally relieved of other duties for several brief periods before leaving in the morning and after returning at night.

Among already weaned babies, mother's work was negatively associated with infant nutritional status when income and the mother's own physical condition were controlled (N=289, F=2.68, p<.05). Early cessation of breastfeeding among employed women was prevalent among those with little postpartum leave in formal sector or unstable occupations. Employed mothers whose infants were at nutritional risk tended to be mothers who earned very little, and whose own physical condition and household appeared rundown according to reports from interviewers. In the ethnographic study, several women in this category ceased to breastfeed unwillingly. They were not comfortable for health and economic reasons with their decision to exclusively bottlefeed, but felt they had no options since they did not have time to adequately establish lactation and were in desperate need of income. As their children grew, they were simply unable to spend more of their scarce income on milk powder. This, coupled with high morbidity, resulted in declining nutritional status of their children.

By contrast, nonemployed and wealthier employed women who elected to terminate breastfeeding early were often very knowledgeable about and comfortable with bottlefeeding, were available themselves or had a competent surrogate to monitor hygiene, and tended to have higher household incomes, which enabled them to bottlefeed more successfully.

In the ethnography, satisfaction with any pattern of infant feeding — exclusive breastfeeding, mixed feeding, or exclusive bottlefeeding — was strongly associated with women's perception of their ability to choose. Notably, among working women, the great majority chose to breastfeed. They did so very consciously and successfully, they perceived health benefits for their infants, and most expressed strong personal satisfaction with the decision.

CONCLUSION

In this population, employment per se is not an impediment to breastfeeding. Neither incidence, duration, nor overall use of mixed feeding differed significantly between employed and nonemployed mothers. Inadequate postpartum leave from employment or from housework did appear to interfere with successful establishment of lactation. The Honduran tradition of forty days of respite after birth is an excellent prescription for successful breastfeeding. In households where mothers are assisted during the first forty days postpartum, successful prolonged breastfeeding seems to be no problem, even for women who work full time outside the home.

Exclusive breastfeeding is attempted for two months by less than 20 percent of mothers regardless of employment status. Mixed feeding is the norm for both employed and nonemployed mothers. Within a mixed feeding pattern, employed women reported in the ethnographic study that, once lactation was well established, they were able to sustain breastfeeding for as long as they chose to do so.

Mixed feeding beginning early in infancy is the rule, not the exception, in this setting. Homemakers perceived themselves as working under difficult time pressures and regarded the hands-off convenience and scheduling of bottlefeeding as a useful element in the organization of their household centered work lives. Unfortunately, to maximize the time savings of bottlefeeding, most infants are fed in bed with a propped bottle, without physical contact or social interaction. Physical and psycho-social stimulation essential to normal development is concentrated in the brief time during which they are breastfed for the majority of infants of both employed and nonemployed women.

The average amount of time spent breastfeeding was approximately 25 minutes per day. Employed women nurse less frequently but for longer periods than housewives, so that total time spent nursing by each group was virtually the same. There did not appear to be significant differences in health or nutrition associated with these different patterns of breastfeeding of mixed fed infants.

The health and nutritional status of infants whose mothers were employed was equivalent to that of infants of mothers who did not engage in income generating activities. However, for very low income households where a network of adults was not available to share child care, mothers' employment was negatively associated with infant nutritional status. A disproportionate number of these mothers were unable to take forty days leave postpartum and did not sustain breastfeeding.

In sum, the ethnographic and survey data demonstrate the feasibility of breastfeeding by employed women in this developing country urban setting. Postpartum leave from employment and household tasks to establish lactation and household support appear to facilitate successful breastfeeding by all women. The forty days postpartum leave, which is traditional in Honduras, appears to be more than adequate for this purpose. Employed women whose leave was less than several weeks, however, experienced the highest rate of early lactation failure, and were least satisfied with their infant feeding practices. Assuring adequate postpartum leave, and encouraging families and communities to support breastfeeding by assisting mothers with household duties during the postpartum period appear to be useful approaches to promoting breastfeeding by employed and nonemployed women alike.

Notes

1. See, for example, the prominence given to maternal employment as a threat to breastfeeding in the 1986 report on the UNICEF "Consultation on Infant Feeding and Breastfeeding".

2. Personal communication, James Shelton, AID, based on Family Health International analyses of 1981 and 1987 Contraceptive Prevalence Survey data on breastfeeding practices in Honduras.

3. It is worth noting that these average costs for breastmilk substitutes are approximately one third the disposable incomes of the nonemployed and low earning women.

References

Fildes, Valerie.
 1986. *Breasts, Bottles, and Babies: A History of Infant Feeding.* Edinburgh, England. Edinburgh University Press.

Martorell, Reynaldo and O'Gara, Chloe.
 1985. "Breastfeeding, Infant Health and Socioeconomic Status." *Medical Anthropology,* vol 9, no. 2, pp. 173-182.

Millman, Sarah.
 1986."Trends in breastfeeding in a dozen developing countries." *International Family Planning Perspectives,* vol 12, no. 3, pp. 91-94.

O'Gara, Chloe and Kendall, Carl.
 1985. "Fluids and Powders: Options for Infant Feeding." *Medical Anthropology,* vol 9, no. 2, pp. 107-122.

World Health Organization.
 1981. *Contemporary Patterns of Breastfeeding.* Geneva: WHO.

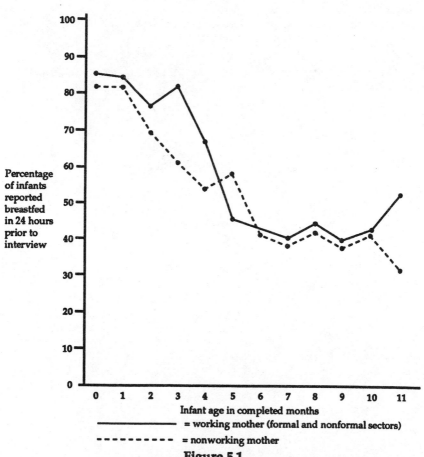

Figure 5.1
Percentage of Infants by Age Consuming Breastmilk.
Tegucigalpa, 1982

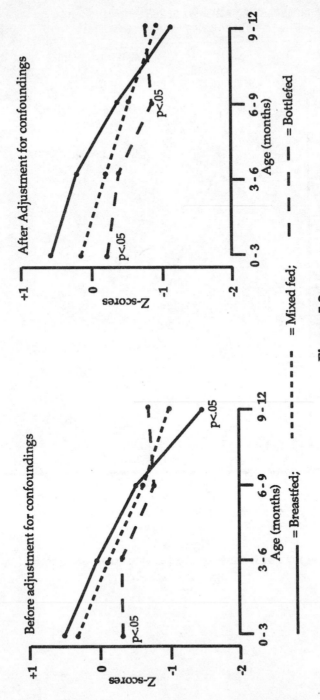

Figure 5.2

Length for Age Z-Score by Category of Infant Feeding

Table 5.1 Income generating activities of 265 employed mothers, Tegucigalpa, 1982

Category	Percentage	Main Income Generating Activities Included in Category
No stable occupation	27	Any of those cited below, but without expectation of continuing ("No Tiene Fijo")
Stable occupation:		
Work in own home	39	Cooking, sewing, washing, ironing
Nonformal sector	22	Housecleaning, domestic services, street or market sales
Formal sector	12	Office or factory, shop attendant

Table 5.2 Disposable household income and earnings of 912 low income mothers of infants, Tegucigalpa, 1982

Income Source	Percentage	Total Disposable Income: $/week	Earned Income
Not currently employed	71	$22/week	0
Work in own home	11	$28/week	$18.5/week
No stable occupation	8	$26/week	$16.5/week
Nonformal sector	6	$48/week	$38/week
Formal sector	4	$53/week	$39/week

Table 5.3   Percentage of Infants fed breastmilk only, breast and substitute milks, or bottle only (substitute milk) by employment status of mother and age of Infant, Teguciagalpa, 1982

Age in Months	Mother Works or Studies Percentage Fed			Mother Does Not Work Percentage Fed		
	Breast	Mixed	Bottle	Breast	Mixed	Bottle
0	21.4	64.3	14.3	34.1	48.2	17.7
1	15.8	68.4	15.8	37.2	45.1	17.7
2	4.8	71.4	23.8	23.2	46.4	30.4
3	10.7	71.4	17.9	15.8	45.6	38.6
4	0.0	66.7	33.3	12.5	41.7	45.8
5	10.0	35.0	55.0	16.2	41.9	41.9
6	9.4	34.4	56.2	13.9	27.8	58.3
7	16.7	23.3	60.0	21.8	16.4	61.8
8	11.1	33.3	55.6	22.6	18.9	58.5
9	21.7	17.4	60.9	12.5	25.0	62.5
10	23.8	19.1	57.1	13.6	27.1	59.3
11	28.6	24.3	57.1	20.0	11.6	67.4

6

Women's Market Work, Infant Feeding Practices, and Infant Nutrition Among Low-Income Women in Santiago, Chile*

Isabel Vial, Eugenia Muchnik and Francisco Mardones S.

Most programs and policies seeking to improve infant nutrition are oriented to increase initiation and duration of breastfeeding practices. Yet, they often fail to achieve their desired impact because mother's time is usually viewed as an underutilized and low value resource that is both plentiful and readily available. In reality, however, women's time is a scarce resource that must be allocated among competing ends, such as household tasks, childbearing and caring, income generation, and leisure. In order to achieve improved child nutrition, there is a need to understand the interactions between these activities, and the ways that changes in mother's time allocation affect the welfare of her children.

Women's participation in the labor force is often a matter of economic survival, particularly among the poorest households. The process of development in Chile has provided economic opportunities for women and access to certain public services. In the long run, this may contribute to the enhancement of family health and nutritional well-being. However, if social support services do not accompany women's participation in the labor force, especially for mothers of low income families, during the transitional stages these development changes may have a negative impact on infant nutritional well-being. The question then becomes: are the infants bearing part of the cost of economic development and urbanization? We hypothesize that infants are, in fact, bearing this cost, and that the answer to this problem is not only through the promotion of breastfeed-

*This study was funded by the Nestle Foundation S.A. and the Kellogg Foundation.

ing, but also through social welfare programs specifically designed to help mothers cope with their responsibilities, both as income earners and child care providers.

The purpose of the study reported in this chapter was to gain further insight into the interaction between women's employment status, infant feeding practices, and infant nutrition among low income urban families. Primary data from a prospective cohort study were collected from a sample of working and nonworking mothers whose infants were observed from birth to six months of age. The focus of the analysis here is on the competing demands on mother's time resulting from her maternal and working activities. Particular attention is given to understanding the choices underlying breastfeeding practices within a social and economic context. The framework for the analysis uses the concepts of human capital and household production of health and nutrition.

CONCEPTUAL FRAMEWORK

A theory of household production has its foundations in the works of Lancaster (1966) and Muth (1966), but it is more commonly attributed to Becker (1965) for his work on the allocation of time. The human capital school at the University of Chicago (Schultz 1973) applied the theory to issues of women's labor force participation and fertility decisions in a large number of settings in developed and developing countries.

The theory acknowledges that not all dimensions of consumer satisfaction are derived from goods and services purchased in the market place. Consumers also obtain utility from goods and, especially, services that they produce at home. In fact, the household is viewed as a production-consumption unit where members use various combinations of inputs, both purchased externally to the household and provided by the members themselves, to produce a combination of outputs that are, in their most basic form, the sources of satisfaction of wants and needs for the household members.

One of the major inputs used in the household production model is the time of household members. An additional component is the recognition of the different levels of education, technical training, and general experience of individual members that add to their human capital. The concept of human capital is essentially an adaptation of the traditional concept of capital where an input in the production process is also an output of some previous production process. In the case of human capital, the inputs used to increase the size or stock of human capital are education (formal and informal), health care, diet and exercise, and whatever other general experience increases the individual's ability to produce and consume more efficiently.

The combination of monetary income and household production introduces the concept of full income. This concept recognizes that the real income available to members of a household is usually greater than the money measures of income earned in factor markets. The value of full income is equivalent to the value of monetary income and the value of the time contributed by household members to the production process.

In this approach, the household is the main environment in which the allocation of human and material resources determines the costs and consequences of nutrition and health for its members. As a rule, mothers exhibit rational behavior in making choices that have economic and other consequences for the household and its community. Breastfeeding exemplifies the nature of economic choices regarding nutritional well-being and health because, to breastfeed, the mother must provide both her milk and her time. Because time always has alternative value in other activities, the productivity of an additional hour that the mother allocates to child care will be affected by the level of her productivity in other activities. Economically the issue is whether or not, at the margin, the mother perceives the value of breastfeeding her child to be equal or higher than the value of the alternative uses of her time (Franklin and Harrell 1983).

It is assumed that improved children's nutritional health is always desired by the household, and that failure to adopt recommended feeding practices must be the consequence of a lack of household resources and/or of constraints on the time of the mother.

BACKGROUND

In 1960, Chile was one of the countries with highest infant mortality rates in Latin America: 120.3 deaths per 1,000 live births. By 1970, Chile had decreased its infant mortality rate by 34 percent, neonatal (less than 28 days old) by 11 percent, and general mortality by 30 percent. Between 1970 and 1980, the infant mortality rate was reduced by 60 percent, neonatal by 48 percent, and general mortality by 23 percent. The fastest decline took place in the 1976-1980 and 1980-1983 period (Castañeda 1985).

According to Castañeda (1985), the fast decline in infant mortality rates is explained by recent increases in rural-urban migration; mothers' education; availability of tap water, sewerage, and electricity; the milk distribution program to pregnant and lactating mothers and pre-schoolers; and health services provided to mothers and infants.

Nationwide information on nutritional status for a considerable number of pre-schoolers has been available since 1975. The records indicate that malnutrition in this age group has been reduced from 15.5 percent in 1975 (among the group of children under control) to 8.3 percent in 1982. Between 1975 and 1982, mild malnutrition has been reduced from 12.1

percent to 7.8 percent; moderate from 2.7 to 0.9 percent; and severe from 0.7 to 0.1 percent (The World Bank 1979).

WOMEN'S WORK AND MATERNAL BENEFITS

Data on women's participation in the labor force show that the percentage of women working has been relatively stable since 1960, fluctuating between 30.9 and 36.5 percent. In 1983, 29.5 percent of housewives participated in the labor force as compared to 34.7 percent for all women (Pardo 1983).

A review of available statistics in Chile points out two relevant facts about poor women's economic needs and working behavior: First, increased low-income women's participation rates in the labor force in periods of economic crisis. In 1975, a year of economic recession with high unemployment, low income women's participation rates jumped from 18 to 22.4 percent, while the participation of middle and high income women decreased significantly (Rosales 1979). Second, increasing women's participation in the two government-created minimum employment programs, the PEM, or minimum employment program, and the POJH, the occupational program for heads of households. This is surprising given women's need to cope simultaneously with child care (while lacking child support systems), but indicative of their need to work in periods of economic crisis. Slightly over 52 percent of the PEM participants in a 1982 survey were women, and 70 percent of these women were between the ages of 18 and 40, a period characterized by a high level of child care responsibilities (Cheyre and Ogrodnick 1982).

The current legislation on maternity benefits and protection for working mothers does not discriminate between women wage-earners, employees, or independent workers. All have access to benefits, provided they can demonstrate a minimum of twelve months of social security payments and up-to-date working status. Three types of legal benefits are available. One example is prenatal leave of six weeks duration and maternity leave for twelve weeks after delivery. During this period, the employer is required to maintain the employment position for the woman; in turn, she is not allowed to engage in any other paid work. In case of maternal and/or child morbidity after the period of legal leave, leave of absence can be extended up to a year when accompanied by a medical certificate. Another type of legal benefit is that during the period of prenatal and maternity leave, pregnant and lactating women receive a monthly subsidy that corresponds to the total monthly salary plus regular benefits received while at work. The third type of legal benefit is day care centers for children under two years of age in firms that employ twenty or more women, located in the work place or nearby, to facilitate breastfeeding during working hours. Alternatively, the employer can pay the expenses directly to a day care center chosen by the mother in the absence of one at the work place. Such centers need to be authorized by the National Board of Day Care Centers (JUNJI). The mother has the right to feed her baby twice during working hours, but she cannot exceed one hour in total. If the day care center is not located in the working place, additional time is given to account for travel time, and the employer is supposed to pay for these transportation costs (Salinas 1985). Mothers who are self-employed, or who are employed by the government minimum wage employment programs, do not benefit from maternity protection or prenatal and maternity leave, but no sanctions are imposed if they take their baby to work.

Additional benefits sanctioned by law include income transfers. For example, mothers working for public or private sector employers who participate in the national social security system are eligible for US$3 monthly per child, from the fifth month of pregnancy and up to 18 years of age, or up to 24 if single and a regular student; in addition, families classified as living in extreme poverty who do not participate in the social security system are eligible for US$3 monthly for each child, from pregnancy up to 14 years of age.

Milk and milk substitutes, and occasionally rice, are distributed by the National Program of Food Distribution, PNAC, to complement the daily consumption of target groups. The food is distributed at no cost to the recipients using the primary health care infrastructure of the health centers belonging to the National Health Service (286 urban health centers, 1,010 rural centers, and 1,281 medical stations). Food recipients must attend the regular health controls established by the Ministry of Health, in accordance with the medical norms for the different age groups. The actual coverage of PNAC among preschoolers and pregnant and lactating women is approximately 70 percent of the target population, and 90 percent among children less than two years of age. A more recent innovation in the program is that malnourished or low-weight pregnant women are given additional food (Ministry of Health 1985).

INFANT FEEDING PRACTICES

In Chile, as well as in many developing countries, there has been an overall decline in breastfeeding resulting from complex cultural, social, and economic changes. However, among the poor and during relatively recent times (1942 - 1977), the proportion of children from low-income urban areas who were exclusively breastfed at three and six months of age has been stable at between 30 to 42 percent and around 20 percent, respectively. Since 1942, there has been no apparent long-term decrease in the number of children breastfed among the low income urban population (Mardones-Santander 1979).

Research findings since 1974 show a strong negative association between breastfeeding and maternal work beyond the third month of lactation (López 1974). This could be due to the duration (three months after birth) of the legally paid maternity leave. Unfortunately, no thorough study has been done of the impact of maternity leave on breastfeeding practices, although it is documented that out of approximately 15 percent of low income urban women who worked in the formal sector of the economy, about 50 percent of them made use of paid maternity leave (Mardones-Santander 1979, 1983). Furthermore, among the population of low income urban mothers working in the informal sector of the economy, the coverage of the social maternity benefits from legal provisions could be significantly lower. The scarce data on the availability of day care facilities in Chile show that in some poor areas of Santiago, only 2 percent of infants under one year of age have access to day care centers (INTA 1982).

In 1981, a partial assessment of the relative impact of the nutritional and educational components of the PNAC program indicated a 61 percent increase in the number of infants exclusively breastfed at 6 months of age in populations where both nutritional and educational components had been implemented and a 41 percent increase when only nutritional aspects had been fully implemented (González et al. 1983).

A later survey in 1982 of a representative sample of pregnant and lactating women of Santiago revealed a clear increase in breastfeeding duration; the percentages of exclusively breastfed infants were 63 percent at three months of age and 44 percent at six months of age. These values were significantly higher than all previous results reported in Chile for the low income urban population (Mardones-Santander 1983).

Nevertheless, recent 1985 figures from a national representative survey by the Ministry of Health revealed that the level of exclusive breastfeeding practices returned to levels recorded for earlier historical periods. Percentages for Santiago were 47.8 and 27.7 percent at three and six months of age, respectively. Percentages for the country were 47.3 and 29.6 percent at three and six months of age, respectively (Ministry of Health 1985).

METHODS

The Sample

A prospective study covering the period July 1984 - July 1985 was conducted among low-income urban women and their infants who participated in the primary health care program of the National Health System, which covers 90 percent of all pregnant and lactating women in urban areas.

From the maternity ward of the hospital Sótero del Rio, an initial sample of 812 mothers was selected according to their working status during pregnancy. Mothers were divided into two groups, those who had worked for pay (or cash) and those who had not, and the sample was drawn intentionally to include approximately half of each group. Retrospective information on maternal weight increment during pregnancy was obtained from the clinic records. The mothers were also weighed when admitted to the maternity hospital (prepartum weight) and between 12 and 48 hours after delivery (post-partum weight). Several variables were recorded at delivery, including birth weight, body length, gestational age, and morbidity. Gestational age was established from the date of the last menstrual period. Body weight and length of the newborn were determined by a nurse using a standardized procedure.

Mothers and infants were studied for six months after delivery to obtain the demographic and socioeconomic characteristics of the household, mother's economic behavior, characteristics of her work, type of support system used for child care, infant feeding practices, family income, and housing conditions. This information was collected at the time of the first home interview. For the following five monthly visits, information on mothers' working behavior, infant feeding practices, and infant morbidity was also obtained. A final follow-up during lactation was completed in July 1985.

Out of the 812 mothers recruited for the study, 767 met the selection criteria during pregnancy. Of the remaining sample, there was an additional loss of cases due to changes of address and incomplete information on infant weight and height. Thus, the final sample size, used in the following regression analysis, was reduced to 612.[1] Of these, only 404 had complete information on all fourteen questionnaires implemented as part of this study (covering pregnancy, birth, six-months' follow-up, and including a 24-hour food consumption recall). This latter sample is the one used in the descriptive tables. Since the work status of some of the women in the sample changed from working to nonworking or vice versa during the six month follow-up, the number of observations in the work and nonwork categories for the different measures is not constant over time.

Basic Model and Methodology

The present application of the theory of household production framework to the study of child nutrition involves two complementary stages: first, the choice of infant feeding practices, and second, the combined effect on infant nutritional status of infant feeding choices with mother's working behavior and other intervening factors.

(A) Infant feeding choices.

The decision of mothers on how to feed their infants was examined considering two dimensions: the duration of breastfeeding and the choice of infant feeding system including breast milk (B), breast milk substitutes (M), and solid foods (S). These choices are clearly not mutually exclusive.

Breastfeeding duration: Several definitions of breastfeeding duration were used in the analysis depending on whether mixed-feeding (using other foods) was allowed or not. Exclusive breastfeeding (B) includes breast milk plus liquids (water or fruity juices); mixed breastfeeding (B + M) includes breast milk combined with artificial (powdered, liquid, or canned) milk (M); "complete" breastfeeding (B + M + S) is breast milk combined with artificial milk plus weaning foods; and breastfeeding plus solids (B + S) is breast milk combined with weaning foods. The model used to assess factors determining breastfeeding duration is:

Duration of breastfeeding = (HC, FSC, PW, IC, TSS) where:

HC = human capital characteristics, such as mother's age and education, mother's nutritional status, and father's education;

FSC = family size and composition, such as family size, number of children [in age brackets 1-5, 6-12, 13-18 years, adults (older than 18)], and sex of household head;

PW = characteristics of parent's work, such as mother's working hours per week and per month, income per hour, maternity leave, type of employment, and father's employment status and income;

IC   = infant's characteristics, such as birth interval; and

TSS = type of supportive child care system for working mothers.

Given that the period observed comprised only six months after child birth, Ordinary Least Square Method (OLS) was used in the estimation of the model for those definitions of breastfeeding in which most mothers had terminated breastfeeding during the observation period, that is, systems (B) and (B + M). On the other hand, the TOBIT estimation procedure was applied for the definition of breastfeeding plus solid foods (B + S) and of complete breastfeeding (B + M + S), given that the observed data is artificially truncated at month 6 (see Maddala 1983).

Infant feeding systems: The approach in this case follows closely that of Akin et al. (1985). A system of derived demand equations is defined, such that the dependent variables: B, M, and S are dichotomous. Each endogenous variable is a function only of a set of exogenous variables, but the endogenous variables are allowed to be correlated with each other, so that the probability that a mother selects one type of feeding method (e.g., B) becomes conditional on choices she makes about using other feeding methods (e.g., M and S).

The following set of equations are estimated, using a multivariate logit method[2]

$$\log \frac{P(B=1/M,S)}{P(B=0/M,S)}_t = X_t \beta + M_t + S_t$$

$$\log \frac{P(M=1/B,S)}{P(M=0/B,S)}_t = X_t \gamma + B_t + wS_t$$

$$\log \frac{P(S=1/B,M)}{P(S=0/B,M)}_t = X_t \phi + B_t + wM_t$$

X_t = represents a 1 x t vector of exogenous variable and ß, γ and ϕ are t x 1 vectors of unknown parameters. X_t contains the following independent variables:

H = human capital characteristics

FSC = family size and composition

PW = characteristics of parent's work

IC = infant characteristics

TSS = type of supportive system

(B) Infant nutrition.

The production of infant nutrition takes place with both household inputs and purchased goods and services, subject to income and time constraints. These include mother's human capital (including her age, education, and health status), the infant's age and health status, the availability of mother's time for child care and of substitutes for her time, and the availability of physical capital used to produce infant nutrition such as potable water and sewerage.

In this second stage, estimated infant feeding systems are used to explain, together with other exogenous variables, the nutritional status of infants. Infant's weight increment is used as a proxy for nutritional status.

The model used to assess factors determining infant's weight increment is summarized as weight increment = f (IFS, HC, FSC, MW, IC, TSS, IM) where:

IFS = estimated infant's feeding system chosen by the mothers from the first stage regressions;

HC = human capital characteristics such as mother's age and level of education;

FSC = family size and composition;

MW = characteristics of mother's work such as mother's working status during the six month period of follow-up, place of work (inside or outside the house), and type of employment;

IC = characteristics of the infant such as birth weight and sex;

TSS = type of supportive system for child care such as maternity leave, access to day care center, and if mother takes the baby to work; and

IM = infant morbidity: the presence of morbidity such as diarrhea, cough and/or temperature during the 30 days that anteceded each of the six interviews, and place of consultation when affected by morbidity. Consultation places were defined as institutional (health center, hospital, or private practitioner) and non-institutional (neighbor, family members, pharmacist, or the mother herself treated the baby without consulting).

RESULTS

Characteristics of the Sample

Table 6.1 summarizes the main demographic characteristics of the families included in the sample. Information is presented comparing the parameters for working and nonworking mothers, as well as the statistical differences between them. Families of working mothers are smaller in size, particularly in number of school-age children, and record a higher proportion of female-headed households, also reflected in the significantly smaller percentage of married mothers. In terms of age, they are on average two years older than the nonworking mothers. No significant differences in terms of average level of education in either mothers or fathers were found between the two cohorts.

Average monthly household income for the group of households with working mothers is comparatively higher: US$129 versus US$110 for the families of nonworking mothers (Table 6.2). Still, both figures represent very low levels of monetary income. Average household income is lower for the cohort of working mothers when excluding mother's income, which implies that mother's work represents an important contribution to the welfare of her family in the low income strata. For the families of both cohorts, food expenditure represents between 62 and 65 percent of total reported household expenditures, followed in importance by expenditures for utilities, almost 14 percent, and next by transport costs to work, 10.5 percent (Table 6.2).

The majority of working mothers in the sample work in the service sector, particularly in traditional female roles such as sewing, hairdressing, crafts and as housemaids. These occupations account for 29.7 percent of the working mothers. Almost 12 percent of working mothers hold jobs in factories; the remaining hold a variety of low level activities, and only one is a professional.

Approximately 35 percent of household cash income (US$40 on average) is derived from mother's market work (Table 6.3). This income is obtained by working an average of 33 hours per week, mostly at a permanent type of job. Nevertheless, only very few of the mothers have access to social security and maternity leave (27.9 percent and 16.9 percent, respectively). Most mothers work outside the home, relying on family members and neighbors as substitutes for the care of their newborns. A fraction of the mothers have to care for their babies while at work (18 percent) and only 11.7 percent have access to institutional child care at work or in a community center.

Infant Feeding Patterns

Tables 6.4 to 6.7 summarize information obtained from the sample on infant feeding practices. Although all mothers in the sample initiated breastfeeding, 2.1 percent of working mothers and 2.3 percent of nonworking mothers stop breastfeeding by the end of the first month after birth (Table 6.4). Most mothers continue with exclusive breastfeeding in the second month, but a significant proportion introduce artificial milk as a complement to breastfeeding (29 percent of working mothers and around 22 percent of nonworking mothers). The use of artificial milk as a breastfeeding substitute becomes fairly common among working mothers in the third month (15.5 percent). By the end of the observation period (6 months), all mothers have introduced weaning foods. In month six, only 34.6 percent of working mothers and 22.4 percent of nonworking mothers have abandoned breastfeeding practices.

Average duration of exclusive breastfeeding (including water and juice) is somewhat higher for the group of nonworking mothers: fewer of them stop exclusive breastfeeding by month three (Table 6.5). However, a higher proportion of working than nonworking mothers introduce artificial milk at month three (Table 6.4).

According to Table 6.6, 36 percent of working mothers initiated the use of artificial milk as a substitute of breastfeeding during the first six months of observation. The highest frequency takes place at month 4, that is, after the end of maternity leave. The corresponding figure for nonworking mothers is 24 percent. Similar results are observed in terms of the initiation of solid foods as substitute of breastfeeding.

The use of artificial milk as a complement to breastfeeding is much more frequent, particularly among working mothers (Table 6.7). Solid foods are widely introduced as a complement to breastfeeding, especially in months three and four after birth.

Table 6.8 presents the results from the multivariate logit estimations of infant feeding choices at four months of age for the total sample. The model includes as dependent variables the decisions by mothers at month four to use or not use breastfeeding, artificial milk, and solid foods (so as to maximize nutritional well-being of the infant), for given household resources and other individual constraints. The method of estimation acknowledges the fact that the use of one or more feeding practices are dependent on each other. For example, a mother can choose to feed her baby combining breast milk with solid foods. Thus, three endogenous variables are included: the choice of using breast milk (B), artificial milk (M), and solid foods (S).

According to the results shown in Table 6.8, the facts that the mother works and that the father is a wage earner negatively affect the probability of breastfeeding at four months of age ($p<.10$). Working mothers have a higher probability of using artificial milk ($p<.001$).

Mother's and especially father's higher education together with a larger number of school age children in the household have a negative effect on the probability of introducing breast milk substitutes, while a shorter interval of child spacing increases the choice of artificial milk ($p<.05$). Finally, the probability of using solid foods at month four is negatively affected by mother's age and positively by mother's nutritional status ($p<.05$).

A significant correlation was found at month four between the use of solid foods and artificial milk. The remaining correlation terms, while not statistically significant, did indicate that breastmilk (B) and artificial milk

(M) are negatively associated (substitutes), while breastmilk (B) and solid foods (S) would be positively correlated (complements), in month four after child birth.

The presence of female heads of household shows a negative effect on breastfeeding and on the use of solid foods, and a positive effect on the use of artificial milk, but this variable was not statistically significant in any of the three equations.

Infant Nutritional Status

The next stage in the analysis relates infants' nutritional status at four and six months of age to both infant feeding practices and the working status of mothers. The proxy for nutritional status is the accumulated weight increment since birth. The analysis was carried out for month four since the greater differences in the use of feeding practices between working and nonworking mothers appeared in this month (at which time the former group had concluded maternity leave). When the nutritional status of infants is explained in terms of breastfeeding duration, accumulated weight increment up to month six is used instead as the dependent variable.

The distribution of infants of both groups of mothers in three categories according to accumulated weight increment is presented in Table 6.9. The first category refers to infants with average monthly weight gains of less than 450 grams, that is, infants at high risk of malnutrition. The second category corresponds to average weight increments of between 450 and 600 grams, which therefore includes infants with low risk of malnutrition. The remaining group includes infants with satisfactory weight increment (over 600 grams per month). Over 90 percent of infants had weight increments above the norm during the first four months (and 81 percent when the entire period is considered). There are no apparent differences in the weight gain of infants of working and nonworking mothers.

In Table 6.10, the estimation of infant's weight increment from birth to four months of age includes as independent variables the first stage estimated use of feeding systems B, M, and S. Separate regressions are presented for the total sample and for working mothers. The positive effects on weight gains for the total sample of using breastfeeding (p<.001) and solid foods (p<.10) are significant, while the use of artificial milk negatively affects infant's weight increment up to four months of age (p<.05). It should be noted that the model captures the choice of breast milk substitute only and not the amounts actually fed to the infants, nor the quality of the food.

Age composition variables are associated with weight increment; the number of children between six to 12 years negatively affects the nutritional status of infants (p<.10), while the number of adults in the house has a positive significant effect (p<.001). This suggests a competition for mother's time and other resources so that additional children tend to increase mother's time constraints, while the presence of other adult family members can augment resources for child care.

As expected, male infants have a better weight increment than female infants; also, infants who are born with higher birth weight have a lower subsequent weight increment, which is not unreasonable if they were born with adequate weight (p<.001). Also, in accordance with the literature, infants' weight gain decreases in the presence of morbidity (p<.001).

According to the results shown in Table 6.10, the fact that the mother worked at month four was positively associated with and had a significant effect on infant's accumulated weight gain (p<.001). This effect of mother's work on infant nutrition is over and above her choice of infant feeding system, which is already captured by B, M, and S. It is hypothesized that because mother's work has a positive effect on family income, thus augmenting food expenses and improving general housing conditions, it favors better infant nutrition. On the other hand, mother's work was also shown to have a negative effect on B and S, while a positive effect on M.

The net effect of mother's work on infant's weight increment can now be assessed. The indirect change (via infant feeding choices of B, M, and S) on infant's accumulated weight gain due to mother's work is -0.71 gm, while the more direct effect of mother's work is 193.2 gm. Thus, the net effect is positive and equal to an average of 192.5 gm during the first four months of life of the infant.

The exogenous variables in the equation for working mothers that yield statistically significant coefficients include number of small children (p<.10), sex of the infant (p<.001), and the presence of infant morbidity (p<.10). The sign of the coefficient for number of pre-school age children is negative, indicating that it imposes an additional constraint on working mother's time allocation between her income earning activities and child care. As expected, the presence of morbidity negatively affects infant weight increment (p<.10). None of the characteristics of mother's work included in the regression were significant in explaining differences in infant's weight increments for the group of working mothers.

The equation estimated using the total sample has a better fit than when only infants of working mothers are considered, as evidenced by the R^2 coefficients in Table 6.10.

Table 6.11 summarizes the results obtained when applying the more traditional method of considering breastfeeding duration as the variable representing household decisions concerning the production of infant nutrition. The total observational period (six months) is considered for the analysis. Two alternative definitions of breastfeeding duration are incorporated in the two-stage regressions: exclusive breastfeeding and breastfeeding complemented with solid foods.[3] Duration of breastfeeding, only when complemented with solid foods, has a positive significant effect on infants' weight gains up to six months of age for the total sample according to these results, (p<.05; equation 2 in Table 6.11).

Within the context of the total sample, equations (1) and (2) show that mother's level of education positively affects infant's weight increment, while the presence of small children (one to five years of age) has a systematic negative impact (p<.05). Infants with a higher birth weight and females have lower weight increments during the observational period (p<.001). Infant morbidity also presents a consistent and significant negative effect on infant's weight gains up to six months of age (p<.05).

Finally, the fact that mother's work has a direct positive impact on infant's weight gain (p<.05; equation 2) is possibly due to the increase in family income, which would result in more food availability.

Equations (3) and (4) were estimated using data only for infants of working mothers. It is hypothesized that because of multicollinearity problems very few of the variables were statistically significant. According to these results, infants carried to work by their mothers have lower weight gains up to six months of age. This may be explained by the difficulties confronted by the mothers to adequately feed their babies at their workplace, particularly due to time constraints and the unavailability of adequate food.

CONCLUDING REMARKS

In the present study infant feeding practices and the achievement of adequate nutrition was seen in the context of more general mothers' issues focusing not only on their maternal role but also incorporating their economic responsibilities as income earners.

The results showed that mothers' work did not affect the decision to initiate breastfeeding, as most mothers did so, but it did affect its duration, shifting working mothers to the use of mixed breastfeeding more frequently than nonworking mothers. On average, a higher proportion of working mothers than their nonworking counterparts had already introduced artificial milk both as a substitute for, as well as a complement to,breastfeeding when infants were three months old. Weaning foods were also introduced earlier in the diets of their infants.

In terms of alternative use of feeding systems — breastfeeding, artificial milk, and solid foods — mother's work negatively affects the choice of breastfeeding but positively influences the use of artificial milk. Among the group of working mothers, none of the working characteristics played a significant intervening role in the duration of exclusive breastfeeding, but some of them did have a significant effect in the choice of combining breastfeeding with solid foods. In fact, working mothers could maintain combined breastfeeding practices either in the presence of day care centers or if they could carry the baby to work. In the absence of the above, working mothers had to substitute breastfeeding earlier with the use of artificial milk.

In analyzing the choices of breastfeeding and other infant feeding practices, the study considers that breastfeeding is not desirable per se, but rather as a mean to achieve better infant nutrition. The analysis also assumes that the use of alternative feeding practices, breastfeeding, artificial milk, and solid foods are not mutually exclusive.

The results obtained showed that exclusive breastfeeding duration did not significantly affect the production of infant nutrition, except when complemented with solid foods. This result may suggest that the appropriate timing for the introduction of weaning foods, rather than exclusive breastfeeding duration per se, is more important in influencing adequate infant nutrition. On the other hand, when artificial milk is used as a substitute for breastfeeding during the infant's first three months of age, the probability of insufficient weight increment is higher.

Mother's work has two opposing effects on infant nutrition: on one hand it implies, at least in the Chilean urban context, an increased use of artificial milk and a more restricted use of breastfeeding, as mentioned above. But on the other hand, it makes it possible for low income households to increase food expenditures and to have better access to other complementary resources such as health, thus improving the chances of better infant nutrition and child development. The net effect of mother's work was unknown on an *a priori* basis. The study has indicated that for the population under study, the positive impact of mother's work outweighed the negative implications of shorter breastfeeding duration.

This result illustrates the fact that breastfeeding is not the only possible means of achieving adequate nutrition. Mothers have been shown to make rational decisions regarding infant nutrition given the time constraints they face in accomplishing their everyday responsibilities.

While society places the main responsibility of child development in the hands of mothers, much still remains to be achieved in terms of social welfare policies and institutional build-up to help women make compatible the maternal role with their income earning activities. This could come about both from changes in the labor market structure, to provide work that is more compatible with infant feeding responsibilities, and from investment in child care facilities.

Notes

1. Only women over 18 years of age and free of medical conditions known to affect fetal growth and/or breastfeeding performance were included in the study. Neither pre- or post-term deliveries nor multiple pregnancies were admitted in the study.

2. See for example Maddala (1983), Guilkey and Schmidt (1979), Schmidt and Strauss (1975), Akin et al. (1985).

3. It should be remembered that the duration of breastfeeding complemented with solid foods is truncated in month six (41 percent of non-working mothers and 18 percent of working mothers were still using this feeding system). Therefore, a Tobit estimation method was used in the first stage regression for such infant feeding system. Variables which positively influenced breastfeeding duration complemented with solids were access to day care centers, mother's care of baby at work, and mother's work at Minimum Employment Programs. Those with a negative effect were mother's work outside the house and distance to work.

References

Akin, J.; Griffin, C.; Guilkey, D.; and Popkin, B.
  1985. "Determinants of Infant Feeding: A Household Production Approach." *Economic Development and Cultural Change*, vol. 34, no. 1, pp. 57-81.

Becker, G.
  1965. "A Theory of the Allocation of Time." *Economic Journal* 75(September 1965): 493-517.

Castañeda, T.
  1985. "Determinantes del Descenso de la Mortalidad Infantil en Chile: 1975-1983." *Cuadernos de Economía*, vol. 22, no. 66, Departamento de Economía, Universidad Católica de Chile.

Cheyre, H. and Ogrodnick, E.
  1982. "El Programa de Empleo Minimo: Análisis de una Encuesta." *Revista de Economía*, Universidad de Chile (November 1982).

Franklin, D.L. and Harrell, M.L.
  1983. "Costs and Determinants of Infant Feeding Practices." Raleigh: Sigma One Corporation.

González, N.; Hertrampf, E.; Mardones S. F.; Rooso, P.; and Verdugo, C.
  1983. "Evaluación Preliminar del Impacto del Programa Nacional de Fomento de la Lactancia Materna." *Revista Chilena de Pediatría.* pp. 36-40.

Guilkey, D. and Schmidt, P.
  1979. "Some Small Sample Properties of Estimators and Test Statistics in the Multivariate Logit Model." *Journal of Econometrics* 10 (April 1979): 33-42.

International Institute of Nutrition and Food Technology (INTA).
  1982. "Una Acción Comunal para la Prevención y Tratamiento de la Desnutrición Materno-infantil; Comuna de la Florida." Working paper.

Lancaster, K.J.
  1966. "A New Approach to Consumer Theory." *Journal of Political Economy,"* vol. 74(1): 132-157

Lopez, I.
  1974. "Duración de la Lactancia Materna y Algunos Factores Condicionantes." Department of Public Health. University of Chile, Santiago, Chile.

Maddala, G.S.
  1983. *Limited-Dependent and Qualitative Variables in Econometrics.* Cambridge MA: Cambridge University Press.

Mardones-Santander F.
1983. "Ampliación del Reposo Post Parto para la Mujer en Chile: Una Medida Necesaria para Fomentar la Práctica de la Lactancia Materna." *Revista Chilena de Nutrición*, no. 11.
1979."Breast-feeding History in Chile." *Nutrition and Food Bulletin*, vol. 1, no. 4.
Ministry of Health.
1985. SISVAN, Consolidados Nacionales.
Muth, R.F.
1966."Household Production and Consumer Demand Function." *Econometrica*, vol 34(3): 699-708
Pardo, L.
1983."La Dueña de casa de sus actividades de trabajo: su valoración en el mercado y dentro del hogar." Serie de Investigaciones no. 59, Departamento de Economía; Universidad de Chile, Santiago.
Rosales, O.
1979."La mujer chilena en la fuerza de trabajo," Documento de Investigación, no. 36, (Julio 1979), Departamento de Economía, Universidad de Chile, Santiago.
Salinas, M.J.
1985."Protección Legal de la Madre y el Niño." Working Document, Santiago, Chile.
Schmidt, P. and Strauss, R.
1975."Estimation of Models with Jointly Dependent Qualitative Variables: A Simultaneous Logit Approach." *Econometrica*, vol. 43, no.4: 745-755
Schultz, T.W.
1973."The value of children." *Journal of Political Economy*, vol. 92,no. 2, Part 2.
The World Bank. 1979. *Chile, An Economy in Transition*. Washington, D.C.

Table 6.1 Demographic Characteristics and Composition of Household Income and Expenditure in the Sample, Santiago 1984-85.

	Total Sample		Working Mothers		Nonworking Mothers		
	Average	SD	Average	SD	Average	SD	T-Test[d]
Family size	6.04	2.65	5.50	2.38	6.24	2.72	<.001
Mother's children under 2 years	1.08	0.28	1.08	0.27	1.09	0.28	
Mother's children under 5 years	1.47	0.68	1.41	0.68	1.48	0.68	
Mother's children 6 - 17 years	0.47	0.87	0.66	1.01	0.40	0.79	<.05
Children under 5 per adult[a]	0.62	0.41	0.65	0.47	0.61	0.38	
Age of mother	25.00	5.04	26.50	5.29	24.50	4.82	<.001
Mother's education (years)	8.41	3.11	8.62	3.37	8.33	3.01	
Age of husband[c]	27.40	5.80	28.30	5.66	27.10	5.77	
Husband's education (years)[c]	8.70	3.18	8.71	3.40	8.70	3.11	
	Percentage		Percentage		Percentage		
Extended family in household	52.0		44.1		54.9		<.10
Female head of household[b]	16.1		21.6		14.0		<.10
Marital status of mother:							<.10
Married	61.0		54.1		63.8		
Unmarried couple	18.1		18.0		18.1		
Unmarried and single	18.1		23.4		16.0		
Separated or divorced	2.7		4.5		2.0		
Sample size	404(100.0%)		111(27.5%)		293(72.5%)		

a   Including children in household that are not mother's children.
b   This does not necessarily mean that mother being studied is the head of household.
c   Sample sizes for characteristics of husbands are total = 320, because some women are single.
d   Significance level of two tailed T-test of difference between working and nonworking mothers.

Table 6.2 Household Income and Expenditure in Month 1: For Working and Nonworking Mothers, Santiago 1984-85

	Total Sample		Working Mothers		Non-working Mothers		T-Test[d]
	Average	SD	Average	SD	Average	SD	
Total Household Income[a]	14,498	9,842	16,297	9,420	13,944	9,902	<.05
Household income less mother's income	13,285	9,586	11,247	8,146	13,912	9,903	<.001
Income per household member	2,527	1,633	3,242	2,091	2,307	1,391	<.001
	Percentage		Percentage		Percentage		
Income from regular jobs	74.6		76.7		73.5		<.05
Income from pensions	8.4		6.2		9.2		
Income from part-time jobs	6.9		6.6		7.0		
Income transfers from welfare programs[b]	4.8		5.3		4.5		
Income from others sources	5.3		5.2		5.6		
	Average	SD	Average	SD	Average	SD	T-Test[d]
Total household expenditure	12,228	6,900	13,033	6,748	11,980	7,031	
Expenditure per household member	2,224	1,373	2,617	1,786	2,103	1,193	<.001
	Percentage		Percentage		Percentage		
Expenditure on food	64.3		62.3		65.0		
Expenditure for utilities	13.9		12.9		14.2		
Expenditure for transport to work	10.5		10.9		10.3		
Other expenditures	11.4		13.9		10.6		
Households reporting expenditure larger than income	39.9		28.4		43.4		<.001
Sample Size[c]	404(100.0%)		95(23.5%)		309(76.5%)		

[a] The exchange rate for December 1984 is Chilean $126.23 per US dollar.
[b] Excludes income transfers from the PNAC program (approximately US$4 per pre-school age child).
[c] In the other tables the mothers are classified as working or not working on the basis of whether they worked in month four to avoid complications with maternity leave. Here the basis is whether the mother was in the labor force in month one because the income and expenditure data were collected in month one. As a result, the sample size for working mothers is slightly different.
[d] Significance level of two-tailed T-Test of difference between working and nonworking mothers.

Table 6.3 Mothers' Working Characteristics in the Sample of Low-Income Households: Santiago 1984-85

	Average	SD
Mother's monthly labor income[a] (in US$ of December 1984)	40.1	29.7
Number of hours worked per week	32.8	19.8
Number of weeks worked per month	3.2	1.2
	Percentages	
Mother's job was permanent	78.4	
Mother had working contract[b]	28.8	
Mother had social security through job[c]	27.9	
Mother had maternity leave[d]	16.9	
Distance to mother's job:		
- mother works at home	16.2	
- less than 1/2 hour	39.6	
- 1/2 hour to 1 hour	31.5	
- more than 1 hour	12.6	
Mother's work category:		
- employer	27.9	
- wage earner	16.2	
- self employed	29.7	
- minimum employment program:		
PEM	6.3	
POJH	19.8	
Supportive system for child care:		
- institutional care[e]	11.7	
- mother works at home	16.2	
- takes baby to work (no day care at work)	18.0	
- family member or neighbor[f]	54.1	

[a] Exchange rate used is Chilean $126.2 per US dollar.
[b] This percentage changes to 65% when self-employed and participants in the minimum employment programs (PEM and POJH) are excluded.
[c] This percentage changes to 63% when adjusted as in [b].
[d] This percentage changes to 39% when self-employed and PEM and POJH participants are excluded.
[e] Day care center at work (10.8%) and day care center in neighborhood (0.9%).
[f] Includes one case where child is cared for by maid.

Table 6.4   Monthly Choices of Infant Feeding Practices[1]: Working[2] (W) and Nonworking (NW) Mothers in the Sample. Santiago 1984-85 (Percentages)

Infant Feeding Systems	Month 1 W	Month 1 NW	Month 2 W	Month 2 NW	Month 3 W	Month 3 NW	Month 4 W	Month 4 NW	Month 5 W	Month 5 NW	Month 6 W	Month 6 NW
breastfeeding + liquid[3]	84.2	81.6	57.0	68.1	22.3	37.2	4.5	8.9	2.7	1.4	0	0
breastfeeding + solid foods	0	0	3.0	2.6	17.5	28.3	26.7	52.1	18.2	52.4	18.3	41.3
breastfeeding + breast milk subst.	13.7	16.1	29.0	21.7	21.4	12.6	2.7	3.4	1.8	0	1.0	0
breastfeeding + breast milk subst. + solid foods	0	0	4.0	2.3	23.3	15.3	37.5	24.3	47.3	28.2	46.1	36.3
breast milk substitute	2.1	2.0	7.0	4.0	8.7	3.3	3.6	0.7	1.8	0	0	0
breast milk subst. + solid foods	0	0.3	0	1.3	6.8	3.3	25.0	10.6	28.2	18.0	34.6	22.4
Total Number	95	309	100	304	103	301	112	292	110	294	104	300

[1] Infant Feeding Practices are mutually exclusive.
[2] Mothers working at each month.
[3] Includes water and/or fruit juices.

Table 6.5   Distribution of Working and Nonworking Mothers According to Duration of Exclusive Breastfeeding. Santiago 1984-85

	Duration Exclusive Breastfeeding (in months) 1	2	3	4	5	Other 6	Average Systems	Duration
Working mothers:								
Number	21	23	12	3	2	0	11	2.27
Percentages	29.2	31.9	16.7	4.2	2.8	0	15.2	
Nonworking mothers:								
Number	55	113	79	19	4	0	62	3.05
Percentages	16.6	34.0	23.8	5.7	1.2	0	18.7	

Table 6.6   Month of Initiation of Artificial Milk and Solid Foods as Substitutes for Breastfeeding for Working and Nonworking Mothers. Santiago 1984-85

	Month 1	Month 2	Month 3	Month 4	Month 5	Month 6
Initiation of Artificial Milk as Substitute for Breastfeeding[1]						
Working mothers:						
Number	2	3	7	17	6	4
Percentage[2]	2.1	3.0	6.8	15.2	5.4	3.8
Nonworking mothers:						
Number	7	14	8	15	15	13
Percentage[3]	2.2	4.6	2.7	5.1	5.1	4.3
Initiation of Solid Foods as Substitute for Breastfeeding[1]						
Working mothers:						
Number	0	0	7	19	8	6
Percentage[2]	0	0	6.8	16.9	7.3	5.7
Nonworking mothers:						
Number	1	3	7	23	16	13
Percentage[3]	0.3	1.0	2.3	7.9	5.4	4.3

[1] Excludes simultaneous use of breastfeeding.
[2] Proportion of working mothers.
[3] Proportion of nonworking mothers.

Table 6.7   Distribution of Working and Nonworking Mothers According to Infant's Initiation of Artificial Milk and Solid Foods as Complements to Breastfeeding

	Month 1	Month 2	Month 3	Month 4	Month 5	Month 6
Initiation of Artificial Milk as Complement to Breastfeeding[1]						
Working mothers:						
Number	12	23	20	14	16	5
Percentage[2]	12.6	23.0	19.4	12.5	14.5	4.8
Nonworking mothers:						
Number	50	40	29	24	16	35
Percentage[3]	16.2	13.2	9.6	8.2	5.4	11.7
Initiation of Solid Foods as Complement to Breastfeeding[1]						
Working mothers:						
Number	0	7	35	38	4	4
Percentage[2]	-	7.0	34.0	33.9	13.6	3.8
Nonworking mothers:						
Number	0	15	120	106	3	3
Percentage[3]	-	4.9	39.8	36.3	10.5	1.0

[1] Excludes simultaneous use of breastfeeding.
[2] Proportion of working mothers.
[3] Proportion of nonworking mothers.

Table 6.8 Logit Estimation of Infant Feeding Choices at Four Months of Age: All Mothers in the Sample

Independent Variables:	Dependent Variables		
	B[a]	M[b]	S[c]
Constant	14.705	13.237	-0.552
	(0.111)	(0.163)	(-3.383)
Mother's education (years)	0.014	-0.058	0.055
	(0.306)	(-1.652)*	(1.220)
Mother's age	0.036	0.025	-0.555
	(1.316)	(1.153)	(-2.030)**
Father's education (years)	0.029	-0.055	-0.011
	(0.886)	(-2.181)**	(-0.330)
Female head of household (D)	-0.212	0.243	-0.054
	(-0.641)	(0.852)	(-0.152)
Per capita family income[e] (excluding mother's)	-0.000	-0.000	0.000
	(-0.438)	(-0.527)	(1.251)
No. of small children (1 - 5 years)	-0.111	-0.125	-0.218
	(-0.677)	(-0.003)	(-1.443)
No. of children (6 - 12 years)	0.030	-0.298	-0.218
	(0.174)	(-2.186)**	(-1.443)
No. of children (13 - 18 years)	0.186	0.051	0.034
	(1.030)	(-0.508)	(0.206)
No. of adults (> 18 years)	-0.027	-0.070	-0.082
	(-0.323)	(-0.075)	(-0.984)
Mother works (D)	-0.437	0.859	-0.011
	(-1.659)*	(3.857)***	(-0.036)
Mother's nutritional status[e]			0.027
			(2.629)**
Birth interval (D) (less than 15 months)	-0.261	0.992	
	(-0.493)	(1.995)**	
Father is salary earner (D)	-0.328	-0.127	-0.171
	(-0.706)	(-0.370)	(-0.382)
Father is wage earner (D)	-0.512	-0.199	0.375
	(-1.595)*	(-0.809)	(1.050)
Correlation terms: B (D)		-13.157	0.148
		(-0.169)	(0.364)
M (D)	-14.750		0.594
	(-0.111)		(1.979)**
S (D)	0.062	0.555	
	(0.151)	(1.867)*	
Chi-Squared (19)	173.4	211.0	23.5
Significance level	0.0000	0.0000	0.075
McFadden R²	0.87	0.92	0.62

t values in parenthesis: (a) = breastfeeding; (b) = breast milk substitute; (c) = solid foods; (d) = measured in Chilean pesos of December 1984; (e) = this is an index which relates to post-partum weight to mother's height

(D) = dummy variable
*** significant at 1 percent
** significant at 5 percent
* significant at 10 percent

Table 6.9   Distribution of Infants According to Average Weight Increment and by Working Status of Mothers: Birth to Month 4 and Birth to Month 6

Average Monthly Weight Increment	Weight Gains from Birth to Month 4				Weight Gains from Birth to Month 6			
	Working Mothers		Nonworking Mothers		Working Mothers		Nonworking Mothers	
	No	%	No	%	No	%	No	%
< 450 grams	1	1.3	7	2.1	0	0	10	3.0
450 to 600 grams	4	5.6	21	6.3	14	19.4	47	14.2
> 600 grams	67	93.1	304	91.6	58	80.6	275	82.8
Total	72	100	332	100	72	100	332	100

Table 6.10   Estimation of Infant's Weight Increment: From Birth to Four Months of Age, Two Stage Least Square Method

Explanatory Variables:	Weight Increment	
	All Mothers	Working Mothers
Constant	27.06 (9.036)***	27.77 (3.710)***
Predicted use of breastfeeding in month 4 (B)	0.200 (5.075)***	0.103 (1.082)
Predicted use of breastmilk substitute in month 4 (M)	-0.109 (-2.283)**	-0.027 (-0.326)
Predicted use of solid foods (S)	0.781 (1.600)*	0.159 (0.282)
Mother's education (years)	0.025 (0.315)	0.211 (1.182)
Mother's age	-0.028 (0.530)	0.042 (0.287)
Number of small children (1 - 5 years)	-0.434 (-1.379)	-1.075 (-1.602)*
Number of children (6 - 12 years)	-0.545 (-1.799)*	-0.023 (-0.037)
Number of adults (> 18 years)	0.389 (2.728)***	0.054 (0.151)
In-house water connection (D)	0.562 (1.133)	-0.194 (-0.182)
Connection to sewage system (D)	0.296 (0.451)	-0.776 (-0.466)
Cooking fuel (D) [a]	1.055 (0.917)	1.283 (0.571)
Boy infants (D)	3.154 (7.177)***	3.701 (3.822)***
Baby's birthweight (100 grams)	-0.002 (-3.192)***	-0.002 (-1.293)

Table 6.10 Continued

Explanatory Variables:	Weight Increment	
	All Mothers	Working Mothers
Presence of infant morbidity (D)	-1.261	-1.454
	(-3.282)***	(-1.806)*
Institutional consultation for morbidity (D)	0.657	0.409
	(1.231)	(0.343)
Mother works at month 4 (D)	1.932	
	(3.750)***	
Mother works outside house (D)		-0.500
		(-0.259)
Mother works in PEM (D)		-1.483
		(-1.280)
Mother's salary (month 4) (b)		0.00007
		(0.633)
Daycare center (D)		-0.241
		(-0.121)
Mother takes baby to work (D)		-0.347
		(-0.178)
R^2	0.23	0.23
R^2	0.21	0.12
F	10.10	2.106
Mean value of dependent variable (100 grams)	26.86	27.23

t values in parenthesis: (a) use of gas, electricity or kerosene for cooking; (b) measured in Chilean pesos of December 1984.
***Significant at 1 percent
** significant at 5 percent
* significant at 10 percent

Table 6.11 Estimations of Infant's Weight Increment from Birth to Six Months of Age. Two Stage Least Square Method: Total Sample and Working Mothers[a]

Explanatory Variables	Total Sample		Working Mothers	
	(1)	(2)	(3)	(4)
Constant	29.38	24.29	21.64	20.45
	(9.39)***	(8.95)***	(3.40)***	(3.34)***
Estimated exclusive	-0.90		0.69	
breastfeeding duration[b]	(-1.09)		(0.68)	
Estimated breastfeeding		0.66		0.72
duration including solid		(2.22)**		(1.23)
foods[b]				
Mother's education (years)	0.15	0.14	0.18	0.15
	(2.19)**	(2.02)**	(1.14)	(0.99)
Mother's age	-0.05	-0.004	-0.02	-0.04
	(-1.07)	(-0.09)	(-0.19)	(-0.46)
No. of small children	-0.49	-0.52	-0.45	-0.25
(1 - 5 years)	(-2.02)**	(-2.20)**	(-0.72)	(-0.39)
No. of children	-0.12	-0.41	0.47	0.46
(6 - 12 years)	(-0.48)	(-1.53)	(0.76)	(0.78)
No. of adults	0.13	0.09	-0.02	0.07
(> 18 years)	(1.05)	(0.72)	(-0.06)	(0.27)
In-house water	0.59	0.60	1.45	1.85
connection (D)	(1.38)	(1.41)	(1.50)	(1.62)*
Sewage system	-0.03	-0.03	2.25	2.17
connection (D)	(-0.01)	(-0.06)	(1.60)*	(1.56)
Cooking fuel (D)	0.38	-0.02	-1.01	-1.16
(gas, electricity or	(0.35)	(-0.02)	(-0.44)	(-0.51)
kerosene)				
Boy infants (D)	2.48	2.46	3.88	3.91
	(6.53)***	(6.52)***	(4.47)***	(4.54)***
Birthweight of the baby	-0.002	-0.002	-0.001	-0.001
(100 grams)	(-3.47)***	(-3.45)***	(-1.002)	(-0.89)
Presence of infant	-0.64	-0.69	-0.94	-0.97
morbidity (D)	(-1.94)**	(-2.09)**	(-1.32)	(-1.37)
Institutional care for	0.26	0.36	0.84	0.88
infant morbidity (D)	(0.56)	(0.79)	(0.84)	(0.88)
Mother works (D) [c]	0.04	1.25		
	(0.08)	(1.92)**		
Mother works in PEM or			-1.17	-1.61
POJH (D)			(-1.06)	(-1.57)
Mother works outside			2.17	3.12
house (D)			(1.21)	(1.56)
Mother had maternity			-0.02	-0.43
leave (D)			(-0.01)	(-0.38)

Table 6.11 Continued

Explanatory Variables	Total Sample		Working Mothers	
	(1)	(2)	(3)	(4)
Distance to work (D) (more than half hour)			-0.75 (0.75)	-0.24 (-0.21)
Day care center (D)			-1.48 (-1.04)	-2.29 (-1.42)
Mother takes baby to work (D)			-2.05 (-1.62)**	-2.69 (-1.91)**
R^2	0.15	0.15	0.32	0.33
R^2	0.12	0.13	0.18	0.19
F	6.16***	6.48***	2.28***	2.36***
Mean value of dependent variable (100 grams)	23.25	23.25	23.48	23.48

***   significant at 1 percent
**   significant at 5 percent
*   significant at 10 percent
(a) The dependent variable is the total weight increment in 100 grams from birth to six months of age.
(b) Predicted duration from first-stage equations.
(c) Mother worked at least the first three months after childbirth.

7

Maternal Employment, Differentiation, and Child Health and Nutrition in Panama*

Katherine Tucker

The effect of maternal employment on the welfare of children is a question of considerable importance to development policy. The relationship is not straightforward, however. On one hand, maternal employment means increased income, which should be beneficial to obtaining food and providing medical care to children. On the other hand, maternal employment means decreased time available to spend with children in the home, a situation generally expected to have a negative effect on child welfare.

Where maternal employment means long hours away from home without adequate substitute child care, and particularly for low wages, an overall negative effect might be expected. If it is assumed, however, that most mothers act rationally and that child welfare is important to them, one might expect that the decision to work would only be made when the mother and/or the family perceived that this action would result in improved family welfare. Most poor women in developing countries, when asked why they join the labor force, reply with some variation of "to help my family" or "to provide for my children." Thus one might expect that

*The study was part of a larger project on Ascaris infection and food intake conducted by Professors M.C. Nesheim and D. Sanjur of Cornell University and D.W.T. Crompton of the University of Glasgow. Support for both projects was provided by the United States Agency for International Development. Other team members who contributed to the collection of the data include Irma Barbeau, Douglas Taren, Celia Holland, Jean Tiffany, Gloria Rivera, and Victoria Valdes. This work benefited greatly from the contributions of Professor Frank Young at Cornell University.

those women who work should have children with better health and nutritional status than those who do not work.

This also assumes complete information and understanding of the factors involved in child welfare, however. Actual decision making is less than perfect and depends on the ability of the mother and the family to access and use information. Given limited resources, this ability is of tremendous importance in maximizing resource use and thus should be a critical factor in determining the effect of maternal labor force participation on child welfare.

This study, conducted in Panama, attempts to contribute to the understanding of the effects of maternal employment on child welfare — particularly nutritional status and parasitic infection — by developing and utilizing a measure of decision-making ability at the household and individual levels based on the sociological concept of "differentiation."

The Sociological Concept of Differentiation

The efficient or maximum use of resources for child welfare depends to a large degree on the "abilities" of the household and the mother, with the latter particularly important in the area of child health and nutrition. In most studies, the indicator of maternal abilities used has been the level of formal education, which has been found to be a strong variable in explaining differentials in child nutrition (Cochrane et al. 1982). However, formal education is limited in its ability to accurately measure maternal decision-making. The number of years of schooling may, after all, have very different meaning in different locations and for different individuals depending on available educational resources and level of individual application.

Turning then to sociological theory, the concept of "differentiation" may provide guidance in the measurement of household and maternal level decision-making abilities. Differentiation is defined by Young (1983) as "level of complexity" or "the ability to process a wide variety of information types." Expanding on earlier thinking on the division of labor in society by Durkheim (1949), Young argues that a social system operates as a whole and that appropriate development measures are a cluster of structural indicators that should correlate because they all develop and change as the system changes (Young 1983). At the community level, for example, indicators of differentiation might include a count of different types of retail establishments, community services, and social organizations, all of which would be simultaneously "differentiating" — that is, becoming more specialized and increasing in number and overall complexity. This concept may be used in the same sense, but with different indicators, at the household or individual levels.

Structural indicators of household differentiation used by Young and Young (1968) include house construction, possessions, social participation, organizational attendance, food consumption, education levels, medical care patterns, family activities, etc. They note that a measure such as income is an indirect outcome of family organization and thus is not as good a measure of the concept of differentiation. Indicators of differentiation in relation to the individual may include education level, use of media and information sources, verbal ability, social participation, and other indicators that also relate to information seeking behavior, or indicate information retention or use, and thus the "complexity" of the individual. As with the community level measures, multiple indicators of household or of material differentiation are expected to increase as a group and, thus, to be intercorrelated.

Household differentiation (increased complexity) should be positively related to family welfare through improved decision-making and use of resources. Because of the special dependence the young child has on the mother, the latter's individual level of differentiation would be expected to be of particular importance to child welfare.

The connection between differentiation and child welfare has been examined by only a few researchers. Larkin (1968), using data from Ghana, showed that measures of maternal education, literacy, meeting attendance, information sources, and nutrition knowledge were correlated with household level measures of housing, possessions, sanitation, and food use. She noted, in particular, high correlations between the maternal measures and the food score (number of different food types consumed the previous day). She also found significant correlations between child nutritional status and mothers' information sources and ability to use them. A health index, including clinical signs of malnutrition, dental hygiene, and minor illness occurrence, correlated significantly with the food scale and with the household possession index.

A second investigator, Engberg (1974), again using Ghanian data, entered measures of household differentiation into a factor analysis procedure and identified two major dimensions, the first focusing on housing and possessions, and the second focusing on land ownership and food production. Maternal measures were analyzed in an analogous fashion with literacy and education defining the first dimension, and religion and tribal prestige defining the second. To explore the relationship with child welfare, Engberg selected the strongest indicator for each dimension. For the household, this was household possessions; for the mother, it was her level of formal education. Engberg found that household possessions was the most significant variable in a regression equation with an index of child illness and death as the dependent variable. Mother's education was not significant in this equation.

The above two studies begin to test the usefulness of the theoretical concept of differentiation in relation to child welfare, but in both cases interpretation is difficult due to the limitations of the measures and of the analysis. Larkin's study uses only correlational analysis. Engberg's study, while utilizing more powerful tools (factor analysis and regression), misses the concept because she uses only single indicators (household possessions and maternal education). A score based on multiple indicators should relate to the concept of differentiation more adequately.

The study discussed in this chapter examines the effect of maternal employment, household differentiation, and maternal differentiation on the nutritional status, dietary intake, and parasitic infection of three- to five- year-old children in Panama.

Research Setting and Sample

The study was conducted in two "health center areas" near David, the capital of Chiriquí Province, Panama. One, the Barriada San José, has a population of approximately 20,000 and is on the outskirts of David. Most of the houses in this community are situated within close walking distance to the main road, and contact with the city is frequent. Some of the residents work in David. Common occupations include construction, transportation services, and factory work at local meat and fish packing plants.

The second area, Chiriquí, is farther from David and extends to include distant rural barrios. In contrast to San José, the people of Chiriquí have little contact with the city and are more widely dispersed. The majority of their employment opportunities are agricultural. Many farm their own land and work as occasional day-laborers for cash income. It is common for those without land to cultivate *tierra prestada* (borrowed land), and to receive a percentage of the harvest. Women rarely work in agricultural production here, but they do grow selected foods near their home for the family's consumption.

The details of the sample have been described elsewhere (Tucker and Sanjur 1988; Tucker 1986). Children, aged three through five years, were selected randomly using vaccination records at the San José and Chiriquí health centers. This sample was supplemented with children selected through a screening process for infection with *Ascaris lumbricoides* for the purposes of the larger study (Nesheim et al. 1985). This difference in the sampling method was not found to affect the relationships examined here, and both groups are included in this analysis.

In all, 207 children received the initial interview, and a randomly selected subset of 137 participated in intensive data collection (food weighing and time use observation). Due to some disqualifications, dropouts, and incomplete data, the final working sample here includes 178 children for general data and 118 for intensive dietary and time use data.

Data Collection and Preparation

Methods of data collection have also been described in detail in Tucker and Sanjur (1988) and will only be briefly discussed here. The data collection was conducted over the course of one year (1983-1984) by a research team consisting of nutritionists from Cornell University working with two trained Panamanian nutritionists. The protocol included three short interviews in the home, two full days of observation for diet and time use, a visit by the mother and child to the health center for physical measurements and blood drawing, and collection of fecal samples for parasite evaluation.

During the observation days, the preschool child was "followed," and all of his/her food was weighed carefully to assess accurate intakes. During the same day, the time use of the mother, and that of the substitute care giver when the mother was out, was recorded.

The nutrient content of dietary data was analyzed using the Ohio State data bank supplemented with values for Panamanian foods located in additional food composition tables (Tucker 1986). Time use was coded and used as number of minutes per twenty-four hours for each of fourteen activities. Both types of data were then averaged for the two days of observation to get a better measure of normal patterns.

Measures of Differentiation

To obtain measures of maternal and household differentiation, structural indicators of the concepts were measured through a questionnaire. For the household these included a house construction index, number of household possessions from a selected list, car ownership, occupation and education of the household head, land ownership, and crop and food production.

Principal Component Analysis was selected as an appropriate data reduction tool to summarize the information from several indicators into one or more variables that measure the overall concept. Based on the commonality in the correlation matrix, this procedure identifies component factors. If all the included indicators are highly intercorrelated, and thus appear to be measuring the same concept, only one strong factor will emerge. If, in fact, several sub-concepts are represented by different clusters of intercorrelations, several strong factors may be seen. Each factor represents orthogonal aspects of the matrix and is a linear combination of the variables, with appropriate "loadings" or weights assigned by the program based on the relationship of each variable to the overall commonality. Those with the highest "loadings" can be said to be contributing the most to that factor. This procedure generates factor scores for each individual case, which are a standardized linear combination of the factor loadings multiplied by the original values for the variables, yielding a distribution of scores that may be used as a single variable that represents the concept.

The results of this procedure for the household indicators of differentiation are presented in Table 7.1. The first and strongest factor includes, in order of importance: household possessions, housing index, education of the household head, car ownership, and occupation of the household head. This factor is used in this analysis as the strongest measure of household differentiation. Additional factors were generated and represent subcategories of the concept. Here, Factor 2 includes agricultural variables and Factor 3 incorporates variables related to home food production. The similarity of these factors to those that Engberg generated with Ghanian data is notable (Engberg 1974). She also found household possessions to be the strongest indicator of differentiation in the first factor.

For mothers, the relevant indicators that were entered into the principal components procedure include years of formal education, number of extra classes taken, nutrition knowledge (based on answers to ten questions), craft production, home decoration, media use, frequency of reading, and social visiting patterns. The first and strongest factor resulting from this procedure for maternal differentiation is composed mainly of four indicators. In order of importance by factor loadings they include: nutrition knowledge score (.77); years of formal education (.73); frequency of reading (.65); and craft activity (.63). Participation in classes contributed only weakly (.23). Taken together, these indicators measure information acquisition, use, and retention and provide a much more powerful measure of "ability to process information" compared to years of education alone. Additional weaker factors were generated that appear to measure different aspects of maternal characteristics. Their interpretation and use are beyond the scope of this discussion. The interested reader is referred to Tucker (1986).

Statistical Analysis

Due to the complex nature of the relationships being examined, a stepwise regression technique was used in order to allow several potential confounding variables and effect modifiers (interactions) to enter the regression equations (Kleinbaum et al. 1982). Independent main effects tested include: maternal employment away from home (yes/no), work for income at home (yes/no), household and maternal differentiation scores, type of substitute care giver (four dummy variables), household income other than the mother's, location (rural/urban), female head (yes/no), household size, number of preschool children, factor scores for agricultural and subsistence food production, child's age and sex, and mother's age and hemoglobin level. Where appropriate, interactions of maternal employment with most of these variables were also tested. This procedure was followed using ordinary least squares regression in SAS for the dependent variables: weight-for-age and kilocalorie and protein intakes. An analogous procedure was run using logistic regression with the LOGIST procedure in SAS (Harrell 1983) for the dependent variables: infection with *Ascaris lumbricoides, Trichuris trichiura,* or hookworm. Final models were run using the REGRESSION and LOGIT procedures of STATA on a microcomputer.

Results

In the total sample, 29 percent of the mothers were employed outside the home — more in the urban (36 percent) than in the rural (14 percent) community. Mothers were found to work an average of 38 hours (± 14) per week and to earn an average of US$48 (±35) per week. Most (44 percent) work as unskilled labor — in the local factories or as housekeepers for other families. A few (8 percent) are self-employed vendors. Twenty-three percent work in retail sales or as office staff, and 25 percent can be categorized as professionals — mostly teachers and nursing aides. Twenty-six percent of the total sample are female heads of household (responsible for children with no legal or common-law spouse present). Not surprisingly, 50 percent of these female household heads are working outside the home as opposed to 21 percent of those with a partner present.

Additionally, 20 percent of the mothers participate in some income activity in the home from which they earn an average of US$14 (±16) per week. The majority of these prepare *tortillas* (flour or maize flat cakes) or other food items for sale in the local community. Those with refrigerators sell ice and/or homemade popsicles. Several of the women raise animals (mostly pigs) for sale; some sell fruit grown on their property; others sell embroidery, crocheted items or other craftwork; some take in laundry and ironing; and a few offer specialized services, such as haircuts, in their homes.

Average time use for the total sample showed that women spend seven hours a day in household production, 1.5 hours on work and income generation, 6.5 on leisure and social activities, and 9 hours sleeping. However, among mothers employed outside the home (who put in, on average, an 8 hour work day) there were significant decreases in time spent on other activities. Mothers employed outside the home spend approximately 4.5 hours less on home production, 1.5 hours less in leisure and social activities, and 1 hour less sleeping.

Within this, maternal care time — specifically time spent on child care and on food preparation — was found to decrease significantly when mothers are working away from home (Table 7.2). When the time of the substitute care giver is included, however, no significant differences remain in time spent on these activities for the household. Substitute child care providers for the working mothers in this sample include: grandmothers (45 percent); older sisters (22 percent); nonrelatives, such as live-in friends or hired child care (18 percent); aunts, usually younger sisters of the mother (10 percent); fathers (4 percent); and older brothers (2 percent).

Additional descriptive information in Table 7.2 reveals that when the income earned by the mother is excluded, no significant difference is found in household income between the two groups. With her income, however, the difference in total household income is highly significant. Additionally, working mothers have a higher level of education and live in better housing — to which their income may be contributing.

For the total group of children, 6.2 percent were more than two standard deviations below the median weight-for-age; 8.7 percent were more than two standard deviations below median height-for-age; and 0.6 percent were more than two standard deviations below median weight-for-height, indicating that stunting is a more common problem than is wasting in this population (WHO 1983). For hemoglobin, 16 percent were found to be below suggested cut-off points, indicating a risk of iron deficiency anemia (Dallman 1977). Mean dietary intakes were found to be 68.0 (±15.1) percent of the RDA for kilocalories and 74.6 (± 25.3) percent of the RDA for protein. Finally, 28 percent of the children selected randomly were infected with *Ascaris*, 34 percent had *Trichuris*, and 14 percent had hookworm infections. Overall, this group of children can be described as having a low prevalence of severe malnutrition, considerable mild-to-moderate malnutrition, with more stunting than wasting, lower than recommended dietary intakes, and high prevalence of parasitic infection. The problem thus appears to be chronic in nature and is likely to result from long periods of low dietary intakes and recurrent infections related to poverty.

Table 7.3 presents a comparison of the dependent variables by work status and reveals that, as a group, children of mothers who work away from home are consuming more kilocalories and protein and are less likely to be infected with parasites. No significant differences were seen for anthropometric measures, but hemoglobin status is also higher among children of working mothers.

Together, this descriptive information indicates that, on average, the positive effect of increased income outweighs the negative effect of decreased time. In terms of quantity, loss of maternal time tends to be compensated for by the inputs of substitute care givers, while the income of the mother appears to be making a significant contribution to total household income and child welfare. The question remains, however, if the effects of these differences in resource patterns on child welfare are affected by differences in quality of substitute child care or by differences in "differentiation" or "ability to process information" for decision making.

The results of regression equations, including the above factors plus additional potential confounders and effect modifiers, are presented in Tables 7.4 and 7.5. As shown earlier in Table 7.3, work status of the mother is an important determinant of kilocalorie and protein intakes and of hemoglobin status, but is not important to anthropometric outcomes in this group (Table 7.4). Plots of these relationships (see Tucker 1986) reveal that kilocalorie and protein intakes are higher, on the average, among children of employed versus nonemployed women. However, these differences are greater in the rural than in the urban community. Hemoglobin levels, again, are generally higher among children of working women but the difference is greater if the substitute care giver is male. The small sample size for male care givers makes this relationship of questionable importance, however.

What is interesting to note is that maternal differentiation is the variable most consistently significant in the equations for different indicators of child nutrition — for kilocalorie and protein intakes and for measures of weight-for-age and weight-for-height. Income (other than the mother's), on the other hand, is significant only for protein intake and for height-for-age. Household level differentiation is, surprisingly, significant for none of these outcome measures with the exception of hemoglobin status. Thus, it appears that maternal "ability to process a wide variety of information types" may be a key factor in determining dietary intake and nutritional status in this group of children.

Table 7.5 presents the results of the logit regression equations for parasitic infection. Maternal employment is a significant variable for *Trichuris* infection (negative relationship) and enters the equation for *Ascaris* infection in two interactions. Plots again revealed an overall tendency for lower prevalence of *Ascaris* among children of working versus nonworking mothers, with a greater effect in the urban area and when a grandmother is the substitute care giver. After controlling other variables, the marginally significant difference between children of working versus nonworking mothers for hookworm infection disappears (seen in Table 7.3).

Interestingly, maternal differentiation is not a significant variable in any of the three equations and was dropped during the stepwise procedure. Here, household differentiation is the variable that is consistently and significantly related to parasitic infection. Children living in more complex households (more different types of possessions, improved household quality, etc.) are less likely to be infected. This is not surprising given the importance of the environment to exposure to parasites. After this variation is controlled, the mother's level of differentiation appears to have little independent effect on likelihood of infection. Although we expect that mothers with both greater access to information, and the ability to process it, would take more precautions with cleanliness and sanitation, this does not appear to be sufficient to prevent infection when the basic household environment is limited.

Other variables important to parasitic infection include location (there are higher prevalences of *Trichuris* and hookworm in the rural areas); household size (significantly related to infection with *Trichuris* and hookworm); and presence of a grandmother as a substitute care giver (with a negative effect on likelihood of infection with hookworm).

Because of the possible importance of situational effects particular to the work situation, several work related variables such as hours worked per week, distance (minutes) to work, and length of time employed (months) were substituted for maternal work in the final analyses for the subsample of working mothers (not shown). None of these variables were found to be significantly related to anthropometric measures. Number of hours worked per week was positively related to kilocalorie (p < .05) and protein (p < .10) intake. Number of months employed was also positively related to kilocalorie intake (p < .05). These findings reinforce the likelihood that the positive income effect of maternal employment outweighs the negative time effect on the dietary intake of these children.

Discussion and Conclusions

In summary, it appears that maternal employment does not have a negative effect on child health or nutritional status for this group of three-through five-year-old Panamanian children. On the contrary, maternal employment is positively related to improved dietary intake, hemoglobin status, and lower prevalence of parasitic infection. Any negative effects of decreased maternal time in child care and food preparation appear to be compensated by the inputs of the substitute care givers. There is some evidence of negative effects of care givers who are nonrelatives (on weight-for-height) or male (on height-for-age), although the sample sizes are small and the lack of consistency of results makes these findings questionable. There is also some evidence that grandmothers as substitute care givers may have positive effects on protection from parasitic infection.

The positive effects of maternal employment are likely to be related to the increased income the mother is contributing to the household. A positive effect of maternal income on household food expenditures is the likely cause of better dietary intake among children of working mothers. Other authors suggest that income earned and controlled by the mother is more likely spent on food and in other ways that improve the child's welfare (Dwyer 1983; Safilios-Rothschild 1980; von Braun, Chapter 9). The reason for a positive relationship between maternal employment and parasitic infection is somewhat less easy to explain, particularly as maternal differentiation is not significant in this analysis. However, it is possible that the increased income under her control is used for test fees and the purchase of medicines and protective equipment.

In addition to these overall positive effects of maternal employment on child welfare in this population, the importance of maternal differentiation is of special note. This variable is significant in the explanation of variation of dietary intake (kilocalories and protein) and in measures of weight-for-age and weight-for-height. As a measure of maternal "ability to process information," differentiation appears to capture an aspect of maternal characteristics important to improved nutritional status of the child. Household differentiation, on the other hand, was found to be more important in explaining differences in parasitic infection and hemoglobin status — which has, in turn, been found to be related to hookworm infection (see Tucker 1986).

It thus appears that maternal employment, in the presence of adequate substitute child care, is likely to have a positive effect on child welfare. This appears to operate primarily through the increased income brought into the household by the working mother, although the increased exposure to new ideas that results from leaving home for employment may also play a role. Additionally, the increased control the mother has over income she earns may be an important factor in increasing expenditures on food and other items important for child welfare.

The independent importance of the composite measure of household differentiation reinforces the overall need for household level development and improvement of housing and equipment for basic protection from disease. The importance of maternal differentiation points to the need for increased efforts to educate women and to provide both formal and informal opportunities to improve decision-making ability through improved information flow.

Reducing the prevalence of malnutrition and infection ultimately depends on the elimination of poverty. The results presented here indicate that the inclusion of women in the process of development is a critical factor in the improvement of the health and nutritional status of preschool children. This study does not address the effects of maternal employment on infants and toddlers, nor in situations where maternal employment, due to severe time constraints and lack of adequate substitute caregivers, may result in genuine neglect. In such cases, the constraints must be identified and given appropriate consideration in policy formulation and program development. In general, however, given the close relationship between mother and child, investment in education, employment, and opportunities for personal development for women (allowing them more control over resource allocation and improved ability to make informed decisions) should translate not only to improvements in their lives but also to improved welfare for their children.

References

Cochrane, S.; Leslie, J.; and O'Hara D.

1982. "Parental Education and Child Health: Intracountry Evidence." *Health, Policy and Education* 2: 213-250.

Dallman, P.R.

1977. "New Approaches for Screening Iron Deficiency." *Journal of Pediatrics* 90: 678.

Durkheim, E.

1949. *The Division of Labor in Society.* Reprinted 1983, Glencoe, IL: The Free Press.

Dwyer, D.H.

1983. "Women and Income in the Third World: Implications for Policy." The Population Council International Programs Working Paper No. 18.

Engberg, L.E.

1974. "Household Differentiation and Integration as Predictors of Child Welfare in a Ghanian Community." *Journal of Marriage and the Family,* (May 1974): 389-399.

Harrell, F.E.

1983. "Logist Procedure." In *Supplemental Library User's Guide,* pp. 181-202. SAS Institute.

Kleinbaum, D.G.; Kupper, L.L.; and Morgenstern, H.

1982. *Epidemiological Research, Principles and Quantitative Measures.* Belmont, California: Lifetime Learning Publications.

Larkin, F.

1968. Household Structure and Children's Health in Ghana. Ph.D. Thesis, Cornell University, Ithaca, New York.

Nesheim, M.; Crompton, D.W.T.; and Sanjur, D.

1985. "Nutritional Aspects of Ascariasis: Report on a Community Study Carried out in Chiriquí Province, Republic of Panama, During 1983 and 1984." Prepared for The U.S. Agency for International Development.

Safilios-Rothschild, C.

1980. "The Role of the Family in Development." *Finance and Development* (December 1980): 44-47.

Tucker, K.

1986. Maternal Time Use, Differentiation and Child Nutrition. Ph.D. Thesis, Cornell University, Ithaca, New York.

Tucker, K. and Sanjur, D.

1988. "Maternal Employment and Child Nutrition in Panama." *Social Science and Medicine,* vol. 26, no. 6, pp. 605-612.

Tucker, K. and Young, F.W.
  1987. "Family Differentiation and Child Nutrition." Paper presented at the Association for the Study of Food in Society Conference, Aquinas College, Grand Rapids, Michigan, April 1987.
WHO.
  1983. *Measuring Change in Nutritional Status.* Geneva: World Health Organization.
Young, F.W.
  1983. *Interdisciplinary Theories of Rural Development.* Greenwich, Connecticut: JAI Press, Inc.
Young, F.W. and Young, R.C.
  1968. "The Differentiation of Family Structure in Rural Mexico." *Journal of Marriage and the Family* (February 1986). vol. 30(1): 154-161.

Table 7.1 Factor pattern for household differentiation variable

	FACTOR 1	FACTOR 2	FACTOR 3
Number of possessions	<u>0.87</u>	-0.06	-0.08
Housing index	<u>0.84</u>	0.00	-0.05
Education HH head	<u>0.66</u>	-0.02	-0.26
Car (yes,no)	<u>0.57</u>	-0.11	0.11
Occupation HH head	<u>0.57</u>	-0.19	-0.24
Land, Sq. meters	-0.07	<u>0.84</u>	0.12
No. plants produced	-0.09	<u>0.83</u>	0.27
No. sacks crops produced	-0.12	<u>0.83</u>	0.07
No. of pigs	0.11	-0.07	<u>0.75</u>
No. chickens	0.04	0.16	<u>0.72</u>
No. fruit trees	-0.17	0.43	<u>0.70</u>
No. different foods produced	-0.17	0.23	<u>0.67</u>
EIGENVALUE	2.65	2.41	2.25
VARIANCE EXPL	0.22	0.20	0.19

Adapted from Tucker and Young, 1987.

Table 7.2 Descriptive Information by maternal work status

	Maternal Employment away from Home			
	no		yes	
	X̄ SD		X̄ SD	t-value
Child's age (mos)	50.0 ± 8.8		51.8 ± 8.8	-1.2
HH income/week	70.5 ± 64.9		124.8 ± 79.6	-4.7[5]
Income w/o mother's contribution	68.8 ± 65.4		74.3 ± 51.3	-0.5
Mother's educ.	6.6 ± 2.4		9.2 ± 3.9	-4.4[5]
Housing score	14.7 ± 3.5		16.7 ± 3.3	-3.4[4]
Mother's time:				
Cooking (mins)	134.6 ± 60.0		48.0 ± 43.4	6.1[5]
Child care	72.1 ± 53.2		35.4 ± 38.9	2.9[3]
Mother + Subs:				
Cooking	137.1 ± 57.9		126.8 ± 51.8	0.7
Child care	74.0 ± 53.1		78.5 ± 60.6	-0.3

[3] p < .01; [4] p < .001; [5] p < .0001.
Adapted from information in Tucker and Sanjur, 1988.

Table 7.3 Dependent variables by maternal work status

| | Maternal Employment away from Home* | | | | |
| | no | | yes | | |
	$\bar{X}$	SD	$\bar{X}$	SD	t-value
KCAL	1372.1	±269.4	1627.9	± 346.0	-3.7[4]
PROTEIN (gm)	34.8	± 10.5	44.3	± 11.3	-3.6[4]
(n)	(98)		(20)		
Weight-age	-0.65 ±	1.0	-0.70 ±	1.1	0.3
Height-age	-0.79 ±	1.2	-0.85 ±	0.9	0.3
Weight-ht	-0.13 ±	1.0	-0.16 ±	1.0	0.1
(n)	(115)		(45)		
Hemoglobin (g/dl)	12.3 ±	1.2	12.7 ±	1.1	-1.7[1]
(n)	(123)		(48)		
	percent infected**				Chi-sq
Ascaris	52.0		23.5		12.0[4]
Trichuris	32.3		15.7		5.0[2]
Hookworm	13.4		5.9		2.1[1]
(n)	(127)		(51)		

[1] $p < .1$; [2] $p < .05$; [4] $p < .001$.
*   Adapted from information in Tucker and Sanjur, 1988.
** Adapted from information in Tucker, 1986.

Table 7.4 Effect of maternal employment on child nutrition

Variable	KCAL	PRO	WA	HA	WH	HGB
Work[mt]	1177.5[3]	47.8[3]				0.11
Workhome					0.51[3]	
Income[wmt]		0.05[3]		0.003[2]		
Diff[hh]						0.33[5]
Diff[mt]	53.2[1]	2.0[1]	0.22[3]		0.27[4]	
Caregiver[nr]					-0.79[2]	
Caregiver[m]				-0.44[2]		-0.40[1]
Location	7.4	0.02				
Sex[ch]	-151.6[3]					
Age[ch]	13.3[4]	0.36[3]				
Age[mt]			0.02[2]			
Hgb[mt]						0.41[5]
Interactions:						
Work[mt] by						
Location	-540.5[3]	-22.1[3]				
Caregiver[m]						1.4[2]
Intercept	947.5	14.5	-1.3	-0.97	-0.20	7.2
F	9.5[5]	9.3[5]	5.2[3]	5.0[3]	7.2[4]	16.0[5]
adj R^2	0.32	0.31	0.05	0.05	0.10	0.32
(n)	(108)	(108)	(161)	(160)	(161)	(163)

[1] $p < .1$; [2] $p < .05$; [3] $p < .01$; [4] $p < .001$; [5] $p < .0001$.
mt = maternal; wmt = without maternal; hh = household; nr = nonrelative;
m = male; ch = child
Adapted from Tucker and Sanjur, 1988.

Table 7.5   Effect of maternal employment on child parasitic infection

VARIABLE	ASCARIS	TRICHURIS	HOOKWORM
Work^{mt}	1.4	-0.81[1]	
Diff^{hh}	-1.2[4]	-0.50[2]	-0.88[2]
Size^{hh}		0.20[3]	0.27[2]
Location	1.8[4]	-1.6[4]	-2.9[4]
Care giver^{g}	0.13		-1.6[2]
Interactions:			
Work^{mt} by: Location	-2.3[1]		
Caregiver^{g}	-2.4[2]		
Intercept	-1.3	-1.2	-2.7
Log likelihood	-93.8	-91.3	-40.2
Chi-square	56.4[5]	27.0[5]	44.7[5]
(n)	(178)	(178)	(178)

[1] $p < .1$; [2] $p < .05$; [3] $p < .01$; [4] $p < .001$; [5] $p < .0001$.
^{mt} = maternal; ^{hh} = household; ^{g} = grandmother

8

Child Care Strategies of Working and Nonworking Women in Rural and Urban Guatemala*

Patrice Engle

The effect of a mother's paid work on the welfare of her young children has been the subject of much debate in the last 30 years. Theorists using a psychodynamic orientation argue that a child not reared primarily by its mother during the first three to five years of its life will suffer various negative consequences from this "maternal deprivation," ranging from emotional damage and lowered intellectual potential to inadequate physical development (Bowlby 1960). Maturational theorists believe that the development of the child is a more robust process, which can proceed well under a variety of family configurations if there is adequate child care. They argue that the effect of maternal paid work depends on conditions such as the mother's hourly wage or the distance between work and home (Scarr 1984). Other factors known to influence outcomes for children are the mother's satisfaction with her chosen role and the amount of time spent on child care for children under two years of age (Schwartz 1983).

While families in all societies promote the health and well being of their children, cross-cultural differences exist in the values and goals associated with child care. As LeVine (1980) points out, parental investment strategies differ if the focus is on child survival and long-term work contribution to the family rather than on school achievement, self-sufficiency, and autonomy (common child rearing goals in the United States). Researchers must be cognizant that in Third World countries the conceptualization of adequate or appropriate child care may refer more to the

*Support for this research was provided through USAID Grant OTR 0096-GSS344600.

provision of physical care, feeding, and socialization instead of the development of socioemotional bonding and intellectual stimulation.

Additionally, the primary caregiver will often be different in non-Western societies than in industrialized countries. In the United States, for example, it is assumed that the mother, or perhaps the father, is the primary caregiver. Yet in developing countries, other family members often provide a considerable amount of child care during the first year of life (Engle 1980, 1986; Ho 1979). Even when the mother is present, she may primarily supervise the older siblings' or family members' care of younger children. In many cases, by the time a child reaches four or five years, he or she may no longer be given much supervision and, in fact, may begin providing care to younger siblings. Furthermore, after the child's first year, the child care patterns of working mothers may differ little from those of nonworking mothers.

Few studies from developing countries have compared the effects of sibling and adult care on outcomes for children, regardless of the work status of the mother. Shah et al. (1979) reported that the age of the caregiver was associated with nutritional status of children; the younger the caregiver, the more poorly the child performed. More attention needs to be paid to the characteristics of the caregivers when evaluating the effects of women's work on children.

This chapter aims to provide further insight into the relationship between maternal work and child welfare in the Third World. Three questions are addressed. First, what child care strategies are used by working and nonworking Guatemalan women? Second, what activities (including caregiving) do women forgo in order to participate in the wage-labor market? Third, what are the effects of these child care strategies on children's nutritional status and morbidity?

This chapter is based on data for mothers and children from a large town near Guatemala City and four small villages in the rural, Eastern section of Guatemala.[1] The data base is both large and complex, having been collected for purposes other than a study of the relationship between maternal work and child welfare.

RESEARCH SETTING

The urban women and children surveyed in the study live in a town and a nearby *colonia* (shantytown) located about 20 minutes by automobile from Guatemala City. Frequent bus transportation connects the town and the *colonia* (hereafter referred to collectively as the town) with Guatemala City. For many residents, this town is a stepping-stone community: migrants often temporarily reside here after leaving a *finca* (plantation) before moving on to the city. Many town residents work in the capital, and have acquired cultural norms similar to those of the urban center. Houses with plastered adobe walls and tile roofs tend to be more permanently constructed than in rural villages. Slightly fewer than half of the houses have dirt floors, while over half have electricity. Almost all of the houses have some type of sanitary facility. There is considerable variation in income level within the town, demonstrated by the presence of areas with dirt roads and very poor houses in contrast with other areas where paved roads and reasonably good houses are found.

In the four rural villages, most families live in two-room houses constructed of local materials, mainly adobe. One room serves as the kitchen and the other as the sleeping quarters for the entire family. Few houses have sanitary facilities, no house has electricity, and all floors are dirt. The pervasive poverty in these rural villages is reflected in the median family income, which in 1975 was approximately US$500 per year. Most of the rural households were engaged to some degree in subsistence agriculture, although 17 percent of the families assessed in a 1974 income and wealth survey were involved in no agricultural activity. Of the farming families, less than 20 percent depended entirely on farming income. Seventy percent of the farming families complemented their income with salaried work, and wages accounted for 40 percent of the total income of farmers (Balderston et al. 1981).

Sample and Methods

The data used here were generated using two distinct methodological approaches implemented in 1975. The first was a time-use survey that asked women about their time spent in income-producing work and child care. The second approach was a Retrospective Life History Questionnaire to record, in addition to fertility history and women's work patterns, the type of child care assistance received by working mothers and the possible effects of this help on their children's nutritional status. This section describes the characteristics of the two data sets and the methods used for each approach. (Table 8.1 describes the sample of each data set.)

Time-use Survey

The time-use survey data were collected for all mothers between the ages of 15 and 49 who had children seven years or younger in the rural villages, or children three years or younger in the urban town. The mothers were interviewed about the previous day's activities every three months for four rounds. Because the data from the first two rounds are questionable, due to a lack of training of the interviewers and difficulties with the form, only the third and fourth rounds are used here. Therefore, the data analyzed here are time-use data collected on two separate occasions in 1975 (summer and fall) with three months intervening. Not all of the women interviewed in the summer could be reinterviewed in the fall, and some additional women were interviewed in the fall (see Table 8.1). Interview days were selected randomly to represent all possible weekdays during the interview process. Estimates of data reliability, based on verification by a second observer, have been discussed elsewhere (Engle et al. 1986; Clark 1981).

Time-use estimates will be influenced by the agricultural cycle. Mejia Piveral (1972) observed for Guatemala that the timing of the important agricultural activities of planting and harvesting was consistent from year to year, except for slight variations due to local weather conditions. In the present study, the four rounds of data collection coincided with minimum agricultural activity, planting, weeding, and harvesting. Rounds three and four, used here, cover the periods of weeding and of harvesting, which are the two more intense agricultural periods. Also, during round four, children were not attending school.

For each activity, the mother was asked: whether she performed it; when she performed it (morning, afternoon, or all day); where she performed it (in the community, on the outskirts of the community, or outside of the community); the distance she traveled (which was coded by the interviewer in terms of blocks); the time she spent (to 10-minute intervals) performing the task; and the number of days the previous week (two weeks for round three) that she performed the activity.

The only information used in the analysis reported in this chapter is the mother's report on her activities the previous day. If the activity involved earning money, the mother was asked how much she had earned the previous day. For activities that took her outside the home, she was asked whether she had taken any children six years or under with her, and whether she had received any adult assistance. Finally, she was asked about the activity performed by each of her children over seven years of age, where he or she performed the activity, the time spent on the activity, and the distance traveled to the activity.

A total of fifteen activities were recorded.[2] These activities were much more appropriate to the rural than to the urban areas, which is reflected in the low frequencies of many of the activities in the urban areas. The interviewer had the responsibility for coding a particular activity into the appropriate category. The only activities for which income earned was recorded were marketing, work inside the home, and work outside the home.[3]

Child caregiving was measured by the woman's statement about whether she watched any children in the morning, the afternoon, all day, or not at all on the previous day. Specific time estimates were not made because in pretests it appeared that mothers, particularly in the rural areas, could not separate the time spent in child care from other activities.

Child care is generally considered a joint activity; that is, it can be (and usually is) performed at the same time as another activity. For example, it is quite easy for a mother to watch a pot of water she has put to boil while at the same time feeding, changing, or simply supervising her child; it would be quite difficult for her to report hours and minutes in child caregiving. However, most mothers were able to estimate whether they spent the morning, afternoon, or all-day on child care.

The variables used in the time-use analyses are whether or not a particular activity occurred and, if the activity occurred, when it occurred (morning, afternoon, or all day), for how long, distance from home, where it occurred, minutes of help provided by other adults, and amount of income earned.

Retrospective Life History Questionnaire

The sample for the retrospective life history data set was children of one to four (age one to three in the urban town) whose mothers were included in the time-use study and whose growth had been measured at a central clinic located in the town or village. The period during which children had been measured was a year and a half (1974-1975) in the urban town, and six years (1969-1975) in the rural villages. Anthropometric measurements of children were taken within a month of their birthdays in both the urban town and rural villages.

Although every effort was made to collect information on identical samples for both the time-use instrument and the Retrospective Life History Questionnaire, there were some differences among the mothers sampled. Some mothers moved or were temporarily away during one of the two interview phases. Also, some children had not been measured within the period of time necessary for inclusion in the sample. For the rural villages, the sample is much larger since it includes children through age four and the measurement period covered is six years (see Table 8.1). The same child may have been measured several times over the period of his or her growth. To avoid having a child enter an analysis twice, all analyses were performed within age cohorts.

In order to be able to use the greatest number of measurements possible, and to relate them to the working status of the mother during the year prior to the measurement of the child's nutritional status, a different measure of mother's work from that in the time-use study was used. The Retropsective Life History Questionnaire also enabled the amount and type of maternal work as a function of her child's age to be documented.

The Retrospective Life History Questionnaire asked mothers to recall each birth, and to relate it to other events that had occurred in their lives between pregnancies, such as changes in living situation or wage-earning activities. In the time-use survey, work for earnings was based on women's report of income-earning activities the previous day. The only categories coded in the survey form were agricultural work, marketing, work inside the home for income, and work outside the home for income. In the Retrospective Life History Questionnaire, specific types of work for earnings were recorded. Women were asked whether they had performed any activities for money, and these responses were coded into 17 categories by the interviewer. These were later collapsed into four: agricultural, domestic (washing clothes, gathering water, etc., for income), informal (selling products, making things in the home), or formal (factory labor, specialized labor such as seamstress, or teaching).

The measurements of children's nutritional status were based on weight and height as measured by trained Guatemalan auxilliary nurses. In the rural villages only, morbidity information was collected from mothers' reports every two weeks in interviews in their homes. The measure used here was the percentage of days ill in bed during the preceding year.

Quality of child care was assessed by the mother's response to a question of whether an adult or an older sibling helped with caregiving during infancy, during the second year of life, or during the third year of life of the target child.

RESULTS

Time-use Study

Table 8.2 shows the percent and number of women engaged in work for earnings in the summer (round 3) and the fall (round 4). Up to 70 percent of rural women and 40 percent of urban women were engaged in some agricultural activity with the highest rates during the (fall) harvest season. Approximately 20 percent of the women reported non-agricultural paid work for both rounds (summer and fall) and in both the rural and urban locations. Work in the home (sewing, craft production, domestic work) was more common than work outside the home or marketing. Both of the latter were slightly more common in the urban setting. It is not certain that these work categories captured all income-earning activities. However, the percentages of workers in each category are similar to figures obtained from other questionnaires on work for earnings (see Engle et al. 1986).

Table 8.3 presents the average number of hours working mothers spent in the income-producing activities of agriculture, marketing, and other work both inside and outside the home during summer and fall. Although the sample sizes are small for some categories, the results are consistent across location and round. Agricultural workers spent less than an hour per day in agricultural work. In contrast, those working outside the home spent an average of seven hours per day in work activities in the rural villages and nine hours per day in work outside the home in the urban town. (From the Retrospective Life History Questionnaire, we know that these women are employed in domestic work such as washing, ironing, and making tortillas in someone else's home, as well as in some formal labor such as factory work.) These long working hours, particularly in the urban town, were unexpected. Typically, a mother working outside the home would arise at 5:00 a.m., feed her children, prepare and leave food for lunch, and board the bus to the city by 6:30. She might arrive at a factory by 7:30 and work until 5:00 with a half an hour for lunch. She would arrive home again at 6:00 or 6:30, depending on the crowding on the buses. She might also have gone to the city to work in a cafeteria as a waitress, or she might purchase food at the central market to resell in another area. Work in the home and marketing are both less time-intensive, requiring about five to seven hours per day in the urban areas, and three to five hours per day in the rural villages.

The time-use data indicate how many women reported spending the morning, the afternoon, or all day caring for their children but not how many hours per day were spent on the activity. Did the percent of women reporting all day child caregiving vary according to work status? This question was asked in several ways. First, were seasonal changes in agricultural production reflected in seasonal changes in child care patterns? The answer appears to be no since between 80 and 85 percent of both urban and rural women reported watching their children all day for both agricultural seasons measured (Table 8.4). Given that women worked, on the average, only one hour per day in agricultural work, this finding is not too surprising. If women were removing the grains from the corn, it could be done while watching the children. Also, many women were observed to take young children with them when they were harvesting crops. Coffee picking, for example, tended to be a family affair, with the whole family camping out in the coffee fields for the day while the parents and the older children picked the berries.

The effect of the other kinds of work on child caregiving, however, is much more substantial. Table 8.4 shows the percent of mothers reporting morning, afternoon, all day, or no time in child caregiving as a function of their work status (agricultural work was excluded). For both rural and urban mothers (in both summer and fall), child care patterns differed significantly between working and nonworking mothers. Urban working mothers were more likely than rural working mothers to report no child care. Rural working women tended to reduce child care to the afternoon rather than to no child care, a reasonable strategy in a hot area in which the typical working day is from dawn to early afternoon, with a rest period following the big midday meal.

The number of women who report full-day child care, despite large number of hours of wage labor, raises the issue of how many hours of work per day a woman can perform before she begins to decrease her time in child caregiving. Figure 8.1 plots the relationship between the number of hours per day that the woman reported working (agricultural work was included in this analysis) and the percent of women reporting full-day child care. These patterns differ for rural and urban women. In the rural villages, the non-parametric correlation between hours per day of work and full day child care (Kendall's Tau β) is not significant for either round. From looking at the graph, it appears that women do not report less than full-day child care until they work eight or more hours per day. On the other hand, in the urban town, child care begins to drop fairly regularly after one hour per day of work, and the non-parametric correlations are signficant both for round 3 (Tau β=-.22. p<.01) and round 4 (Tau β=-.15, p<.01).

Wage employment appears to be more compatible with child care in the rural than in the urban areas. One possible explanation is that more women work in their own home for money in the rural area (see Table 8.2). Also, many of the agricultural workers, who are much more numerous in the rural villages, probably work inside the home, although specific information on location of agricultural work was not obtained. For those working outside the home, many more rural than urban women worked inside the community (90 percent of rural women compared to 61 percent of urban women). For all women who worked outside the home, there was a significant association between distance to work and likelihood of reporting less than full day child care. The farther away the mother worked, the less likely she was to report spending all day in child care.

If these working women, particularly the rural women, are not significantly reducing their time in child care as a function of work, either they are simply increasing their labor time or they are reducing some other home production activity. Do women who work for earnings spend as much time in other activities as those who do not work for earnings?

The answer appears to be that working women are simply working more hours rather than significantly reducing the time they spend on non-income earning activities. Table 8.5 shows that there was a significant difference in total hours spent in productive activities (income earning and household activities) between working and nonworking women. However, they spent similar amounts of time on household activities. The only significant difference in time spent on such an activity was washing clothes during the fall round in the rural villages. Clothes washing is a very time-consuming and social activity in several villages, requiring a day-long trip to a nearby river to wash and dry the clothes, and the time spent was clearly shortened.

Finally, women reported receiving very little help (less than half an hour a day) from other adults. Among urban women there was no significant difference in the amount of help received between working and nonworking women. For rural women, working women reported significantly more help from other adults in the fall round, but nonworking women reported significantly more help in the summer round.

In sum, mothers who work for earnings spend more total time in household plus income earning activities, and are less likely to report full day child caregiving, although at least 50 percent of women working for earnings still report full days of child caregiving. These women receive little additional help in child care or other activities from other adults in the household.

Retrospective Life History Questionnaire

Questions concerning occupation from the Retrospective Life History Questionnaire showed that in the rural areas most of the women who report having an occupation were informal workers, many of whom were involved in a home craft project of weaving mats for sale. In the urban areas, half of the women were in domestic work, and approximately 25 percent were employed in the formal sector. In both the urban and rural areas, the number of women who were engaged in informal work increased with the age of the child, whereas the number in the other categories were constant after the infancy of the child. The percent of women who reported working for earnings in this survey was slightly lower than that in the time-use survey in the rural villages, but very similar in the urban town. Because the definitions of work differed in the two surveys, it was not possible to determine the percent of overlap in particular work categories. The number of hours per day that women reported working for earnings on the Retrospective Life History Questionnaire are consistent with the time-use findings; women who worked for earnings (nonagricultural) reported on the average 10 hours of work per day in the urban areas, and 6.2 hours per day in the rural areas.

Figures 8.2 and 8.3 show the amount of caregiving help working and non-working mothers received from siblings or adults. Rural working women consistently reported more child care help than non-working women at all three age levels. For urban women, however, more help was provided only during the first and second years of the child's life. As in the previous analysis, over half of the women, regardless of their work status, reported no help in child caregiving. Clearly, for many women, children are simply taken along to the work site, or work is performed at home while children are being watched. In the urban areas, relatively little help is provided by siblings, and the amount of help did not vary by the age of the child. For both urban and rural areas, the extra help provided to the mother who worked for earnings comes from adults, not from a sibling.

The independent effects of child care strategies and women's work on the health and nutritional status of children at ages one, two and three in the town, and up to age four in the villages, was examined with a 2 X 3 analysis of variance of work status (working or not working) by child care help (none, sibling, or adult).[4] Results of the analyses of variance indicate that there are almost no main effects of type of child care on child health or nutritional status. None were found in the urban areas, while in the rural villages only two main effects were seen: morbidity from age one to two ($F=5.04$, df=2,406, $p<.01$), and height for age at four years ($F=2.79$, df=2,562, $p<.06$). In both cases, children appeared to be doing better with adult help and worse with sibling help.

Maternal work status was unrelated to child nutritional status in the rural villages. In the urban areas, infants with working mothers were slightly shorter ($F=2.29$, df=1,125, $p<.10$) and lighter ($F=3.01$, df=1,125, $p<.10$), whereas in the second year of life, children of working mothers were heavier than those of non-working mothers ($F=4.56$, df=1,125, $p<.05$). No main effects of work status were seen in the third year. However, there was a significant interaction between work status and child care strategies for weight for age for children two to three years old from urban areas ($F=3.19$, df=1,125, $p<.05$). Examination of the cell means suggests that children of working mothers who were taken care of by *either* siblings or adults were lighter than those taken care of by the mother herself.

A second method for examining the effects of maternal work and child care on children's nutritional status was through multiple regression analyses, controlling for other economic and demographic variables. Results are shown in Tables 8.6 and 8.7 for the urban sample and Tables 8.8 and 8.9 for the rural sample. In Tables 8.8 and 8.9, villages which had received the calorie-only supplement (FRESCO) were separated from those that had received the protein supplement (ATOLE). In general, these results are consistent with those from the analyses of variance reported above. The lower height for age of infants with working mothers found in the analysis of variance (for the urban sample) appears to be due primarily to a significant negative association between domestic work and height. Domestic work was also found to have a negative but only marginally significant effect on weight for age. Among children one to two years old, the significantly greater weight for age of children of working mothers seems to be due primarily to a positive effect associated with women working in formal or informal sector jobs. Although the associations of outcome measure with method of child care are not large, when they are found, they are more positive for adult help and more negative for sibling help. The exception is the negative effect of adult care on height among the four year olds in the FRESCO villages. An analysis (not shown) of effects of maternal work and child care patterns on morbidity showed no significant effects except for a positive association of maternal care on morbidity for children in the second year of life.

DISCUSSION

These above results suggest that there is no consistent relationship across ages of children between who provides child care and the health or nutritional status of the child. When differences were found, however, it appeared that adult caregiving had positive associations for children, whereas sibling caregiving was negative for children. The effects on the child of the mother receiving "no help" fell somewhere in between. The main effects were found in the crucial second year of the child's life.

The fact that any differences were found at all might be considered noteworthy, since the data were not gathered to specifically investigate this relationship, and the measure of caregiving was simply the mother's report as to whether she had anyone who helped with her child. More detailed and appropriate measures of the amount of time caregiving or the location would help build a firm basis for investigating specific linkages in this relationship.[5]

The apparent inconsistency of the effects by age should be remarked upon. Social scientists without specific training in developmental psychology tend to aggregate children for analyses, for example, from birth to six years of age. This grouping ignores certain important changes in children's functioning within the first three years that can influence the way the mother's work might affect the child.

During the first year, a child tends to be more dependent on the mother's physical condition and presence; environmental factors such as the family's income are less related to nutritional status (see Engle et al. 1986). The data analyzed here from Guatemala suggest that, during the first year, the category of individual who helped in child care did not appear to influence outcomes for children. However, in the urban area, maternal work status did influence outcomes. Further investigations suggested that the negative effect was limited to domestic workers, who worked many hours per day at very unskilled, poorly paid jobs. These women were the poorest of the urban mothers (Engle et al. 1986). They worked many hours a week and may have been unable to provide a minimum level of attention to the child as well as being undernourished themselves.

In the second year of life, children normally begin to walk, which creates a substantial change in their mobility, although they are not yet able to perceive and respond appropriately to dangers. This is the period during which children are most prone to accidents, vulnerable to illnesses, and most in need of supplementary feedings of high protein and energy dense foods as well as more time to insure proper feeding. Thus, during this period, extra adult help could be extremely valuable, as it appeared to be here for height for age of urban children (marginally significant) and morbidity among rural children. The positive effects of maternal work for earnings on child nutritional status seen in the urban areas could be a function of the availability of extra income to purchase higher-quality, toddler-appropriate foods (see Engle et al. 1986 for a fuller discussion of this point).

During the third year of life, language begins to develop and children are a little more capable of assessing dangers in their environment, and caregiving may be less crucial. Thus one might not expect to see significant effects of a caregiver during this period. Although these data do not provide a definitive answer, they suggest that age differences among children less than three years old may be important to include in examining the effects of maternal work for earnings on children's health nutritional status.

A clear conclusion from this study is that income-earning women in both rural and urban areas work many hours a day with little help from other adults. Although, in the retrospective survey, rural women who report work for earnings also stated that they received more regular help in caregiving than those who do not work. This difference, however, was not found when mothers were asked in the time-use study to report on help given the previous day by other adults. For both estimates, the majority of mothers working for earnings are still performing child caregiving all day long. A study of poor urban women workers in Lima found that the biggest problem the women reported was what to do with their children while they worked other than taking them along (Bunster and Chaney 1985). In future research more attention should be directed to assessing the effects on children of being taken with mothers to the workplace, or the effects of concurrent work and child care in the home.

Notes

1. The four rural villages were participants in a longitudinal study of the effects of protein supplementation on cognitive development in children conducted by INCAP from 1969-1977. Two villages were selected as experimental villages, and a protein-calorie supplement was made available daily (ATOLE). Two other villages were provided with calorie-only supplement (FRESCO). For this analysis the effects of the nutritional intervention have been statistically controlled.

2. The coded activities are: prepare food, watch children, make purchases, fetch water, gather firewood, wash clothes, take lunch to husband in fields, agricultural work (plant, harvest, weed, process, etc.), sell, work outside the home for wages, work inside the home for income, non-income producing activities within the home, non-economic activities outside the home, attend school or training center, and visit health or nutrition center.

3. The interviewers were all Guatemalan women who were trained to administer this questionnaire and were responsible for asking the mothers about their children's illness every two weeks. Therefore, they were quite familiar with the mothers, particularly in the rural villages where the study had been underway for five years prior to the administration of the time-use survey.

4. Several potentially confounding variables were controlled for, in particular, birth order and socioeconomic level. Because a first- or second-born child in a family will be unable to receive help from an older sibling, and because birth order may be associated with nutritional status, it is a potential confounding variable controlled for by entering it as a covariate. Another possibly confounding variable that was covaried was the economic indicator "house quality."

5. Two studies specifically designed to investigate the relationship between child care and child welfare of working and nonworking mothers were carried out in the same urban town in 1986 and 1987 and have been initiated in the rural villages.

References

Balderston, J.B.; Wilson, A.B.; Freire, M.E.; and Simonen, M.S.
　1981. *Malnourished Children of the Rural Poor*. Boston: Auburn Press.
Bowlby, J.
　1960. "Separation Anxiety." *International Journal of Psycho-analysis* 41:
　89.
Bunster, X. and Chaney, E.M.
　1985. *Sellers and Servants: Working Women in Lima, Peru*. New York:
　Praeger.
Clark, C.A.M.
　1981. "Demographic and Socioeconomic Correlates of Infant Growth
　in Guatemala." RAND Note N-1762-AIDIRF.
Engle, P.L.
　1986. "The Intersecting Needs of Working Mothers and Their Chil-
　dren: 1980-1985." Report prepared for the Carnegie Foundation.
　1980. "The Intersecting Needs of Working Mothers and Their Chil-
　dren: A Review of the Literature." Report prepared for the Ford
　Foundation.
Engle, P.L.; Pederson, M.; and Smidt, R.K.
　1986. "The Effects of of Mother's Income Generation on Children's
　Nutritional Status and School Enrollment in Rural and Urban Guate-
　mala." Final Project Report to USAID/PPC (Revised), Grant ORT-
　0096-GSS344600.
Ho, T.
　1979. "Time Costs of Child-Rearing in the Philippines." *Population and
　Development Review* 5: 643-662.
LeVine, R.
　1980. "A Cross-Cultural Perspective on Parenting." In *Perspectives in
　Parenting in a Multicultural Society*. Edited by M. Fantini and B. Carde-
　nas. New York: Longman.
Mejia Piveral, V.
　1972. "Características Económicas y Socioculturales de Cuatro Aldeas
　Ladinas de Guatemala." *Guatemala Indigena* 7: 5-300.
Scarr, Sandra.
　1984. *Mother Care/Other Care*. New York: Basic Books.
Schwartz, P.
　1983. "Length of Day-Care Attendance and Attachment Behavior in
　Eighteen-Month Old Infants." *Child Development* 54: 1073-1078.
Shah, P.M.; Walimbe, S.R.; and Dhole, V.S.
　1979. "Wage-Earning Mothers, Mother-Substitutes, and Care of the
　Young Children in Rural Maharashtra." *Indian Pediatrics* 16: 167-173.

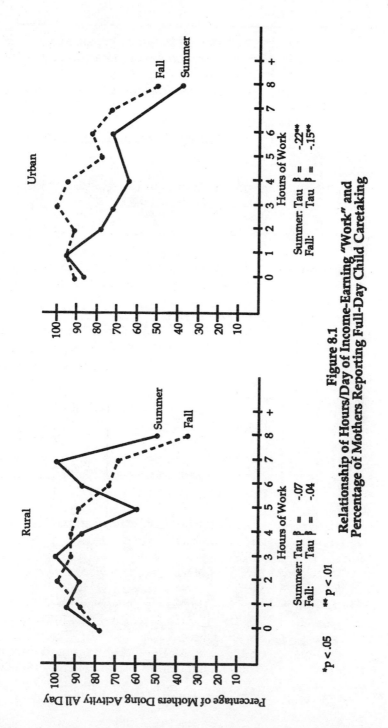

Figure 8.1

Relationship of Hours/Day of Income-Earning "Work" and Percentage of Mothers Reporting Full-Day Child Caretaking

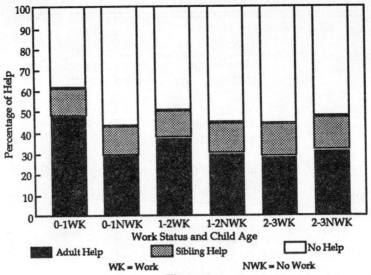

Figure 8.2
Percentage of Child Care Help by Mother's
Work Status and Child Age for Urban Town

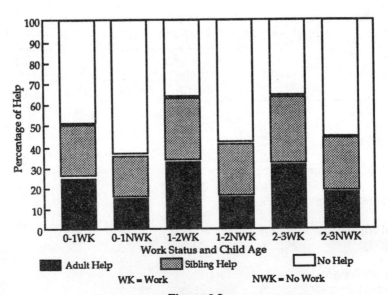

Figure 8.3
Percentage of Child Care Help by Mother's
Work Status and Child Age for Rural Villages

Table 8.1   Description of the samples for the two surveys

	Time-Use	Retrospective Life History
Rural Subsample	Mothers with children ≤ 7 yrs.	Children age 0-4 with growth data
	n = 419 (summer) n = 413 (fall)	n = 962
Urban Subsample	Mothers with children ≤ 3 yrs.	Children age 0-3 with growth data
	n = 343 (summer) n = 461 (fall)	n = 322

Table 8.2   Percentage of women in the time-use study who reported working for earnings by location and season

Type of Work		Rural		Urban	
		Summer (N=419)	Fall (N=413)	Summer (N=343)	Fall (N=461)
Agriculture	%	58	70	17	43
	N	(245)	(289)	(58)	(198)
Marketing	%	7	2	5	5
	N	(29)	(10)	(16)	(53)
Work Outside Home	%	2	3	9	6
	N	(8)	(13)	(32)	(26)
Work Inside Home	%	13	14	8	10
	N	(53)	(58)	(26)	(45)
Total Working for Earnings	%	80	90	38	70
	N	(335)	(370)	(132)	(322)
Total Working for Earnings (Excluding Agriculture)	%	21	20	22	27
	N	(90)	(81)	(74)	(124)

Table 8.3 Average number of hours per day spent on different types of work by location and season (working mothers only)

	Rural				Urban			
	Summer (N=419)		Fall (N=413)		Summer (N=343)		Fall (N=461)	
	X	SD	X	SD	X	SD	X	SD
Average Time Working for Earnings (N in parentheses)								
Agriculture	0.91 (245)	1.68	1.01 (289)	1.51	0.47 (58)	0.88	0.54 (198)	1.09
Marketing	3.13 (29)	4.3	2.62 (10)	4.45	4.94 (16)	4.00	5.42 (23)	4.35
Other Work Outside Home	6.75 (8)	3.22	7.58 (13)	4.29	9.02 (32)	5.09	8.74 (26)	4.39
Other Work in Home	4.35 (53)	3.32	4.26 (58)	3.40	7.68 (26)	5.68	7.35 (45)	4.79

Table 8.4 Percentage of mothers who reported spending morning, afternoon, all day, or no time in child caretaking by location, season, and work status of mother (Chi Square analysis)

	Rural				Urban			
	Summer		Fall		Summer		Fall	
Mother's Work Status:[a]	No Work (N=331)	Work (N=88)	No Work (N=334)	Work (N=79)	No Work (N=272)	Work (N=71)	No Work (N=368)	Work (N=93)
Child Caretaking[b]								
Not Done	10	16	10	11	10	34	6	23
AM Only	1	2	2	2	1	6	1	5
PM Only	1	9	1	10	1	8	2	3
All Day	88	73	87	77	88	52	91	69
X^2	23.3**		15.0**		47.8**		32.9**	

[a] Work = nonagricultural income-earning work only.
[b] Columns sum to 100 indicating percentage of mothers within each work status category performing the activity in the morning, in the afternoon, all day, or not at all.
** $p < .01$

Table 8.5 Average Hours/day spent in household activities as a function of mother's income-earning work by location and round

Mother's Work Status:		Rural				Urban			
		Summer		Fall		Summer		Fall	
		No Work	Work	No Work	Work	No Work	Work	No Work	Work
Total Time (including income earning activities)[a] hrs/day	X	3.79	7.26	3.67	6.88	2.48	9.10	1.82	8.32
	SD	3.15	3.67	3.13	3.70	2.72	4.76	2.38	4.39
	N	331	88	334	79	272	71	368	93
	t	-8.88**		-7.14**		-11.27**		-13.78**	
Amount of Help Received from Others[b]	X	0.63	0.21	0.11	0.51	0.04	0.36	0.08	0.31
	SD	2.35	0.96	0.60	1.55	0.28	1.39	0.51	1.40
	N	331	88	334	79	272	71	368	93
	t	2.42*		-2.25*		-1.95		-1.57	
Time Shopping	X	1.08	1.24	0.88	0.69	1.55	1.31	0.78	0.77
	SD	2.01	1.42	1.29	0.51	1.85	1.31	1.14	0.93
	N	198	57	189	50	206	29	252	44
	t	-0.64		1.64		0.65		0.06	
Time Getting Water	X	0.75	0.74	0.69	0.76	0.61	0.25	0.66	0.58
	SD	0.54	0.47	0.48	0.66	0.52	0	0.37	0.24
	N	221	44	210	36	22	1	35	4
	t	0.20		-0.61		0.68		0.40	
Time Getting Wood	X	1.99	2.75	2.55	1.15	2.67	0	2.18	3.08
	SD	1.34	1.53	1.51	0.86	0.92	0	1.43	1.41
	N	14	3	26	5	6	0	10	2
	t	-0.27		1.99				-0.81	
Time Washing Clothes	X	3.32	2.76	4.30	1.83	2.58	0	3.33	1.42
	SD	2.70	2.72	3.60	0.86	0.71	0	2.02	0.58
	N	50	15	52	10	2	0	5	
	t	0.71		4.34**				1.56	
Bring Food	X	1.87	1.08	1.80	1.64	2.67	0	2.26	0
	SD	1.10	0.71	0.98	1.26	1.32	0	1.27	0
	N	10	2	10	3	6	0	11	0
	t	0.95		0.24					
Agricultural Work	X	0.90	0.95	1.06	0.78	0.48	0.28	0.56	0.40
	SD	1.68	1.74	1.60	0.93	0.92	0.18	1.17	0.36
	N	204	41	239	50	53	5	169	29
	t	-0.15		1.64		1.34		1.48	
Social Activities Outside House	X	2.14	2.09	1.89	1.25	5.09	3.99	3.38	2.12
	SD	2.89	3.42	2.86	0.86	5.81	2.96	3.81	1.78
	N	126	27	122	14	53	6	89	12
	t	0.07		1.84		0.76		1.92	

Continued

Table 8.5   Continued

Mother's Work Status:	Rural				Urban			
	Summer		Fall		Summer		Fall	
	No Work	Work	No Work	Work	No Work	Work	No Work	Work
Visit Clinic								
X	0.96	0.85	0.79	0.79	3.48	7.58	1.87	3.58
SD	0.97	0.82	0.73	0.51	4.60	0.71	1.85	2.12
N	207	45	156	31	28	2	9	2
t	0.69		-0.03		-1.24		-1.17	

Note: t-test compares time spent by "workers" and "nonworkers."
N = Numbers of participants in a given activity.
ª = Time spent on child care and food preparation is not included because it was not measured in hours per day.
ᵇ = Time spent by other adults.
* p <.05; ** p <.01

Table 8.6   Variables predicting height for age of urban children by age of the child (b values from OLS regression)

	Age of Child (years)		
	0-1 b (N = 110)	1-2 b (N = 153)	2-3 b (N = 124)
Variables			
Formal and Informal Work (0,1)	-.29	.12	.12
Domestic Work (0,1)	-.74*	.07	.03
House Quality (0-16)	-.004	.04	.15**
Sibling Help (0,1)	.30	-.20	-.38
Adult Help (0,1)	.32ª	.31ª	.13
Marital Status (1,2,3)	.26	.15	.30*
Mother's Education (grades)	.04	.08**	.07*
Weaning Age (months passed)	.001	-.0004	.0008
Birth Order	-.02	.02	-.23
Sex (1 = male; 2 = female)	.10	-.21	-.20
F	1.51	2.53**	6.24**
R^2	.13	.15	.36

ª p <.10; * p <.05; ** p <.01

Table 8.7   Variables predicting weight for age of urban children by age of the child (b values from OLS regression)

	Age of Child (years)		
	0-1 b (N = 110)	1-2 b (N = 153)	2-3 b (N = 124)
Variables			
Formal and Informal Work (0,1)	-.34	.62*	-.15
Domestic Work (0,1)	-.70ª	.31	.14
House Quality (0-16)	-.04	-.004	.14**
Sibling Help (0,1)	.36	-.46ª	-.36
Adult Help (0,1)	.14	.18	.01
Marital Status (1,2,3)	.17	.03	.12
Mother's Education (grades)	.04	.10**	.07*
Weaning Age (months)	-.0008	-.0010	.0008
Birth Order	.02	.05	.005
Sex (1 = male; 2 = female)	.21	-.09	-.27ª
F	1.22	3.20**	4.87**
R²	.11	.18	.30

ª p <.10; * p <.05; ** p <.01

Table 8.8   Variable predicting height for age of rural children by age of child (b values from OLS regression)

	Age of Child (Years)							
	0 - 1		1 - 2		2 - 3		3 - 4	
	FRESCO b (N=205)	ATOLE b (N=237)	FRESCO b (N=248)	ATOLE b (N=273)	FRESCO b (N=257)	ATOLE b (N=300)	FRESCO b (N=251)	ATOLE b (N=286)
Variables								
Mother's Work (0,1)	.30	-.61	.17	-.14	.40*	-.21	.18	.04
House Quality (0-16)	.04	.03	.06	.07	.02	.11*	.06	.10*
Length of Lactation (mos.)	.002	.001	.005**	.003*	.003*	.002*	.003*	.003
Child Care:								
Adult (0,1)	-.01	.03	.15	.11	-.09	.06	-.35*	-.05
Sibling (0,1)	-.42	-.09	-.22	-.16	-.36**	.01	-.40**	-.15
Marital Status (1-3)	-.17	.32*	-.17	.06	-.13	-.08	-.19	.06
Natural Child (0,1)	2.00**	-.57	2.15**	-.23	2.07**	-.87	1.63**	-.81
Birth Order	-.04	-.007	-.03	.02	-.02	.00	-.03	.001
Sex (1 = male; 2 = female)	.11	.07	-.23	-.20	-.38**	-.16	-.54	-.15
Mother's Education	-.004	.05	.08	.01	.08	.07	.10**	.06
Supplement (K cal/day/yr)	-.001	.004	.002	.0006**	.002**	.0008**	.002**	.0006**
F	3.07**	1.33	4.00**	1.82*	4.65**	4.67**	4.68**	2.86**
R²	.15	.06	.16	.07	.17	.15	.18	.10

ª p <.10; * p <.05; ** p <.01

**Table 8.9   Variable predicting weight for age of rural children
by age of child (b values from OLS regression)**

	Age of Child (Years)							
	0 - 1		1 - 2		2 - 3		3 - 4	
	FRESCO	ATOLE	FRESCO	ATOLE	FRESCO	ATOLE	FRESCO	ATOLE
	b	b	b	b	b	b	b	b
	(N=205)	(N=237)	(N=248)	(N=273)	(N=257)	(N=300)	(N=251)	(N=286)
Variables								
Mother's Work (0,1)	.18	-.11	.12	-.05	.14	-.01	.02	.16
House Quality (0-16)	.04	.03	.04	.03	.01	.04	.05*	.03
Length of Lactation (mos.)	.003	.0004	.004**	.0005	.002	.001	.002	.001
Child Care:								
Adult (0,1)	.09	.04	.12	.08	-.12	-.02	-.17	-.04
Sibling (0,1)	-.29	.02	-.05	-.11	-.06	-.02	-.11	-.49
Marital Status (1-3)	-.10	.24*	-1.00	-.03	-.06	.08	-.07	.08
Natural Child (0,1)	1.97**	-.61	2.03**	-.86	.99*	-1.47**	.25	-.90
Birth Order	-.02	-.01	-.0004	.04	-.03	.02	-.002	.005
Sex (1 = male; 2 = female)	.11	.18	-1.00	.07	-.34**	-.16	-.14	-.04
Mother's Education	.04	.03	.06	.08*	.06*	.06*	.05	.05
Supplement (K cal/day/yr)	.005	-.0003	.003	.0006**	.001**	.0004**	.001**	.0004**
F	2.23**	1.32	3.56**	2.46*	3.80**	2.87**	3.32**	1.81*
R²	.11	.06	.14	.09	.15	.10	.13	.07

* p < .05; ** p < .01

9

Effects of New Export Crops in Smallholder Agriculture on Division of Labor and Child Nutritional Status in Guatemala

Joachim von Braun

Many developing countries promote the increased production of export crops. The primary objectives of such a policy are to generate foreign exchange earnings and fiscal revenues. Increasingly, attempts are made to use export crop promotion for raising the income of small landholders, and to provide employment for the rural poor. Critics of these policies, however, argue that, in fact, the potential benefits have never materialized. They claim that in many cases, where cash crop production has increased, it has been accompanied by adverse consequences, such as increases in women's workload without due remuneration, decreases in household food consumption, and deterioration of children's nutritional status. A comprehensive review of the existing literature on the issue shows mixed results (von Braun and Kennedy 1986). Given the great variety of both cash crops and production conditions, which makes generalizations about the process of commercialization and its effects difficult, it is not surprising that conclusive findings have eluded researchers.

At the macro level, it appears that the effects of increased commercialization on food consumption and nutrition may be either positive or negative, depending on factors such as the resulting price and wage rate effects, the impacts on foreign exchange earnings, and the actual allocation of incremental foreign exchange. At the micro level, the effects depend on such factors as the actual increase in real income from cash cropping and its distribution, income composition, preferences of decision makers in the household, and changes in income control. Changes in any of these determinants may reinforce or counteract each other and translate into food consumption and time allocation effects for household individuals.

The research for this study focused on the micro-level effects of commercialization of agriculture, in particular, the introduction of new export crops. The approach used traces the consequences for different types of households and different individuals within the household. The particular focus of the results presented in this chapter are the changes in men's and women's labor allocation and the resulting nutritional outcomes for children. It is not *a priori* assumed here that incremental employment and income from the new crops leaves household utility functions unchanged or that households necessarily maximize a joint utility function in this largely patriarchal system of the rural Western Highlands of Guatemala. It is by now widely recognized that farm households are not necessarily homogeneous decision-making units (Folbre 1986). Changes in the income-earning opportunities on the farm — be it through new technology or new market outlets — may have profound implications for the division of labor and the relative control of income, which in turn may change budget allocations within the household, over and above the pure income effect. This study attempts to trace the effects of increased commercialization of traditional agriculture and to quantify the impact on food consumption and nutrition. Understanding these relationships is crucial in identifying policy options that both minimize adverse effects and enhance positive effects of commercialization on consumption and nutrition in poor households.

This case study of the commercialization of smallholder agriculture in Guatemala looks at the introduction of nontraditional vegetables (specifically broccoli, cauliflower and snow peas) for export and its effect on household division of labor, decision-making power, and child nutritional status. The practice of growing nontraditional vegetables for export reached the Guatemalan small-farm sector in several steps. Production of these vegetables first moved from a single multinational company in the mid-1970s, to medium-sized farms (20-30 hectares) in the form of contract growing, to the smallest farmers (average 0.7 hectare) in the Western Highlands. The new export vegetables were rapidly adopted by even the smallest farmers. Today, much of the nontraditional export vegetable production is done by small farmers. The experience of the *Cuatro Pinos* cooperative, which specializes in export vegetables, is the focus of this study.

This chapter will review the process of commercialization of traditional agriculture and evaluate the impact of changes in the labor supply (on-farm/off-farm), the division of labor (male/female), and the control (male/female) of incremental cash income at the household level. From the changes in income control, the effects on a household's resource allocation to food and nonfood expenditures are traced. Food expenditures and food (energy) consumption receive special attention. Finally, changes in child nutritional status will be examined as an outcome of the changes in the above variables. A simplified overview on the relationships, as affected by commercialization at the household level, is provided in Figure 9.1.

Data and Methods

The cooperative *Cuatro Pinos* is active in six villages in and around the *municipio* (county) Santiago Sacatepequez located about 35 kilometers to the west of Guatemala City. Santiago is the base of the cooperative where the storage and processing facilities for the export vegetables are located. The community is connected to the paved road of the Pan-American Highway, which is five kilometers away. The general socioeconomic environment, and the health and nutrition situation in the *Cuatro Pinos* villages, do not appear to be particularly different from the general situation in the Western Highlands. Some special features of their economic environment, such as closeness to the capital city and good infrastructure, facilitate market integration of fresh vegetables and are therefore noteworthy. Average farm size is below the mean for the Western Highlands. Also, there are no big farms in the location. This has two implications: there were no serious conflicts over land, at least in the 1970s, and the influence of non-indigenous farmers on the social organization and economic activities in the municipality was small. Thus, there was neither an important social force to oppose the local development of the cooperative nor landowners who considered the promotion of the profitable labor-intensive crops as a threat to their control over the labor market (Hintermeister 1986).

The sample of the INCAP/IFPRI survey specifically designed for this research is based on a census in the villages done in 1983 by INCAP (INCAP 1985). A roughly equal number of cooperative members (n=195) — that is, growers of the new export crops — and nonmembers (n=204) were drawn at random by village from the census information. To assure a reasonable coverage of the situation in the smaller villages, the sample was biased toward the four small communities among the six villages. This brings the sample closer to the prevailing village pattern in the Western Highlands. The proportional adjustments of the sample by village size led to a coverage of 38 to 75 percent of the cooperative members in each community (47 percent average) and 8 to 17 percent of noncooperative member households (11 percent average) in these communities.

The households were visited between November 1983 and January 1984 and two years later in the same months. The fact that the surveys were done during the same time of the year avoids seasonal effects. However, the composition of the 1985 sample is affected by changes in household characteristics since the 1983 survey. Some households split into two when the younger generation started its own households, some members quit the cooperative, and some nonmembers became members. Also, some households could no longer be interviewed because of long-term absence. The sample includes both early and late adopters of the new export crop. Forty-two percent of the sampled member households had participated in the cooperative for as long as five to seven years. Newcomers are distributed over all six communities, while early adopters are all in the four founding villages of the cooperative.

The field data collection for the 1983 and 1985 surveys was done by experienced INCAP survey staff. The agricultural production data collected covers the crop years 1982-1983 and 1984-1985 (May-April); the off-farm income covers the 12 months preceding the surveys. Food and non-food expenditures are for the one-month period immediately preceding the surveys (October 1983, October 1985). Recollections of annual nonfood expenditures (especially durable goods) were collected in the 1985 survey (more detailed discussion of the data, methods, and the specifics of the questionnaires is found in von Braun, Immink and Hotchkiss 1987).

Effects of New Export Crops on Employment and Women's Work in Agriculture

The new export crops create employment both directly, through forward and backward linkages of the specific new crops, and indirectly, through multiplier effects due to related income and employment effects. The substantial forward and backward linkages are significant for employment since the operation of the first stage of marketing is quite labor-intensive (selecting, screening, and packing of produce). There are indirect employment effects from potentially higher incomes spent on goods and services with an employment content. The following discussion focuses on the direct employment effects.

The inability of family labor to meet the increased labor requirements of the cash crops forces members of the cooperative to purchase additional labor. The hired labor input is used in both subsistence crops and the introduced export vegetables. As Figure 9.2 shows, the allocation of hired labor varies according to the specific crop types. The most significant finding is that snow peas require substantially more hired labor per unit of land than other new export crops and traditional vegetables. Not surprisingly, maize, the traditional staple, requires the smallest amount of hired labor.

Member farms employ hired labor as a complement to their own substantial labor inputs to agriculture. Most family labor in agriculture is provided by men, but this varies by crop type. Women are responsible for

9 percent of family labor in maize, 25 percent in traditional vegetables, and 31 percent in snow peas (Table 9.1). In addition, the division of family labor between men, women, and children in the production of crops is not uniform across farm size. While men's share of total family labor remains quite stable across farm size, women's share decreases and children's share increases (Table 9.2). With increasing farm size, women's labor is relatively replaced by hired labor and child labor. This is not true for men's labor. The high substitution between women's labor and hired labor is a phenomenon observed widely across countries of the Third World (Boserup 1970). It is probably related to the increasing opportunity cost of women's labor in the field when the household and farm enterprise expands. Returns to female household labor, including activities such as meal preparation for hired labor, increase and lead to higher degrees of specialization within the integrated farm-household unit. This still means that absolute levels of family labor input by both men and women may increase with farm size.

To better evaluate the impact of the new export crops on women's labor, a cross-sectional comparison of farms of the same size in the area with similar agroeconomic conditions was undertaken. The comparison used the average 0.7 hectare farm and the respective labor-use data of farms within the 0.5 to 1.0 hectare range. It was found that the introduction of the new export crops increased women's work in agriculture (crop production) by 78 percent, while men's work increased by only 33 percent (Table 9.3). In absolute terms, men provided more incremental work (21 days) than women (15 days); children's incremental labor input is also significant and high with 15 more days of work per household.

It would be misleading to assume that the incremental work in agriculture — largely due to export vegetables — is incremental to total household workload. Much of it is in fact substituting for earlier off-farm work by men and women. For women, however, partial withdrawal from off-farm work into new export vegetable production leads to important changes. In contrast to their off-farm work (e.g. marketing), women's work in agriculture requires them to relinquish primary responsibility for production decisions. Traditionally men have always made the major agricultural decisions. It seems that the presence of the cooperative has not altered this relation, at least not in the short-term. In a case study on 21 households, which constituted a subsample of the INCAP/IFPRI survey in 1985, it was found that the decision to join the export crop cooperative was, in all 21 cases, prompted by the male head of the household (ICRW 1987).

Effects on Income and Consumption

Since nontraditional export crops are substantially more profitable to farmers than traditional crops, farm household incomes have increased. For example, net returns (gross margins) per unit of land of snow peas — the most important new crop — are on average five times those of maize — the most important traditional crop. Returns of the new crops per unit of family labor were about twice as high as for maize and 60 percent higher than for traditional vegetables produced for local markets in 1985. The input costs for snow peas, however, are on average about 1,600 Quetzales/hectare, while they are only Q430 for traditional vegetables and Q120 for maize.

Export crop producers spend on average 64 percent of their total expenditures on food compared to 66.8 percent among the other households (including value of own-produced food consumed by households). However, the absolute per capita budget spent for food is, on average, 18 percent higher in export crop-producing households. Proportion of total expenditures spent on food decreases with increased income but, as expected in a poor population, this decrease is not very rapid. A 10 percent increase in total income decreases the budget share to food by only 1.4 percent (von Braun et al. 1987). It is noteworthy that, at the same income levels, export crop-producing farm households spend less of their additional income on food.

In addition to income source, control over the income from new export crops influences consumption. Holding income constant, an increased household income share from new export crops (male-controlled) has a negative effect on the budget share spent on food. Among the nonmember households, a similar relationship for food expenditures is observed in the case of male-earned nonagricultural income.

More than half of the energy (calories) consumed in households comes from maize, but this share decreases with increasing income. Accordingly, there is a higher price per calorie and more diverse diet with rising income in both the export crop producing and other households. Additional income increases calorie acquisition significantly, but at decreasing rates at the margin. (At the sample mean, a 10 percent increase in income increases household calorie consumption by 3.1 percent.)

The effects of export crop production on spending patterns also influence food energy consumption. Joining the export crop scheme apparently reduces the above mentioned positive income effect on energy consumption but does not eliminate it. Member households in the lowest half of the income scale increase their energy intake by 2.8 percent with a 10 percent increase in income, while nonmember households increase by 4.4 percent. The next question is, how do these income, expenditure, and consumption effects of the new export crops translate into effects on nutritional status of children?

Effects on Nutrition

Despite the relative proximity of Guatemala City and the improved infrastructure facilities of some of the sample villages, the general nutritional status in the study area is as poor as in other, more remote, rural Guatemalan regions. The above analysis suggests a clear relationship between income and food energy consumption. What follows is a multivariate analysis of the income-nutrition relationship. The model measures the nutritional effects of changes in income control and income composition resulting from increased commercialization. The total household income variable includes subsistence food income.

The following hypotheses were tested:

1) increased per capita income improves children's nutritional status but less so at the margin;
2) an increased share of male nonagricultural income and/or an increased income share from export crops (which is male-controlled) may have a negative effect on child-welfare related spending, holding household income constant; and
3) an increased share of income received and controlled by females will lead to increased child welfare related spending and nutritional improvement.

The model is based on the following formula:

1) $S_{ij} = f(DEM_{ij}, INCOME_{j}, INCOMP_{j})$

where

S_{ij} = nutritional status of child (i) in household (j) in 1985;

DEM_{ij} = demographic variables of child (sex, age in months, age squared, birth order);

$INCOME_{j}$ = income per capita of household$_{(j)}$ per year (and the respective squared term); and

$INCOMP_{j}$ = composition and sources of income for household$_{(j)}$ (shares from new export crops, male- or female-earned nonagricultural income).

The results of this model (Table 9.4), applied to the three nutritional status variables of 1985, show that the level of income (approximated by the 1985 per capita expenditure) is statistically highly significant for the weight/age, height/age, and weight/height indicators. At higher levels of income, the marginal effect is reduced as hypothesized and this is indicated by the negative sign for the squared income term. This means that increases in marginal income improve nutrition more in poor households than indicated by sample means.

The multivariate analysis also reveals that higher shares of off-farm nonagricultural income improve the nutritional status of children regardless of whether it is female- or male-earned. The respective parameter values, however, indicate different levels of impact for male-and female-controlled income. Children's weight-for-age improved more for any additional percentage of women's income over total income compared with men's income. In the height-for-age model, which depicts the long-term effects, female-controlled income continues to have a more positive effect than men's nonfarm income, although the difference is less pronounced. For short-term nutritional status (weight-for-height), male versus female income control within the household does not appear to be an issue (the parameters are not statistically significant).

Finally, a higher share of income from the new export crops has a low positive effect on nutrition, over and above the general income effects in the weight-for-age and height-for-age model, but is not significant in the weight- for-height model. However, this (male-controlled) export coop income has a substantially less positive effect for nutritional improvement than female controlled income.

Conclusions

It was clear at the outset of the *Cuatro Pinos* study that the commercialization of a subsistence agricultural economy would have substantial effects on household division of labor and income generation. Yet, the specific effects on income utilization, energy consumption, and nutrition were not clear. The principal concern was that the expansion of an export crop in an area with a well-known nutrition problem might adversely affect the availability and security of food. A number of studies had shown that the positive effects of increased cash income on energy consumption may be quite small, even among the poor (von Braun and Kennedy 1986).

A less than expected increase in consumption and nutrition, due to the introduction of a cash crop, may be due to changes in division of labor, income composition, and income control within the household. The results presented in the preceding sections offer insights into these linkages by focusing on the productive contribution of women and the possible effects on the nutritional welfare of children.

As indicated above, participation in export crop production in *Cuatro Pinos* affected women's labor allocation in both agricultural and nonagricultural activities. For the average small farm, the introduction of the export crop increased women's participation in agriculture by 78 percent (Table 9.3). Although member farms purchased hired labor to meet the additional labor demands of the export crops (Figure 9.2), women provided about 40 percent of the incremental family labor used for new crops.

Increased participation in agriculture due to export crop production requires women to reduce time spent in nonagricultural income generating activities (e.g. marketing). Women substitute agricultural work for nonagricultural work, which removes them from their traditional sources of income. Men continue to make the major decision in agriculture and control the income generated.

Women's participation in nontraditional export crop production contributes to an overall increase in household income and consumption. Export crops are profitable and lead to increased household income. However, the expenditure and food consumption analysis showed that the incremental income earned from nontraditional crops is related to a tendency to spend less of that income on food than income from other types of work, and this is also reflected, although to a lesser extent, in energy consumption. Although absolute increases in food expenditures and food consumption (calories) were found, relative food consumption and expenditure increased less than expected.

The division of labor and income-consumption analyses raise the issue of whether the removal of women's labor from traditional nonfarm income producing activities, and its incorporation into the male-controlled export crop production, at least partially explains the lower than expected food consumption benefits. The nutrition-income multivariate analysis explores the relationship of consumption effects on anthropometric measurements of children and allows a comparison of increased shares of income from various sources (male nonagricultural, female nonagricultural, and male-controlled export crop). As the results discussed above suggest, increases in income controlled by women lead to short-term nutritional increases significantly greater than equal increases from male-controlled income (Table 9.4). Furthermore, for both short-term and long-term measures of nutritional status, incremental income controlled by women has a more positive effect than a higher share of income from the new export crops.

Participation in the export crop scheme does increase household income and nutrition. However, the analyses and interpretations presented here indicate that potential benefits of the new export crops for food consumption and nutrition are deviated due to complex intra-household dynamics in the division of labor and income control. Women's labor patterns are altered and their control over income reduced. If women had more control over income from the new export crops, the result might be additional improvements in nutritional status of children over and above the benefits already realized from the new export crops.

References

Boserup, Ester

1970.*Women's Role in Economic Development.* London: George Allen Ltd.

von Braun, Joachim and Kennedy, Eileen.

1986.*Commercialization of Subsistence Agriculture: Income and Nutritional Effects in Developing Countries.* Working Papers on Commercialization of Agriculture and Nutrition, No. 1. Washington, DC: International Food Policy Research Insitute.

von Braun, Joachim; Immink, Maarten; and Hotchkiss, David.

1987."Non-traditional Export Crops in Traditional Smallholder Agriculture: Effects on Production, Consumption, and Nutrition in Guatemala." Washington, DC: International Food Policy Research. Photocopy.

Folbre, Nancy.

1986."Cleaning House — New Perspectives on Households and Economic Development." *Journal of Development Economics.* vol. 22, no. 1, pp. 5-41.

Hintermeister, Alberto.

1986."Report on 'Cuatro Pinos'." Guatemala City. Photocopy.

ICRW.

1987."An Exploratory Study of Intrahousehold Resource Allocation in a Cash-Cropping Scheme in Highland Guatemala." Washington, D.C.: International Center for Research on Women. Photocopy.

INCAP.

1985.*Evaluación de Características Sociales y Nutricionales de Seis Comunidades Participantes en la Cooperative Cuatro Pinos, Departamento de acatepequez, Guatemala, 1983-1984.* Guatemala City: INCAP, División de Clasificación Alimentario y Nutricional.

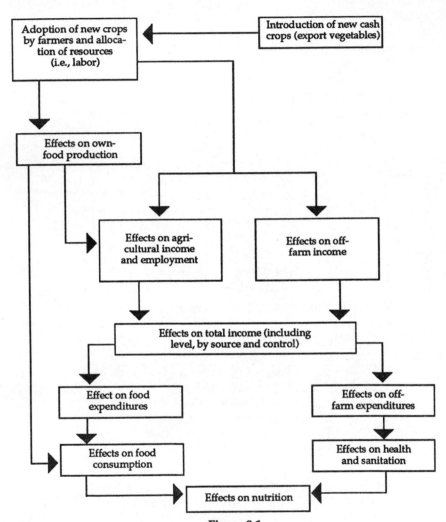

Figure 9.1
Flow of Analysis for Evaluation of Effects of the
Commercialization Process at the Household Level

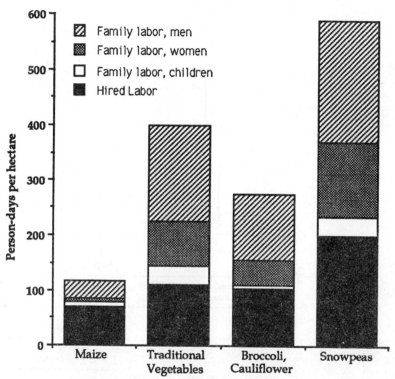

Source: Institute for Nutrition in Central America and Panama/International
Food Policy Research Institute survey (1985).

Figure 9.2
Labor Inputs in Traditional Crops and New Export Vegetables
(Co-op Members' Farms)

**Table 9.1   Shares of men, women, and children
in total family labor by crop (co-op members)**

| | | | Export Vegetables | |
	Maize	Traditional Vegetables	Broccoli Cauliflower	Snow peas
		Percentage of Family Labor		
Women	9	25	20	31
Children	6	14	10	10
Men	85	61	70	59
Total	100	100	100	100

Source: Computed from INCAP/IFPRI survey (1985).

**Table 9.2   Relative divisions of family labor in agriculture between men,
women, and children by farm size**

| | Percentage of Family Labor | | | |
Farm Size	Women	Children	Men	Total
<0.25	39	2	59	100
0.25 - 0.50	33	7	59	100
0.50 - 1.00	32	10	58	100
>1.00	26	15	58	100

Source: INCAP/IFPRI survey (1985).
*   farm size measured in square hectares.

Table 9.3 Changes in division of family labor in agriculture due to new export vegetables[a]

	Days of Work in Crops, 1984/85 Per Household		
Crops	Men	Women	Children
Export crop producers			
Maize, beans	18.2	2.1	2.5
Traditional vegetables, etc.	9.4	3.2	5.3
New export vegetables	56.9	28.1	14.9
Total	84.5	33.4	22.7
Other farmers (nonexport crops)			
Maize, beans	27.2	3.6	0.8
Traditional vegetables	36.2	15.2	7.2
Total	63.4	18.8	8.0
Difference in percentages between totals for export farmers and other farmers	+33.3	+77.7	+183.8
Difference in person days	+21.1	+14.6	+14.7

Source: INCAP/IFPRI survey (1985).

[a] Data refer to average 0.7 hectare farm in each group.

**Table 9.4   Effects of income and income source and composition on the level
of nutritional status: multivariate analysis
(children aged 6 months - 10 years)**

Explanatory Variables	Weight-for-Age Z-Scores Estimated Parameters	T-Values	Height-for-Age Z-Scores Estimated Parameters	T-Values	Weight-for-Height Z-Scores Estimated Parameters	T-Values
Age in months	-3.489E-03	-0.85	-0.0156	-3.03	-9.485E-03	-2.28
Age squared	3.497E-05	1.14	1.397E-04	3.64	1.053E-04	3.39
Birth order[a]	1.706E-04	0.01	-0.0240	-1.37	0.0220	1.55
Sex (male=1, female=2)	7.083E-03	0.12	0.0379	0.52	-0.0562	-0.96
Duration of breastfeeding[b]	9.663E-05	2.03	1.894E-04	3.17	-3.063E-05	-0.63
Income per capita[c]	8.231E-04	3.20	7.807E-04	2.41	5.162E-04	1.98
Income squared[c]	-3.930E-07	-2.74	-3.489E-07	-1.93	-2.625E-07	-1.80
Share of male non-agricultural income	0.1613	2.00	0.3291	3.24	-0.0531	-0.67
Share of female non-agricultural income	0.4953	2.20	0.4895	1.73	0.3140	1.37
Share of income from export crops	0.1569	1.88	0.1958	1.81	0.0640	0.73
Constant	-2.1165	-12.89	-3.110	-15.08	0.0549	0.33
R^2	0.032		0.073		0.028	
F-value	3.590		7.280		3.290	
Degrees of freedom	785		785		785	

[a] Birth order: first-born child = 1, second = 2, etc.
[b] Duration of breastfeeding: variable only for children above 24 months of age (else = 0).
[c] Expenditure per capita per year is used as proxy for income.

10

Women's Agricultural Work, Child Care, and Infant Diarrhea in Rural Kenya

Michael Paolisso, Michael Baksh and J. Conley Thomas

The problems confronting agricultural development in sub-Saharan Africa will not be resolved without addressing the concerns of women farmers. Not only do women comprise one-third to one-half of the region's agricultural labor force, but they are also responsible for many food-related agricultural activities indispensable to the household (Dey 1984).

Increasing the productivity of women's agricultural work in sub-Saharan Africa is one challenge where recent progress has been achieved through policy and program recommendations supported by a growing body of research (Creevey 1986; Davison 1988; FAO 1985; Moock 1986; Poats, Schmink, and Spring 1988). Still, agricultural development projects, particularly those that target the small farm, need to be more cognizant of women's dual productive and reproductive responsibilities, and acknowledge that changes in women's agricultural work may impact on other responsibilities traditionally held by women, such as family health and child care. The issue requiring further attention is whether women spend additional time in agriculture at the expense of other activities essential to household social and economic reproduction, and, if so, does this work trade-off affect overall family health and development.

This chapter analyzes the relationship between women's agricultural work and child care, and the subsequent effect of different child care practices on infant diarrhea. The data were collected among the Embu, a rural agricultural group in Kenya. Time allocation data on women's work patterns and child care practices are used to explore the first part of the research question. An epidemiological study of the influence of caretaking practices on the risk of infant diarrhea addresses the second part of the question. The results from these two facets of the study suggest that women's time in caretaking is influenced by corresponding increases in agricultural work, that decreases in caretaking increase the risk of infant diarrhea, but that participation of older children in caretaking responsibilities can reduce the risk of diarrhea among infants in the family. To provide a background for interpreting these data and the results of the analyses, an ethnographic description of the Embu is first presented.

THE EMBU

The Embu are a Bantu tribe occupying the southeastern slopes of Mt. Kenya, an area that forms part of the country's fertile highlands. Similar to other indigenous groups in Kenya, the Embu population is increasing rapidly. Haugerud (1984), using available census data, calculates that the Embu population has tripled over the past 60 years. The most recent national census estimates the Embu population to be 180,400 (Republic of Kenya 1981). This problem of rapid population growth is made even more acute by a situation of high population density, currently ranging between 200 and 400 individuals per km^2 in Embu District.

The Embu live at an elevation ranging from 3,800 to 4,850 feet above sea level. The principle unit of residence is the extended family compound, consisting of two to three semi-autonomous nuclear families linked through patrilineal descent to a senior male elder. Most production and consumption decisions are made at the nuclear household level, although interhousehold exchanges of labor, material goods, and food occur at the compound level. Land is inherited through men, and women reside in their husband's compound after marriage.

At the community level, households are organized according to both traditional and recent political structures. Chiefs and subchiefs, who work closely with government commissioners, are the most important administrative officials within locations and sublocations. The clan structure continues to exert influence on social proceedings, especially in the case of land transfers, although land is increasingly held by individual title rather than communal arrangement. The opinion of the elders remains important, although their power base is restricted due to the government administrative structure headed by the chief.

The Embu of Kyeni South Location, the research site, are smallholder agriculturalists producing both subsistence and cash crops. The principle food crops are maize, beans, millet, sorghum, arrowroot, bananas, potatoes, and cassava. The main cash crops are coffee, tobacco, and cotton, plus small amounts of foodstuffs occasionally sold in local markets. Of the cash crops, coffee is by far the most important. Irrigation is rain-fed, with hoes and machetes used as the main tools in all stages of the agricultural cycle; wealthier farmers, however, often hire men with teams of oxen to plow fields. Although agriculturalists, Embu households also keep small numbers of cattle, goats, and chickens. As is the case throughout sub-Saharan Africa, during times of famine these livestock are particularly valuable to the household directly as food and indirectly as sources of wealth.

In addition to agriculture and animal husbandry, the Embu also engage in both temporary and permanent remunerative labor. Most cash labor involves work in either the agricultural fields of larger Embu landowners, the local industries such as carpentry, blacksmithing, and tailoring, or the rural service sector of shops and restaurants. Other income-earning opportunities in the informal sector include the selling of locally-produced commodities such as charcoal, milk, wood, and honey.

METHODS

Study Population and Sample Selection

The data used in this study were collected as part of a collaborative research effort between the University of California, Los Angeles (UCLA) and the University of Nairobi. Known as the Nutrition Collaborative Research Support Program Kenya Project (hereafter referred to as the Kenya Project), this multidisciplinary project investigated the biological and social consequences of chronic mild-to-moderate malnutrition (Neumann and Bwibo 1987).[1] The data were collected in the Kyeni South Location of Embu District (Eastern Province), in the sublocations of Kathanjure, Karurumo, and Kathunguri. The three sublocations contained a total of 11,810 people residing in 2,059 households, averaging 5.7 people per household (Republic of Kenya 1981).

The Kenya Project selected a cohort of 289 households nonrandomly to represent various levels of nutritional status (as determined by anthropometry) and to maximize the number of women expected to have pregnancies during the study period.[2] Sixteen (5.5%) of the selected households dropped out before completing their time in the study and 24 (8.3%) became ineligible due to a change in one or more of the inclusion criteria (e.g., monogamous marriage, local residence of household head for at least six months of the year). Thus 249 (86 percent of the initial sample) were studied for a minimum of one year between January 1, 1984, and March 31, 1986.

Time Allocation

To study how household members allocate time to distinct activities, a technique of random spot observations was employed (Baksh and Paolisso 1987; Johnson 1975).[3] In this method, households were visited unannounced and activities being performed by all members at the moment of the investigator's arrival were recorded. Such "on the spot" observations offer a number of advantages over other techniques for studying time allocation in that (1) the data are collected more quickly and for a larger number of participants than with continuous observations; (2) direct observations are used rather than the less-reliable techniques of recall or reporting by participants; (3) there is little influence on participant behavior, since the times of observation are unpredictable and of short duration (five to ten minutes required); and (4) observations are recorded in a coded fashion, facilitating computer key entry and subsequent analysis. A potential disadvantage is that households may not welcome the unpredictable, though brief, appearances of investigators. This, however, was not the case in the Kenya Project.

Time allocation data were collected for 12 months, from March 1985 through February 1986. The sample included all of the 169 households enrolled in the Kenya Project as of March 1985. These households were evenly distributed among the total sample of households participating in the Kenya Project. Sixty-five visits were made to each household, yielding approximately 79,000 separate observations of individuals. The majority of the data (91 percent of the observations) were collected on weekdays from 7:00 A.M. through 6:00 P.M. and Saturdays from 7:00 A.M until midday. The remaining data were collected weekday nights from 6:00 P.M. through 9:00 P.M. and Sundays from 7:00 A.M. through 6:00 P.M.

The quantitative results on women's agricultural work and child care practices are based on analyses of all daytime observations, excluding Sundays. Of the 169 women studied, 132 (78%) consistently either had or did not have an infant (under 24 months of age) present for the full 12 months, and were not one of the five full-time school teachers (who had markedly atypical work and child care patterns). Ninety-one (69%) of the 132 mothers had a infant, while 41 (31%) did not.

The statistical significance of mean differences in time allocation between women with infants and women without infants was assessed using an independent t-Test. Pearson correlation coefficients were used to determine covariation of women's activities. The cultural context for interpreting the numerical description of women's agricultural work and child care practices was obtained through standard ethnographic field observations and interviews.

The Epidemiology of Infant Diarrhea

A cross-sectional sample including all 237 children in the Kenya Project households under 36 months of age in May 1985 was used to obtain information on the prevalence of diarrhea. Diarrhea was defined as three or more loose or watery stools in a 12-hour period. However, since stool frequency was not independently observed, the functional definition of diarrhea was the perception and report of diarrhea by the mother. The prevalence of diarrhea was estimated by asking mothers if their child or children experienced diarrhea "yesterday."

Physical contact with others was measured several times for each child studied in the Kenya Project. The child was observed with a standardized protocol by a trained Embu observer for two continuous waking hours randomly selected between 8:00 A.M. and 5:00 P.M. on weekdays. The amount of physical contact with others, expressed as the percent of total minutes observed, was found not to vary with the time of day. Holding was defined as physical contact in which another person supported the child's weight (usually with the child's feet off the ground). Touching was defined as any physical contact other than holding.

The observation of the child which most closely preceded the day of the cross-sectional diarrhea study was used in the analysis of the prevalence data. Thirteen (5.5%) children were excluded from the analysis because observations of their physical contact were first made after determination of the prevalence of diarrhea. The observation periods used for the 224 (94.5%) remaining children preceded the diarrhea survey by a median of 65 days. The data on these children are more useful for examining the causal association between physical contact and diarrhea because the measurement of the hypothesized cause (physical contact) precedes the measurement of the effect (diarrhea), providing a stronger causal inference than usual cross-sectional data in which the cause and effect are measured simultaneously. Reanalysis using all 237 children resulted in negligible differences.

The strength of the relationship between prevalent diarrhea and measures of physical contact is measured with the prevalence odds ratio, or POR (i.e., the odds of diarrhea among persons with the risk factor divided by the odds of diarrhea among those without the risk factor). When the duration of illness is not influenced by the risk factor, the POR approximates the person-time incidence ratio (or rate ratio), the parameter of interest for making causal inferences with cross-sectional data (Kleinbaum 1982). The PORs were obtained through logistic regression. Variables in the logistic model included the mother's level of education and knowledge of diarrhea, the household size, the presence of neighboring children and contact by holding and touching (Thomas 1987). Therefore, the effect of a given factor (expressed in a POR) is independent of the effects of the other factors included in the model. Statistical significance was assessed using two-tailed tests at an alpha level of 0.5, and is expressed in the results with 95 percent confidence intervals (CI). The 95 percent confidence interval is the range of values within which one is 95 percent certain that the "true" POR lies, assuming the absence of other biases. A POR of 1.0 signifies no association between the potential risk factor and the outcome. A 95 percent confidence interval which includes the value of 1.0 within its limits signifies no statistical significance at an alpha level of .05.

RESULTS

Women's Work and Child Care

Embu women are charged with attending to the day-to-day activities of the farm household. Their responsibilities are wide-ranging and affect every dimension of household life. Not surprisingly, a primary responsibility for women is the preparation of foods consumed in the household. This is particularly true for the traditional meal of cooked maize and beans (*githeri*), which, taken with tea, is the most common dish consumed in Embu households.

Household labor, a category of women's work that consists of a number of specific tasks, is the other major activity in the compound requiring large amounts of women's time. As evidenced by the results of the time allocation study and even more by field observations, the activities comprising this category are wide-ranging: women manufacture sisal rope, repair floor mats, wash dishes and kitchen utensils, clean house and clothing, sweep compounds, and sew or knit clothing. Two important household activities that require women to leave the compound are drawing water and collecting firewood. Only a few households have a water tap in the compound or a good source of firewood nearby, or, in the latter case, rely extensively on purchased charcoal for cooking fuel. Rather, women must walk long distances, often over hilly terrain, to collect water and firewood. That the water canisters or tied bundles can weigh up to 25kg explains why women consider this type of work to be particularly exhausting.

Although food preparation and household labor require substantial time inputs from women, these activities are secondary to two other major activities: agricultural production and child care. As will be described in more detail, women are involved in three types of agricultural work. The first and most important is the production of food, principally for home consumption. Food production includes the entire range of subsistence activities from planting, weeding, and harvesting to in-field processing and home storage. Women do not, as a rule, do the heavy clearing of the field. Women engage in cash cropping activities, such as weeding, picking, and processing coffee, cotton, or tobacco. Women are also involved in intermittent wage labor in agriculture, working for other households in any of these activities.

Embu mothers are constantly attentive to the needs of their young children and spend substantial amounts of time caring for infants. The most visible and frequent type of care involves prolonged physical contact with the child. If seated, a mother may hold an infant upright on her lap or cradle the child lengthwise between her outstretched legs. If a mother is standing or walking, the child is arm-carried on the hip or wrapped in a *kanga*, the colorful cloth used by women as a work apron or sling, and firmly secured on the mother's back. This latter position is preferred both by infants, who apparently feel secure, and by mothers, who can continue with many of their other activities.

Holding is a major component of the total care provided by a mother for her infant. Other activities, although less frequent and of shorter duration than holding, have equal impact on infant well-being. The more important among these other activities are feeding (which includes breastfeeding, usually until an infant reaches 18 to 24 months of age), washing, dressing, treatment of illness, and entertaining the infant by either singing or talking.

Relative to Western culture, child care practices among the Embu are more frequently performed within view of others and are shared by family and friends. A mother who is negligent of her child care responsibilities soon experiences social pressures from others, inducing her to correct her behavior or allow another relative, usually a maternal grandmother or aunt, to care for the child. These social pressures and resources for child care help to minimize the instances of inadequate care.

Given the multiple responsibilities of Embu women, one would anticipate some trade offs in time spent in productive and reproductive activities. Women with infants spent an average of 21.0 percent less time in food production activities and 32.5 percent less time in cash crop activities than women without infants (Table 10.1). Mothers of infants spent instead an average of 96 minutes per day caring for their infant. These care activities included holding, washing, feeding, and treating of illnesses. Infant care was the third most time-consuming activity for these women, following food production and household labor.

The difference in time allocation between women with and without infants is greater for cash crop activities than food production activities. The overall time spent by either group of women attending to cash crops, however, is relatively small; less than one-quarter of that for food crops. The difference in food production time consists of more minutes, and therefore should be seen as more important.

Among the various activities performed by women with infants, infant care and food production have the strongest negative correlation ($r=-0.438$, $p<.001$), indicating that women compensate for time in child care primarily by decreasing their work in food production. Alternatively, food production demands may result in a decrease in child care time.

Women frequently participate in planting, weeding, and harvesting for others as part of reciprocal labor exchanges. This social form of agricultural labor was included in the construct of the variable "social activities." When analyzed separately, it too is negatively correlated with infant care (r=-0.251, p<.01). When added into the "food production" construct, the latter's correlation with infant care increases in magnitude from -0.438 to -0.509, further strengthening the estimated association between agricultural work and child care.

Low correlations among the remaining variables (e.g., cash cropping, food preparation, eating, social, inactive) suggest that allocation of time to these activities is less critical and more discretionary when compensating for time caring for an infant. For example, some cash crop activity can be maintained while caring for a child because the fields containing cash crops are often located next to the household compound, enabling a mother to switch easily between caring for her infant and working on her cash crop. In contrast, fields containing food crops are often farther from the household, making concurrent child care impractical or impossible.

Maternal infant care among the Embu occurs in a social context that includes other household members, adult relatives, and nonkin. Of particular importance are young daughters who, from as young as four years old, are expected to assist mothers with the care of younger siblings. The care provided by young daughters consists predominantly of holding, entertaining, and watching, tasks undertaken as they play and visit with other children. An older daughter, when there was one, was the most frequent holder of the infant other than the mother (Figure 10.1).

The role of other family and nonfamily members in child care is best seen in the seasonality of time allocation. The seasonal variation in time allocated to food production and infant holding by mothers and older sisters of the infant is presented in Figure 10.2. Infant holding by the mother varied inversely with food production from March through October, and directly from November through February. Infant holding by the older sister was consistently inversely related to food production. Decreases in time allocated by the mother to holding were matched by increases in holding by the infant's sister. This remained true in December when mothers decreased work in both food production and child care. Young girls in the family are thus a valuable caretaking resource for mothers, widening their options for allocating their time to agriculture and other economic activities.

Holding by either the mother or sister generally decreased over the study period. This may have been due to aging of the infants during the year, resulting in less need for holding. The three peaks in time allocated to holding by sisters correspond to school holidays lasting for the entire month. During the remaining months, girls five years and older attend school from 8:00 A.M. until late afternoon (depending on the grade level and school).

A correlation or co-variation between two variables indicates association between the variables, but does not indicate the degree to which one variable or action leads to the other. Therefore, there are several reasonable explanations for the inverse correlation between infant holding and food production, including (1) women decrease food production work to compensate for time in child care, (2) women decrease time devoted to child care when spending more time in food production, and (3) women increase time allocation to food production when free of child care responsibilities. These scenarios are not mutually exclusive and each may be in force at different times or in different situations. If a mother decreases time in necessary child care without delegating this responsibility to another, the child is likely to suffer the consequences. The increased risk of illness in the child resulting from less time being held is addressed in the next section.

Infant Care and Diarrhea

Diarrhea is the second most common illness in most developing countries, following respiratory infections (Black 1982; Kamath 1969). Diarrhea is a more serious illness than respiratory infections, however, resulting in more hospitalizations (Black 1982). In Kenya, for example, diarrhea is estimated to account for 15 percent of all deaths (Leeuwenburg 1978). Those most susceptible to diarrhea are children under 36 months of age who suffer growth and development consequences due to decreased nutrient intake and absorption (Leslie 1987; Martorell 1975). The presence of a child with diarrhea is thus a relevant indicator of the current health status of a household.

The large majority of diarrhea in developing countries results from infectious organisms transmitted by the fecal-oral route. Direct contact with contaminated hands or ingestion of food prepared with contaminated utensils or hands are sufficient to transmit the organism and result in diarrhea in a susceptible person. Diarrhea organisms also have been identified in the feces of domestic animals (Blaser 1982). The presence of feces from these animals in a household compound thus presents children with an increased risk of infection. Though organisms causing diarrhea can be transmitted in drinking water, the dose in water sources is usually so dilute that infection from food and physical contact are more common (White 1972). Water's most important effect on diarrhea is its capacity to reduce transmission through hand washing.

Twenty-one (9.4%) of the 224 children included in the epidemiological study experienced diarrhea on the prior day.[4] In designing the study of the effect of physical contact on diarrhea, it was anticipated that physical contact, especially by young caretakers, would provide more opportunities to transmit infectious organisms to an infant, and thus cause more diarrhea. The opposite was found, however, with less physical contact resulting in more diarrhea. This relationship is most clearly seen in Figure 10.3 for holding by caretakers other than the mother. A child aged 0-23 months held less than 20 percent of the time was 13.4 times more likely to experience diarrhea than one held 60 percent or more of the time (95% CI=0.7, 275). This effect was consistent for all ages within this group.

The odds of diarrhea among children held less than 20 percent of the time by their mother was 40 percent greater (POR=1.4, 95% CI=0.3, 6.0) than among children held 20 percent or more of the time. The most probable explanation of why the preventative effect of mother's holding is not as strong as the effect of holding by other caretakers is because a mother's holding, more than any other caretaker, involves feeding of breast milk and supplementary foods. While breast milk is protective against diarrhea, supplementary foods represent opportunities for ingestion of diarrhea-causing organisms. The relationship between holding and diarrhea, apart from the mixed effects of feeding, is thus best represented by that seen for nonmother caretakers.

Essentially all Embu children have stopped breastfeeding by the age of 24 months. Among the 108 children aged 24-35 months, 76 (70.4%) were held by anyone for any length of time during the observation period. The odds of diarrhea among those never held was 6.3 (95% CI = 0.8, 50.0) times greater than among those ever held.

Touching, as distinct from holding, had a similar effect on diarrhea. Children aged 0-23 months who were touched less than five percent of the time were 5.5 (95% CI = 1.1, 28.6) times more likely to experience diarrhea than those touched 5-14 percent of the time. Those touched for a longer period experienced slightly more diarrhea (POR=1.2, 95% CI = 0.2, 6.9). Contact by touching did not have an effect on diarrhea among children aged 24-35 months.

The strength of the associations between physical contact of either type and diarrhea were not affected by the amount of time between the observed contact and the diarrhea survey. Thus, the PORs were the same whether three or 60 days elapsed between the contact observations and the diarrhea interview, indicating consistency of contact behaviors during this time of the study. Relatively wide confidence intervals around POR estimates resulted from analyzing the effects of risk factors in separate age groups, as opposed to the sample as a whole. The smaller number of children within a subgroup reduced statistical power. The consistently positive effects, though of varying magnitude, among the two age groups and for the (lack of) two types of physical contact, however, reinforce the validity of the results obtained.

Observations of children for 12 consecutive daylight hours in 38 households revealed that an absence of physical contact by holding or touching frequently meant the child was left unattended. Children aged 0-23 months and 24-35 months spent an average of 65 and 76 waking minutes unattended, respectively (Thomas 1987). While unattended, children were observed to crawl around the household compound, which was often soiled with the feces of domestic chickens and goats, among other potential sources of diarrhea-causing organisms. Child caretaking, even by young siblings, may achieve some of its beneficial effect by limiting the contact of infants with such potential sources of infection in the household.

DISCUSSION AND CONCLUSIONS

Among Embu women, time spent in child care is affected by time allocated to food production. This is evidenced by (1) the time allocation differences between women with infants and women without infants, (2) the negative correlation of these activities among women with infants, and (3) the seasonal interactions of child care and food production activities. Child care, in turn, affects a child's physical health. This is seen in the increased risk of diarrhea for children of all ages studied who were held or touched less than other children.

The older sisters of infants help out with the child care, thereby enabling the mother to spend more time in food production. A young family without older children, however, has fewer caretaking resources, and thus fewer time allocation options. Such a family risks undernutrition from inadequate food production and/or a sick infant from inadequate child care.

Agricultural development projects that increase the demand for woman's time in food production must also address the mother's child care responsibilities, if such projects are not to be frustrated by this competing demand and are not to result in a negative effect on the mother's infant. Within this context, at least three programmatic considerations are relevant. First, that women farmers have access to technologies (e.g., crop varieties, tools, new techniques) that increase the efficiency of their agricultural labor, which in turn can lead to a decrease in time allocated to agriculture while maintaining the same level of food production. Second, that the productivity and income-earning possibilities of those farm activities most compatible with child care, such as the marketing of crops or in-compound small animal husbandry, be improved and integrated with efforts targeted at in-field crop production. And third, that alternative micro- or small-enterprise activities (e.g., local products and services) that can be undertaken in or near the household be promoted.

In a high-birthrate population such as the Embu, the large number of children increases the demand for food production while also requiring that mothers spend less time in food production and more in child care. This is of special concern where the older children do not contribute to the food production work because of time in school. Increasing child spacing and/or decreasing the number of children per family in these situations will lessen the demands for child care, free mothers' time for other economic activities, and reduce the child care responsibilities for young daughters attending school.

Development projects must also consider the apparent conflict between the goals of educating young women and of increasing the agricultural productivity of small farms. Mothers rely on their daughters to attend to child care and other household responsibilities in order to have time to work in the household's fields. Sending girls to school removes this option for the mother. For this reason, girls are not infrequently kept home from school to attend to the household work. Some (as yet unknown) creative child care programs may enable girls to attend school unencumbered by competing household demands, and enable mothers to attend to food production. Two possible alternatives for such a child care program might be remunerated child care using "professional" caretakers, who might be unemployed women with minimal additional economic responsibilities, or the use of indigenous women's organizations consisting of groups of women who, on an individual rotation basis, could take care of each other's children.

Finally, the preceding analyses have shown that although infants are at increased risk of diarrheal infection during periods of peak agricultural work by their mothers, young siblings can provide a form of care — holding — that is effective in reducing the risk of this infectious disease. One should not discount the positive health effects that can arise from well-targeted public health information dissemination. Health education programs that illustrate the positive health benefits of keeping infants and toddlers away from sources of infectious organisms, and also train household members in ways to better maintain compound sanitation and hygiene, can go a long way toward reducing infant diarrhea and freeing women's time for productive work, both of which are important development goals for the 1990s.

Notes

1. The Kenya Project is part of a larger research undertaking funded by the United States Agency for International Development. In addition to the Kenya Project, the AID-funded Nutrition Collaborative Research Support Program (CRSP) included research in central Mexico by the University of Connecticut and the Nutrition Institute of Mexico and research outside Cairo by the Universities of Purdue, Kansas, and Arizona and the Nutrition Institute of Egypt. AID funded these collaborative efforts through grant number DAN 1309-G-SS-1070-00.

   The authors would like to thank Drs. Charlotte Neumann (UCLA) and Nimrod Bwibo (University of Nairobi), the Kenya Project's Principal Investigators, for their support of our research efforts; Mr. Duncan Ngare, the field sociologist who collaborated with us, and Dr. Dorothy Cattle, field anthropologist who designed the child care survey instrument used in the infant diarrhea study; and the Embu field staff, particularly the time allocation study's supervisors—David Mvinju, Charles Murega, Elijah Mbiriani, and the late Eliphas Ireri.

2. Based on the Kenya Project's initial demographic survey of the Kyeni South population, it was determined that an overall sample of approximately 300 households would be required to provide adequate numbers of target individuals to test the study's hypotheses on the functional consequences of chronic mild-to-moderate malnutrition. The target individuals included the lead male, lead female, infants (0-6 months), toddlers (18-30 months), and school-age children (7-9 years). The collection of nutrition and health data focused on these target individuals, while socio-economic information collection targeted the household. The selection of study households was biased in favor of those households that could supply target individuals. This resulted in a sample with demographic characteristics slightly different from those of the base population. The Kenya Project sample had comparatively more women in their reproductive years, more school-age children, fewer older adults, and slightly larger household size (Neumann and Bwibo 1987).

3. Given the physical characteristics of the study area and the spatial distribution of the study households, a variation of the random spot observation method was used. A purely random selection of times for visiting households would have resulted in excessive travel for fieldworkers. For example, random selection might designate a household in the upper region of the study area for a visit at 7:00 A.M., a household in the lower region for a visit at 7:15 A.M., and another

household in the upper region of the study area for a visit at 7:30 A.M. Given the size of the study area (55km2) and the hilly terrain, such an observation schedule would have been impossible for field staff traveling by bicycle.

A more feasible method for randomizing household observations was developed. A set route for visiting study households was established, and each household was observed in the same order during each completion of the route. The route was begun again after all households had been visited. Over the study period of one year, the route was completed 64 times.

While visiting households along the route, factors such as varying length of visit (5 to 10 minutes), differences in travel time due to weather, delays due to bicycle repairs, and other unforeseen situations removed any systematic biases in when a household would be visited. The time that a household was visited varied during each completion of the route. Frequency distributions of visit times by household and subregion of the study area show no discernible biases in the coverage (Baksh and Paolisso 1987).

4.   The cross-sectional data on diarrhea represent the diarrhea "picture" at one point in time, and therefore are not influenced by seasonal trends. The Kenya Project collected data on diarrhea incidence (i.e., new episodes) every two weeks for the duration of the study. Seasonal fluctuations were apparent in these data. The cross-sectional data on diarrhea were found to be more reliable, however, and thus were used for assessing the relationship between caretaking and diarrhea.

References

Baksh, Michael and Michael Paolisso
1987. "Time Allocation Methods." Unpublished manuscript. School of Public Health. University of California, Los Angeles.

Black, Robert E. et al.
1982. "Longitudinal Studies of Infectious Diseases and Physical *American Journal of Epidemiology*, vol. 14, no. 115, p. 305.

Blaser, Martin J.
1982. Camplylobacter Infections. In *Bacterial Infections of Humans.* Edited by A.S. Evans and H.A. Feldman. New York: Plenum Publishing Corp.

Creevey, Lucy E. (ed.)
1986. *Women Farmers in Africa: Rural Development in Mali and the Sahel.* Syracuse, NY: Syracuse University Press.

Davison, Jean (ed.)
1988. *Agriculture, Women and Land: The African Experience.*Boulder, CO: Westview Press.

Dey, Jennie
1984. *Women in Food Production and Food Security in Africa.* Rome: Food and Agriculture Organization of the United Nations.

FAO
1985. *Women in Developing Agriculture.* Rome: Food and Agriculture Organization of the United Nations.

Haugerud, Angelique
1984. "Household Dynamics and Rural Political Economy among Embu Farmers in the Kenya Highlands." Ph.D. Dissertation, Northwestern University.

Johnson, Allen
1975. "Time Allocation in a Machiguenga Community." *Ethnology* 14: 301-310.

Kamath K.R. et al.
1969. "Infection and Disease in a Group of South Indian Families: II. General Morbidity Patterns in Families and Family Members." *American Journal of Epidemiology* 89: 374-383.

Kleinbaum, David G.; Kupper, Lawrence L.; and Morgenstern, Hal
1982. *Epidemiologic Research.* Belmont, CA: Lifetime Learning Publications.

Leeuwenburg, J. et al.
1978. "Machakos Project Studies: VII. The Incidence of Diarrhoeal Disease in the Under-Five Population." *Tropical Geographic Medicine* 30: 383-391.

Leslie, Joanne
    1987. "Interactions of Malnutrition and Diarrhea: A Review of Research." In *Food Policy: Integrating Supply, Distribution and Consumption.* Edited by J.P. Gittinger, J. Leslie and C. Hoisington. Baltimore: Johns Hopkins University Press.
Martorell, Reynaldo et.al
    1975. "Acute Morbidity and Physical Growth in Rural Guatemalan Children." *American Journal of Disease in Children* 129: 1296-1301.
Moock, Joyce Lewinger (ed.)
    1986. *Understanding Africa's Rural Households and Farming Systems.* Boulder, CO: Westview Press.
Neumann, Charlotte and Nimrod Bwibo
    1987. "The Collaborative Research Support Program on Food Intake and Human Function, Kenya Project." Final report submitted to United States Agency for International Development.
Poats, Susan; Schmink, Marianne; and Spring, Anita (eds.)
    1988. *Gender Issues in Farming Systems Research and Extension.* Boulder, CO: Westview Press.
Republic of Kenya
    1981. Kenya Population Census, 1979. Volume 1. Nairobi: Central Bureau of Statistics, Ministry of Finance and Planning.
Thomas, J. Conley
    1987. Risk Factors for Diarrhea among Young Children in Rural Kenya. Ph.D Dissertation. University of California, Los Angeles.
White, Gilbert F.; Bradley, David J.; and White, Anne U.
    1972. *Drawers of Water: Domestic Water Use in East Africa.* Chicago: University of Chicago Press.

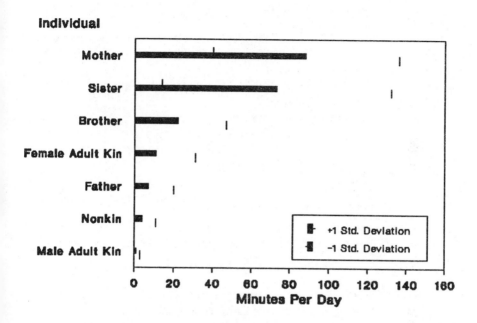

Figure 10.1
Average Number of Minutes per Day Infants
are held by Family and Non-family Members.
Based on 5,278 Observations of 91 Infants.

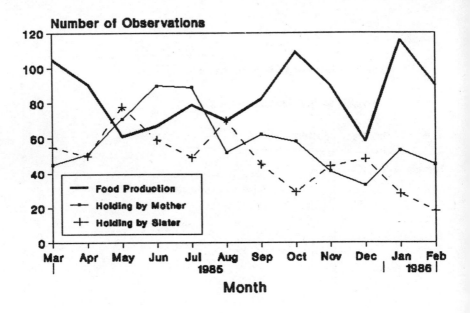

Figure 10.2
Food Production and Infant Holding by Month.

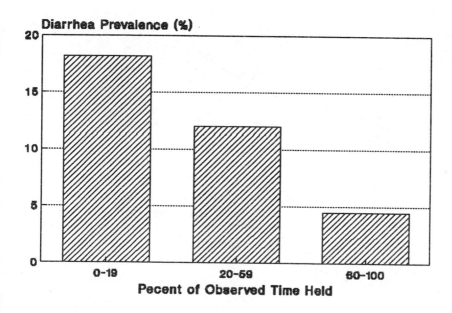

Figure 10.3
The Prevalence of Diarrhea Among Children
0-23 months Old For Three Levels of Contact
by Holding by Non-mother Caretakers.

Table 10.1 Time Allocated to Work and Care Activities by Women with and without Infants[1]

Activity	Average Time per 11 hour day (minutes)			
	Women with Infants (n = 91)	Women without Infants (n = 41)	Percent Difference	p
Food Production	128	162	-21.0	.004[2]
Cash Cropping	27	40	-32.5	.025
Infant Care	0	96	—	—
Self Care	14	20	-30.0	.05
Other Care[3]	14	22	-36.4	.05
Household	104	118	-11.9	.08

1. Minute calculations are based on percentage of each category's observation out of total number of observations.
2. t-Test used to determine p values; df=130; alpha=.05.
3. Includes care provided to children greater than two years of age and adults.

11

Women's Community Service and Child Welfare in Urban Peru

Jeanine Anderson

The point of departure for this chapter is the death of a ten-month-old baby girl in Leoncio Prado, a shantytown bordering Lima, Peru.[1] The child was the youngest of three daughters of Alicia Guzman, a woman who some ten years earlier had been among the first wave of squatters who established Leoncio Prado. Alicia's baby became ill one Saturday afternoon when the father, who earned a relatively high income as an informal construction contractor, was out drinking with his friends and Alicia herself was at a meeting of the community women's council.

As the elected delegate from her housing block, Alicia was responsible for reporting to the weekly council session the decisions and needs of families on the block, and for taking news of the council's activities back to the block. As usual, the most committed delegates to the women's council had arrived at 4:00 p.m., the appointed hour, while others, with the idea of preventing prolonged discussion prior to any formal vote, planned their arrival for much later. Alicia stayed through the end of the session, which continued until 10:00 p.m. The council was staging an important event the following day — a food fair intended to raise money to be distributed as social assistance over the coming year to particularly needy families.

While she attended the meeting, Alicia left her 12-year-old daughter in charge of the household. When she returned home after the session she found the baby fretful, with fever, and refusing to take a bottle. This child had never been breastfed because Alicia claimed she didn't have the "patience" for it, although one suspects the decision to exclusively bottlefeed the infant was strongly influenced by the financial contribution from her husband, which allowed her to buy formula and evaporated milk. Because she was expected at the community center to help prepare the food for the next day's festival, Alicia went out again after making her baby as comfortable as possible.

The fever seemed to have risen even higher by the time she returned in the early hours of Sunday morning. She administered drops of Novalgin and rubbed the infant's body with vinegar and oil, but by Sunday afternoon the child was vomiting and continued to have high fever. Alicia, however, had to supervise ticket sales and serve food at the community center, so again she left her oldest daughter with the baby. She tried to monitor the situation by running back home whenever there was a lull in the sales or when another council member could be pressed into substituting for her. By Sunday evening the baby was seriously dehydrated and refused all liquids. Alicia took recourse to her child's *comadre* (godmother), who advised seeking the assistance of a local *curandero* (healer).

The end of this episode is sadly predictable. By midday Monday, Alicia's child was convulsing. At this point the decision was made between mother and godmother to take the baby to the hospital. While the godmother ran home to find money for a taxi, the baby died in her mother's arms.

The chain of events that, in one fatal weekend, took the life of Alicia's daughter highlights many of the issues discussed in this chapter. Alicia is exceptionally active in her shanty settlement's projects and organizations. Because of her reputation for enthusiasm and reliability, she is invited to participate in community organizations, including the primary health promoters' group. The purpose of such groups and their projects is to raise community health and welfare. How could so severe a conflict arise between Alicia's community activities and her mothering role as to occasion a baby's death? Did over a year's training as a health promoter not prepare her to respond quickly enough to clear symptoms of dehydration and to use the therapies she had learned? Or did Alicia feel that her obligations to the women's council and the community in general could not be ignored, even in a situation of high risk for her infant? To a large degree, these questions cannot be answered with complete certainty, not by the author and probably not by Alicia herself. They are raised to highlight, in ethnographic relief, the themes of this chapter: first, that community work should be taken into consideration in the analysis of poor women's work; and, second, that community service can create severe problems for women already balancing too many responsibilities.

Community Service Work: A Necessary Category

To understand the competing demands on women, so well illustrated by a case such as Alicia's, work in community service must be added to the more familiar categories of market work and household reproductive work, particularly in settings like the burgeoning shantytowns of major

Third World cities. These urban communities develop in an atmosphere of limited shared cultural understanding, few neighborhood organizations, and a complete lack of infrastructure. The new residents' task is one of forging the social ties that enable the establishment of health, education, provisioning, recreation, and other services. Neighborhood committees, charged with carrying out local development projects, are typical of newly-formed, poor urban communities (additionally, they are increasingly found in rural communities affected by various development projects). In Peru, they build on Andean communal traditions, although the proliferation of organizations beyond a single male hierarchy of traditional authority is a product of the last decade.[2]

The multiple organizations one now finds in any urban shantytown have a diversity of origins. Frequently, new community organizations form part of the operational framework of large schemes for social and economic development. One of the best known examples is the spread of primary health services throughout the Third World since the 1978 Alma-Ata conference. Although sponsored by a private organization rather than the Ministry of Health, Alicia's health promoters' group followed Alma-Ata philosophy of training, organizing, and empowering individuals from the local community to provide health services to their neighbors. Similarly, the municipal government of Lima has sought to address problems of infant and child malnutrition via a milk distribution program that operates through 7,000 committees distributed over the city's approximately 450 shantytowns and poor inner-city neighborhoods.

Community committees have also been formed in spontaneous response to rising food prices under economic crises. Women (and the occasional man) cook collectively, with most of the ingredients supplied through food donation programs. However, the community groups that place the biggest demand on women like Alicia are those charged with creating basic infrastructure and services — electricity, piped-in water, health posts, schools, and so on, down a long list of necessities and amenities taken as givens in middle- and upper- class neighborhoods.[3]

The social burden of such community activism is overwhelmingly shouldered by women. In Lima's massive municipal milk program, women pick up the sacks of powdered milk at drop-off points, carry them on foot or microbus to storage rooms in the community, organize fund-raising events for buying cooking fuel and the ingredients (sugar, rolled oats, *quinua*, or cocoa) considered necessary to make the milk more appetizing, and, finally, take weekly turns in preparing the milk-based mixture. The preparation is a time-consuming process that involves carrying water, obtained from a distant spigot, that is brought to a boil before dissolving the powder. Then there is the long wait for the children of 20 or so neighbors to present themselves with their cups. The first may arrive at

6:00 A.M., while the last may drop by on the way home from an early session at school. This work of preparing and serving the milk is never done by men. The few men that participate in the program do so in administrative posts.

Men, in fact, are far more active in shantytown organizations in Lima when the shantytown experience is younger and needs are more "basic." They lead the campaigns for water, electricity, and transportation services that will facilitate housework and alleviate constant health problems ("women's sphere"), but also provide the men with easier access to jobs outside the community or even permit them to establish a workshop within it. Once the struggle moves to an arena of food programs, day-care, refuse collection, or safety on the streets, however, the women are left to champion these remaining causes.

Several factors help explain why women take on a disproportionate share of community-improvement activities. The first is the much observed fact that women tend to spend more of their time in the local neighborhood. They may be exclusively dedicated to housework and child care, or, if working for pay, they may use the household and/or community as a base. Governments and development agencies frequently assume that women's opportunity costs as executors of community service activities are lower than men's opportunity costs. Therefore, they can be paid little or nothing without household welfare being adversely affected. The administrators of community-improvement projects, similar to many women's employers, may also find women to be a more docile and manageable work force than men.

Women may be less able to resist the calls to neighborhood solidarity that underpin community volunteerism. Their socialization for caretaking at the family level may transfer readily to higher-order groups under the pressure of invitations that stress the needs to be filled through collective action. Just as women are not expected to count the personal cost of being the first to rise and the last to rest in the household, so their investments of time and energy in community service may come to seem part of their natural role. Other female-socialized traits, such as self-effacing leadership styles and attention to immediate practical results, may further reinforce the use of women in community development roles.

In Peru, the task of creating a community and provisioning it with services is made especially difficult by the lack of an accepted optimal path or model for the acquisition of needed services. A potable water system can be financed through different agencies on different terms. Objective expert advice on what is best for a particular community may be impossible to obtain because of the vested political interests that vie for the loyalty of the shantytowns. All decisions over models and service providers, then, are inevitably accompanied by conflict. However, regardless of the perceived need for a particular service, decisions sometimes cannot be made.[4]

In these circumstances, women take on roles of mediation and reconciliation, similar to roles they assume in the maintenance of an affective balance within the family. The effort they expend on such activities could easily be miscoded in the time-budget studies as "visiting" or "leisure." But a high social investment is required in order for a community to coalesce around a plan for obtaining its infrastructure and services. Shantytowns in Lima do not emerge as integrated, functioning communities simply because peasant communities in the Peruvian Andes once were.

While the need for self-help construction of a community is a principal motive for the great investment of time that women in the shantytowns make in service projects, their counterparts living in long-established, inner-city poor neighborhoods also devote large amounts of time to managing human relations among close neighbors. They organize door-to-door collections and fund-raising activities to assist in emergencies that befall one or another family, and coordinate Independence Day and New Year's festivities that integrate the neighbors in all-night dancing on a crowded inner patio. Their most formidable task, however, is smoothing daily relations among the 30 to 50 children, teens, and adults who share a single toilet, two or three water spigots, and a single passageway to the street.

The above helps clarify the impetus for women to take on community organization work, but says nothing about the impact community service has on women's workloads, the costs and benefits it entails, and, in particular, its implications for child welfare. A better understanding of these issues has important implications for government policy towards poor communities and for development project planning where women's availability as agents is often taken for granted. Organizing community improvement projects on the basis of unproven assumptions is poor management in any case, but if there are indeed costs for the women who act as promoters, and for their children, the projects will be self-defeating as a means of improving social welfare.

The Data

The discussion of women's community service work in the shanty settlement of Leoncio Prado will draw on three different studies carried out there at different points in time. The first was a study of child care needs of urban Peruvian women undertaken in 1978 as part of a six-country, Agency for International Development (AID) Office of Nutrition project (Anderson et al. 1979). The second was a study of child development that I directed for the Peruvian Ministry of Education in 1980 (Anderson et al. 1982). The third was a study of women's informal social networks and participation in community organizations carried out in the early 1980s.[5] Although the data analysis in the last case is as yet incomplete, a special objective of the research was to investigate to what extent the women of Leoncio Prado actually rely on community services and community-based social networks to resolve practical problems such as the health emergency that Alicia confronted. The findings from these three studies have been supplemented by extensive fieldnotes and observations made during my eight year involvement in development projects in Leoncio Prado.

This wealth of information, including a time-depth that is lacking in the vast majority of studies of Third World urban poverty, is still not completely adequate for the purpose of this analysis since none of the studies focused directly on community participation as an independent variable and child welfare as the outcome. The arguments in this chapter will thus be somewhat indirect and not entirely conclusive on many points. Quantitatively measuring the time poor women spend in community projects in the city of Lima and relating that directly to indices of child nutritional status and psychological development now seems a clear research priority. Its importance was not clear to me, however, when I began work on women and children because I, like most development planners, underestimated the weight of community volunteerism and, further, accepted the common assumption that all women's participation outside the household entails unambiguous benefits (social, educational, recreational and integrative).

An Urban Shanty Community

In 1978, Leoncio Prado was an array of small precarious dwellings on the sandy hill of Pamplona Alta. Its approximately 900 families were organized in block communities that sent male representatives to a central committee whose principal role was to lobby the municipal utilities for electricity, potable water, and sewers. The women were organized in a parallel structure of block delegates to the women's council.[6] The only collective infrastructure available for meetings was a barn-like community center and a small preschool donated by a German development agency.

The women's council performed ceremonial roles at community celebrations, worked to motivate women to take a greater interest in the world around them, and occupied itself with problems of social assistance through its capacity to distribute small amounts of money. Each year a special commission solicited two practice teachers from a teacher-training institute. The council's secretary for education was responsible for monitoring their work and facilitating their relations with parents and the community.

A core group of the officers of the women's council received training in parliamentary procedure, accounting, interpersonal relations, community organizing, and even assertiveness from a nun who was their self-appointed advisor. In contrast, the block delegates to the council perceived their participation as socially satisfying, mildly informative, but rather unimportant (Bogdanovich and Castillo 1978).

By 1980, the date of the Ministry of Education study of child development, there were several new women's voluntary groups operating in the community of Leoncio Prado. A religious congregation had started a health center and meals program that involved a number of women as assistants. A private development group had signed an agreement with the central committee to organize a primary health care program aimed at training a woman health promoter for each block. In protest against the men for having infringed on their sphere of authority, some of the former members of the women's council were creating an independent new mothers' club.

Also, during this time, residents of shantytowns, in a desperate response to poverty, increasingly relied on food obtained through participation in food-for-work programs. Several brigades, each of 50 to 60 women, functioned in three-month cycles in Leoncio Prado throughout 1980. Like many other organizations, the brigades emphasized training. The women involved typically spent one afternoon a week learning how to cook the imported food products they received.

Community Participation and Child Welfare

Despite the modest pretensions of the women's council and the limited role women were taking in the affairs of Leoncio Prado at the time of the earlier 1978 child care study, one of the hypotheses tested in this study was that the mother's greater participation — defined as her being a block delegate and/or demonstrating knowledge about community problems — would be related to more favorable weight-to-age ratios for children under the age of five. This hypothesis had to be rejected (Anderson et al. 1979: 51-52). Nor was any relationship found, either positive or negative, between the children's nutritional status and the mothers' work for pay. Only 18 of 74 women interviewed were working even a half-day schedule, since all the families studied had at least two preschool children and child care alternatives outside of relatives were practically nonexistent (Anderson et al. 1979: 46).

The 1980 study in Leoncio Prado again tested the hypothesis that participation by the mother in community organizations would be related to superior child development. The broadened social network, greater access to information and services, and perhaps heightened self-confidence of participating women seemed, as they had earlier, self-evident reasons why these women should be better mothers than women with less involvement with community groups.

The specific relationships explored were between both mothers' participation in community organizations and mothers' income-generating work and child development (as assessed by the Bayley and McCarthy child development scales[7] in Leoncio Prado and in two other poor communities that served as points of comparison in the Ministry of Education investigation.[8] According to the 1980 findings, neither a mother's working nor her belonging to community service groups showed any significant relationship to the development of one- and three-year-old children in Leoncio Prado, although there was some evidence of a negative relationship for these age groups in the other two communities. Of even more interest is the finding that older preschool children in the Cuzco and inner-city Lima communities seemed to benefit from their mother's participation in community organizations and activities as well as their participation in remunerated work. In contrast, five-year-old children in Leoncio Prado seemed to be adversely affected, at least in terms of gross motor development, by mother's participation in community organizations and mother's paid work.

The Fluid Boundaries Between Community Service and Market Work

It is frequently difficult to draw the line between community service work and paid work in settings such as Leoncio Prado. Most community work is unpaid and may even entail high direct and indirect costs. Nonetheless, community projects in Peru are occasionally remunerative in the form of a *propina* (tip), while certain informal-market activities (for example, food vending on the street) may produce returns only in kind. Monetary reward for work rendered is not a consistent distinguishing criterion separating community and market activities.

Labor on community projects paid in donated food epitomizes the difficulty of distinguishing between these two categories of work. A food-for-work brigade project may consist of meeting five afternoons a week to knit or weave. Each woman provides her own materials and can use or sell what she makes as she wishes. In addition to the weaving and knitting, the brigade may also spend three months eliminating clandestine garbage dumps. In general, these types of brigades will alternate between projects that benefit the community (e.g. cleanup) and activities that promote personal income generation. Interestingly, Peruvian women use the same terminology to refer to their participation in the brigades as they use to refer to paid work.

Other community volunteer activities can easily turn into a paying job. In Leoncio Prado a subsidized meals program, sponsored by a distant wealthy parish, was staffed in the first stage by members of the women's council, who took turns doing the buying, cooking, and washing. As differences among them in management and cooking skills became clear, the parish priest offered contracts to two women at salaries near minimum legal wage — a fact to which the men's central committee objected strenuously when it was duly informed.

A final case further illustrates how volunteer service can become remunerated work without sacrificing goals of the service project. Most of the individuals in Alicia's health promoters' group were also most of the local door-to-door sales force for a cosmetics company that produces minuscule vials of perfume and tiny makeup kits for the low-income market.

Participation in community groups is not always an alternative survival strategy, distinct from seeking remunerated work, with each group operating as a separate economy: an economy of benefits in services, donated goods, and community recognition versus a salary that can be invested in child welfare (among other possibilities). The ties women establish through community groups are bridges to job opportunities. Although the above examples show jobs based in the community, there is evidence that through their connections to community service projects, women may also gain employment opportunities outside the shantytown.

Neither jobs nor community projects are permanent. Observations of women in Leoncio Prado over eight years show a high degree of volatility in both kinds of commitments. Jobs prove to be less profitable than expected, and/or the conditions of work are less attractive than believed, or a child's illness forces a mother to temporarily stop working. Community groups, for their part, set fixed terms for their officers and rotate their delegates frequently in recognition of the fact that no poor family has sufficient reserves to maintain a high level of volunteer activity for extended periods. Despite such mechanisms for distributing community service responsibilities among households, there are periods for women when involvement in remunerative work and community activity coincide, and children are caught in a situation of acute competition for their mothers' time and attention.

Any assessment of child welfare at a given moment in time must show the mixed effects of community service and paid work. Small children experience many different types of child care arrangements and many different levels of mother's attention, depending on the mother's position in the complex cycle of work and community participation. Thus, one possible explanation for the ambiguous effects of women's community service activities on child development is the confounding of those effects with the effects of remunerated work.

Networks and Community Service

Social networks — the set of special neighbors, kin, and friends that forms a unique constellation around each individual — clearly bear some relation to the various factors we have been examining. It is highly likely that the size and composition of women's social networks are related to their child care and child-feeding practices. It has occasionally been suggested that the restricted range of poor women's networks — the relatively few people they tend to know and associate with, and their origin in a single social class — limits their effectiveness as aides in problem solving (Warren 1981). Community development practitioners almost universally assume that "getting women out of the home," in order to broaden and diversify their immediate social world, should be an end in itself.

The data on social networks in Leoncio Prado confirm that women who participate in community groups have larger social networks than those who do not (Table 11.1).[9] The participatory women count an average of 15 persons in their social networks; those who do not participate in community groups have an average of ten. The social networks of the participatory women are also somewhat less tied to the place of residence. Thus, these women have close associations with eight persons who do not live in Leoncio Prado and seven who do. The women not involved in community organizations associate with an average of five persons from outside and five from within the shanty neighborhood. Most community organizations in Leoncio Prado have external advisors or receive financial support channeled through agencies that periodically send their representatives to the shantytown. In addition to these advisors, other outsiders who figure in the social networks of the participatory women include former employers, wealthy and prestigious godparents, relatives living in other districts, and friends that resulted from a variety of occasional contacts.

The data in Table 11.1 suggest an association between the size and composition of women's social networks and their degree of community participation. This association, albeit a tentative one, raises two related questions regarding the role of these networks in helping Leoncio Prado women respond to problems or emergencies. The first question sets the stage for the second by asking whether the problems confronting women with different levels of participation are the same. The second question asks whether the increased size of social networks of community-active women leads to increased opportunities for assistance from community or noncommunity sources.

Table 11.2 compares responses from Leoncio Prado women regarding the types of problems they normally encounter. This comparison suggests that the problems faced by participatory and nonparticipatory women are not notably different. When asked to recall the most serious problem in the last few months before the interview, both groups put problems related to their husbands in first place (participatory 28 percent, nonparticipatory 25 percent). Also for both groups of women, approximately one-fifth of the emergencies were related to children, of which most were concerned with serious health problems.

Not only were the problems confronting these women similar, but also the types of individuals called upon in time of need (Table 11.3). Those most frequently asked for assistance were relatives, followed by neighbors. The proportions of participatory and nonparticipatory women who went to these two categories of individuals were almost identical. It appears that women, both active and inactive in community organizations, reach out to the same group of community residents through their social networks. Of interest is the fact that 19 women mentioned service institutions as a second line of defense, after having first mobilized a member of their social network.

More nonparticipatory than participatory women mentioned using local community services such as the Leoncio Prado health post (16 percent of the total 44 nonparticipatory respondents; 9 percent of the total of 57 participatory women) in resolving problems. The only women who took recourse to service institutions outside the community were seven (12 percent) of those who participated in community groups. A close examination of these seven cases leaves no doubt that the participatory women were using their extensive extra-community networks to identify bridges to more specialized services — sophisticated health facilities and legal expertise, for example — that will probably never be available in the shantytown.

There often exists an important difference between the way social networks are used to meet emergencies and the way they are employed to solve life's minor problems.[10] To investigate whether such a difference existed, a sample of participatory and nonparticipatory women of Leoncio Prado was analyzed to determine who assisted the mother in routine child care (Table 11. 4). Again, both groups relied on neighbors — usually a single next-door neighbor — for the majority of child care assistance. A slight difference appears in the greater proportion of participatory women who could count on more than one neighbor for such help (27 percent participatory women; 15 percent nonparticipatory women). The women who did not participate in community service groups were also somewhat more likely to use older siblings when forced to leave young children with a caretaker (12 percent participatory; 25 percent nonparticipatory).

The Rewards of Community Service?

If community service projects and community development groups do, in fact, create the basic infrastructure and local integration that are their ostensible justification, it is reasonable to expect benefits to accrue to women who participate in such efforts. The evidence discussed in this chapter, however, raises doubts about such benefits, or at least suggests that there may be short-term costs to be weighed against the longer-term benefits.

The Leoncio Prado case suggests that local community participation is not enough to ensure access to the information and adequate services women need in order to promote the well-being of their children in the setting of a large and heterogeneous city. The variable that was most powerful in explaining the Leoncio Prado children's performance on the scales of development administered in the Ministry of Education study in 1980 was a variable of "cultural integration" (Anderson et al. 1982). This reflected the access their parents had to abilities and practices associated with the dominant national culture: literacy, Spanish language, a history of travel in Peru, higher levels of formal education, and urban sophistication in general. Where parents, in particular mothers, were simultaneously well-integrated in the Andean culture, the effects were even more beneficial.

The education that women need to gain expertise and self-confidence in the dominant culture is not likely to take place in Leoncio Prado, however. The community development experts are right in their calls to end poor women's isolation in their domestic enclosure, but they should also recognize that the shantytown itself is another kind of enclosure. No amount of activism within its boundaries will give the women the range of experiences they need in order to gain a greater measure of control over that outside world.

It is significant that the Leoncio Prado children scored lower on the 1980 tests of child development than children from an inner-city Lima slum neighborhood, whose material conditions of life were in some respects worse than those of the shantytown. The gap between the two groups of children widened progressively with age: there was no difference among one-year-olds in cognitive development and a very slight difference in favor of the slum children in motor development. By age five, however, the slum children out-performed the shantytown children in verbal skills and on the memory and general cognitive scale of the McCarthy testing instrument.

For the urban poor, part of achieving a good child care outcome is being able to negotiate benefits and advantages from the dominant society and to instill appropriate negotiating skills in one's children. These are the skills that will, for example, permit a mother — once she has decided to seek a solution to a child's illness through the modern health system — to overcome the obstacles of receptionists and nurses, registries and medical histories, and to obtain, from a busy and often indifferent doctor, a competent diagnosis and intelligible recommendations. Such skills are founded on taking an accurate reading on the risks and opportunities of urban life in the slum or shantytown. In this respect, inner-city slum children — their families not recent migrants but the product of generations of urban poverty — also enjoy the advantage of what seems to be better protection from some particularly grave dangers: they are less likely to suffer sexual abuse, and less subject to what in the shantytowns is a strikingly high frequency of children getting lost.[11] In the slums, should a father die or abandon the mother, one of her male relatives is likely to step in to support the family; whereas in the shantytown a mother in these circumstances usually takes on a full breadwinning role (Anderson 1983).

Conclusion

It is clear that for the women of Leoncio Prado, participation in community services is an important responsibility, one which is in many ways similar to participation in remunerative work. It entails costs in terms of time and energy, but at the same time offers the benefits of increased status, access to services (particularly outside their immediate community), and occasionally direct financial rewards. It is probable that, on average and in the long run, family welfare in shantytowns is increased by women's participation in community services. However, the case study with which this chapter opened and the limited evidence presented concerning a relationship between mother's community service participation, child care, and child development raise a real concern that mothers' dedication to community activities may even be negatively related to child welfare.

Mothers in new urban communities such as Leoncio Prado face the difficult challenge of developing successful child care strategies in a setting for which their own heritage of child-rearing knowledge has not fully prepared them. To do this, they need accurate information about, and direct experience in dealing with, the larger society beyond the confines of the shantytown. Their participation in community groups and projects could give them that kind of information and experience. But the conception that underlies such groups and projects (community self-help with a minimum of outside "alienating" intervenors and a corresponding minimum of outside resources) and their mode of operation leave little room

.for that at present. For women's community service work truly to benefit them and their children, its potential as a mechanism for integration beyond the local neighborhood must be recognized and abetted. When this begins to happen, researchers may find the positive effects of mothers' community service on child development I once so confidently anticipated in Leoncio Prado.

Notes

1. The death occurred in February 1983. Other observers during the aftermath of these events were Leslie Salzinger and Maria Eugenia Mansilla.

2. "Mothers' clubs," specifically for women, are among the new organizations to have appeared in Peruvian peasant communities in the last decade. Mixed organizations of men and women are rare in poor urban or rural communities, although women may frequently have reason to attend the sessions of a "male" organization, and men may sit in on the sessions of a women's group.

3. The Peruvian urbanologist, Gustavo Riofrio, has pointed out that the poor "invaders" of tracts considered to be worthless and undesirable by everyone else are not simply house-builders with each family concerned with completing the progression from straw shack through brick-and-cement house as best it can; rather, they are urban developers concerned with planning and servicing the new neighborhood according to similar standards applied by government or private developers in wealthier neighborhoods.

4. In Lima, a deadlock over competing bids for potable water installations kept the enormous district of Canto Grande without water (except that delivered by unhygienic trucks) through the unusually hot summer of 1983, despite a general recognition of the likelihood that the lack of water would lead to a high incidence of infant diarrhea and death.

5. This study was a follow-up to a study of women's social networks and survival strategies in three neighborhoods of Lima, including Leoncio Prado, carried out with Ford Foundation support in 1982.

6. The existence of a parallel men's and women's organization is rare in shantytowns of Peru. In Leoncio Prado, it was a male general secretary of the central committee who brought the women's council into being.

7. Though it has many precedents, the application of U.S.-standardized instruments (whose validity in Peruvian populations has not been firmly established) was not an ideal procedure. In this case, it was the decision of the Ministry of Education psychologists who participated in the project.

8.   The two other communities studied were a poor urban community in the capital of Cuzco Province and a "deteriorated" inner-city district of Lima.

9.   This comparison uses a sample of 35 nonparticipatory women of the 60 interviewed in Leoncio Prado in 1985. A total of 79 participatory women were interviewed. They were members of the women's council, mothers' club, health promoters' group, family day-care group and the cooperative in formation at the handicrafts center. Except for a small number of refusals, the 79 women represent the universe of Leoncio Prado women who participate in community service groups. The nonparticipatory women were selected from households situated between the households of participatory women, in an effort to map neighborhood-based networks over the entire community.

10. Barry Wellman has written extensively about the characteristics of neighborhood and social support networks in industrialized countries (Wellman 1982: 61-80).

11. The risks to physical safety of young children in squatter and shanty communities of Lima have frequently been underestimated not only by parents but also by social scientists (Anderson and Panizo 1984: 15-35; Schmink, Bruce and Kohn 1986).

References

Anderson, Jeanine and Panizo, Nelson.
 1984. Limitaciones para el uso de los servicus urbanos por mujeres de bajos ingresos: transporte y seguridad". Working Paper. Lima Working Group on Women, Low-Income Households and Urban Services.
Anderson, Jeanine.
 1983. "Redes y estrategias." pp. 63-67. Manuscript.
Anderson, Jeanine *et al.*
 1982. *El desarrollo del niño en contextos de transición cultural: Un estudio de cuatro zonas en el Perú.* Lima: National Institute for Educational Research and Development (INIDE).
Anderson, Jeanine; Figueroa, Blanca; and Mariñez, Ana.
 1979. "Child Care in Urban and Rural Peru." Washington, DC: Overseas Education Fund.
Bogdanovich, Mafalda and Castilo, Mariela.
 1978. "Factores que influyen en la participación femenina en Pamplona Alta." B.A. Thesis. Lima: National Pedgogical Institute.
Schmink, Marianne; Bruce, Judith; and Kohn, Marilyn, eds.
 1986. *Learning about Women and Urban Services in Latin America and the Caribbean: A report on the Women, Low-Income Households and Urban Services Project of the Population Council.* New York: The Population Council.
Warren, Donald.
 1981. "Problem Anchored Helping Networks: A Key Social Bond of Urbanitos." Paper presented to the Annual Meeting of the American Association for the Advancement of Science, Toronto, January 1981.
Wellman, Barry.
 1982. "Studying Personal Communities." In *Social Structure and Network Analysis.* Edited by Peter V. Marsden and Nan Lin. London: Sage Publications.

Table 11.1 Social network size, women of Leoncio Prado, according to participation in community service organizations*

	Total social network	Community based segment	Segment living outside Leoncio Prado
Participatory women N = 79			
Average number of network members	15	7	8
Range	5 - 28	2 - 19	2 - 16
Nonparticipatory women N = 35			
Average number of network members	10	5	5
Range	3 - 19	1 - 11	1 - 13

* Social networks were essentially of the "helping" kind, according to the question used to elicit names of network members.

Table 11.2 Women's perception of most serious problem they faced in recent months

	Respondent's community participation			
	Nonparticipatory		Participatory	
	N	Percentage	N	Percentage
Problem related to:				
Children	14	23	15	19
Husband	15	25	22	28
Respondent herself	10	17	14	18
Other	9	15	11	14
No serious problem	12	20	17	21
Total	60	100	79	100

Table 11.3 Person from whom help was sought to deal with this serious problem

	Respondent's community participation			
	Nonparticipatory		Participatory	
	N	Percentage	N	Percentage
Help sought from:				
Respondent alone	1	2	4	7
Husband	3	7	6	11
Relative	16	36	21	37
Neighbor(s)	11	25	15	26
Other/Nobody	<u>13</u>	<u>30</u>	<u>11</u>	<u>19</u>
Total	44	100	57	100

Table 11.4 Who helps with child care, according to mothers' participation in community service organizations

	Nonparticipatory		Participatory	
	N	Percentage	N	Percentage
Assistance from:				
1 neighbor	25	41	32	40
2 neighbors	8	13	14	18
3 or more neighbors	1	2	7	9
Only older siblings	15	25	10	12
Relatives*	1	2	4	5
Domestic servant	1	2	0	0
Nobody	6	10	6	8
Not relevant (no children or only grown children)	<u>3</u>	<u>5</u>	<u>6</u>	<u>8</u>
Total	60	100	79	100

* Relatives that were simultaneously neighbors (i.e., living on the same block) are classified as neighbors.

Index

About the Authors

John S. Akin is a professor of economics at the University of North Carolina, Chapel Hill. He specializes in health economics and has researched, published, and lectured on topics relating to health financing, primary health care in the Third World, and contraceptive demands in Thailand and Jamaica. He organized and chaired the International Seminar on Health Insurance, 1985, and he helped to organize the WHO World Health Assembly of 1987 and the Infant/Mother Nutrition Project in the Philippines. He received a Ph.D. degree from the University of Michigan.

Jeanine Anderson is program officer for the Women's Program of the Ford Foundation. Her expertise includes social anthropology, gender studies, and Latin American studies. She has researched and published on issues of child development, daycare service, women's social networks, neighborhood links to family survival, women and development, and the anthropology of gender in Peru. She has extensive background in the development of daycare models appropriate to the conditions of Lima shantytowns. She received a Ph.D. degree from Cornell University.

Michael Baksh is a research anthropologist with the School of Public Health at the University of California, Los Angeles. He specializes in sociocultural anthropology. He was field director of the Nutrition CRSP Kenya Project and is currently analyzing data from that project and preparing papers for publication. Topics of special interest include time allocation, agricultural production, and cultural change. He received a Ph.D. in anthropology from UCLA.

Mayra Buvinic´ is the founder, director, and a member of the board of directors of the International Center for Research on Women. She has also served as president of the Association for Women in Development, is a member of the board of trustees for the International Institute for Tropical Agriculture in Ibadan, Nigeria, and was a scholar in residence at the Bellagio Study and Conference Center in Italy. Among her publications is the volume *Women and Poverty in the Third World*, co-edited by M. Lycette and W.P. McGreevey (Johns Hopkins University Press, Baltimore, 1983). She received a Ph.D. in social psychology from the University of Wisconsin, Madison.

Patrice L. Engle is associate professor in the Department of Psychology and Human Development at California Polytechnic State University. She specializes in developmental psychology, childcare, the effects of malnutrition on mental development, and the social context of development in Latin America. She has served as a consultant and conducted research on the interrelationship of childcare, nutrition, development, education, women's work, and family planning. She has published and presented numerous papers on these topics, particularly as studied in Guatemala and other developing nations. Among other honors, she was awarded a Fulbright scholarship to study in Guatemala. She received a Ph.D. in Child Development/Educational Psychology from Stanford University.

Wilhelm Flieger is director of the Office of Population Studies at the University of San Carlos in Cebu City, the Philippines. His area of expertise is demography, and among the volumes he has published is *A Demographic Path to Modernity*, co-edited by Peter C. Smith (University of the Philippines Press, Manila, 1975). He is president of the Philippines Population Association. He received a Ph.D. in sociology from the University of Chicago.

Scott B. Halstead is acting director of the Health Sciences Division at the Rockefeller Foundation. His areas of specialization include infectious diseases, preventive medicine, epidemiology and international health. He has served as a consultant or advisor to numerous health organizations and on the editorial boards of major journals. He has published widely on the epidemiology of a number of infectious diseases and on international health in general. He received his M.D. from Columbia University.

Susan P. Joekes is a research fellow at the Institute of Development Studies at the University of Sussex, England. Her areas of special interest include women and development, trade and employment, and the international economy, with a focus on the Middle East. She has published a book, *Women in the Third World Economy* (Oxford University Press, New York, 1986), as well as articles, evaluation research, and policy studies on female employment in developing countries and on the impact of structural adjustment programs on women in developing countries. She received her Master's degree from the University of Oxford, England.

Francisco Mardones S. is associate professor of public health and nutrition at the Family Health Unit of the University of Chile's Institute of Nutrition and Food Technology. He has written for some 30 publications relating to public health and nutrition, mainly on epidemiological topics of breastfeeding, birthweight, and the evaluation of nutritional programs. He received his M.D. degree from the University of Chile and a Master of Science from the University of London.

Joanne Leslie is a health and nutrition consultant to the International Center for Research on Women. While a staff member at the Center, she served as director of the Maternal Nutrition and Health Care Program. Her research interests include child nutrition, women's health, and maternal work and child welfare in the Third World. Among her publications is the volume *Food Policy: Integrating Supply, Distribution, and Consumption*, co-edited with J.P. Gittinger and C. Hoisington (Johns Hopkins Press, 1987). She received her Sc.D. from Johns Hopkins University.

Chloe O'Gara is international education advisor at the Bureau of Science and Technology in the Agency for International Development's Office of Education. She is a specialist in development, learning, instruction, and communications. She has written journal articles on cultural perceptions of breastfeeding and on child growth. She received an Ed. D. degree from the University of Rochester.

Michael Paolisso is an anthropologist with the International Center for Research on Women. His research interests include agricultural development, time allocation, gender, and health. He has undertaken long-term fieldwork in Venezuela and Kenya, and provided short-term technical assistance to development organizations in both Latin America and Africa. He has written journal articles on culture change, ecology, and time allocation. He received his Ph.D. in anthropology from the University of California, Los Angeles.

Barry M. Popkin is professor of nutrition at the University of North Carolina, Chapel Hill, and fellow of the Carolina Population Center. His primary interest includes the microeconomic determinants of nutrition and health behavior, and women's roles; time allocation; and household welfare. He has researched the relationship between women's market and home production activities, infant feeding, and infant health, and he is principal investigator of several research projects on maternal work, infant care, and child welfare in China and the Philippines. Among his recent publications is the volume, *The Infant Feeding Triad: Mother, Infant, and Household* (Gordon and Breach, New York, 1986). He received a Ph.D. degree from Cornell University.

Eugenia Muchnik de Rubinstein is director of the Department of Agricultural Economics at the Catholic University of Chile. She contributed a chapter on nutritional concerns in the establishment of commodity priorities in the volume *International Agricultural Research and Human Nutrition*, edited by Pinstrup-Andersen, et al. (IFPRI/SCNN, 1984). She has also written articles on women's work, labor supply, and birthweight. She has belonged since 1986 to the WHO steering committee on social and economic research in tropical diseases, and she is a fellow of the Kellogg International Fellowship Program in Food Systems. She received a Ph.D. in economics from the University of Minnesota.

J. Conley Thomas is an epidemiologist with the Acute Communicable Disease Control Division of the Los Angeles County Department of Health Services. His principal interests are epidemiological methods, infectious diseases, maternal and child health, and health and development. He has undertaken field research in Kenya to study the health and sociocultural causes of infant diarrhea. He received his Ph.D in Public Health from the University of California, Los Angeles.

Katherine Tucker is assistant professor in the school of Dietetics and Human Nutrition at McGill University. Her area of special interest is international nutrition. She received her Ph.D. from Cornell University.

Isabel Vial is a sociologist and professor in the Family Health Unit of the University of Chile's Institute of Nutrition and Food Technology. Her expertise is in the areas of women's work and its effect on family welfare, determinants of women's employment behavior and its changes through time, and the evaluation of health and nutrition programs. She has participated in seminars and on committees dealing with nutrition programs and women's work and has written various journal articles on the relationship between family nutrition, women's work, education, and family planning and formation among low-income Latin American households. She received a degree in sociology from Catholic University in Santiago.

Joachim von Braun is a research fellow at the International Food Policy Research Institute. His focus of interest is food policy analysis and research on food security and poverty alleviation. He has published on the topics of consumer-oriented food subsidy policies, the effects of technological change in agriculture on consumption and nutrition in Africa, and commercialization of agriculture and nutritional improvement. He received a science award from the Eiselen Foundation for research contributions towards alleviating hunger, and he received a professorial title from the University of Goettingen in Germany. He received a doctoral degree in agricultural economics from the University of Goettingen.

Emelita L. Wong is a graduate research assistant and doctoral candidate at the Carolina Population Center at the University of North Carolina, Chapel Hill. Her specific area of study is biostatistics and quantitative epidemiology. She has been involved in research on maternal and child health in developing countries.